NOTHING VENTURED

NOTHING VENTURED

The Perils and Payoffs of the Great American Venture Capital Game

Robert J. Kunze

HarperBusiness
A Division of HarperCollins*Publishers*

International Standard Book Number: 0–88730–461–3

Library of Congress Catalog Card Number: 90–23334

Printed in the United States of America

Library of Congress Cataloging-in-Publication Data

Kunze, Robert J., 1935-
Nothing ventured / Robert J. Kunze.
p. cm.
ISBN 0-88730-461-3 : $19.95
1. Venture capital—United States. I. Title.
HG4963.K86 1990
332'.0415'0973—dc20 90-23334
CIP

90 91 92 93 CC/HC 9 8 7 6 5 4 3 2 1

For Tim

Contents

Acknowledgments

With thanks and appreciation to Eileen Rafter Thomas who provided invaluable assistance in preparing my manuscript, to Betsy Nolan, my literary agent who showed me what it takes to write a worthy book, and to Michael Powers.

Robert J. Kunze
San Francisco
September 1990

1

Venture Capital—A Catalyst for Creating New Business

Don't we all, at least once in a while, dream of having our own business and being our own boss? Bob Swanson realized this dream when he created Genentech. So did Bill Gates with Microsoft, Steve Jobs with Apple Computer, and Mitch Kapor with Lotus. In each case, these men were helped by a formal process known as venture capital, a system created to build new companies.

The venture capital process not only invests risk capital in a new business but also nurtures that fledgling company until it grows and becomes profitable. This combination of equity participation plus active involvement in the development of the company distinguishes venture capital from all other investment vehicles. The money for venture capital investments comes from financial institutions such as trust funds or endowments, and from wealthy individuals, all hoping to make a killing or at least beat the market averages. Most of these investors put their money in a venture fund to be invested in a portfolio of baby companies, with no more than 10 percent of their cash going into any one enterprise. The investor thus offsets the losers and can provide a superior return on investment as his reward for taking the risk.

The fund concept was established because the high failure

rate among start-up businesses makes owning a stake in only one company too risky. Spreading the investment risk over ten or more companies makes hitting a few winners more likely. Two or three winners out of ten is about average, resulting in a profit for the investor. A monster hit like Apple or Genentech would offset a hundred failed start-ups and generate huge profits.

Venture investors need patience. The average venture-backed company takes six years to develop to the point where the stock has tangible value. Investor patience is further tested by early disappointments. The venture capital cliché, "Lemons ripen before the cherries," means that investors hear of company failures and write-offs long before they get any news of dividends from winners.

Entrepreneurs are vital to the venture capital process. These are the men and women with the guts and vision to create and build new businesses. They don't just dream, they bet their livelihood, energy, comfort, and security that they will succeed. Unlike the investors who are able to spread their risk over a portfolio of several companies, entrepreneurs have to succeed in their single enterprise or be written off. Statistics make it clear that less than half of venture-backed companies succeed, but all the entrepreneurs who founded them believed that, despite the odds, they would succeed. Many entrepreneurs have little or no general management or business experience. They are often fleeing from the structure of a large corporation. And then they find themselves living with capital restraints, operating losses, setbacks, and disappointments but must still rapidly build a business.

When the venture-backed company is formed, the entrepreneurs are given generous stock awards as their principal economic incentive as well as compensation for irrevocably transferring to the business their ideas, technology, and patents. Successful investors have found that venture capital works best when all the company's employees are granted stock in the company thereby giving them a stake in its success.

The facilitator in the venture process is called a venture capitalist. He or she represents the investors' interest, deciding where and how much to invest. The venture capitalist must then "add value" to each company in which he has invested. During the first year or two in the life of a company, a venture capitalist is part of the company's management, helping to fill vacancies and participating in hiring key employees. Venture capitalists have traditionally served as advisors to management either formally as a member of the company's board of directors or informally through telephone calls and visits. Another vital venture capitalist role is to raise the additional cash needed to build the business.

As a result, a venture capitalist is not merely a money manager for investors' funds but also a full partner with the entrepreneur, sharing a mutual goal of creating a valuable company. The venture capitalist, like the investors, has the advantage of spreading risk throughout a portfolio of companies and doesn't live or die on one investment. However, he or she must shoulder the heavy burden of daily dilemmas, decisions, disasters, and disappointments that arise out of simultaneous involvement in five to ten companies. Investors hear only tidbits about the companies once or twice a year during formal portfolio reviews. Entrepreneurs have only their own company's problems to deal with. The venture capitalist has the responsibility for the full load.

Venture capital isn't available to every entrepreneur wanting to start a business. It is usually restricted to companies with potential sales of at least $25 million within six years and where cash invested can at least triple in value. (Some monster winners have shown increases of more than one hundredfold.) Nor is a venture capital fund available to every investor. Most funds require a $500,000 minimum investment with some as high as $5 million. In addition, investors in venture capital funds must be "qualified," meeting net worth and sophisticated investor standards designed to prevent them from betting their houses on this risky business.

Today there are only about 500 venture capitalists in the

United States and, consequently, only a handful of job opportunities at any one time. I receive hundreds of truly impressive résumés every year from people seeking to become venture capitalists. I offer some encouragement but must remind them that few if any will land a job.

Despite these obstacles to participating in the process, venture capital plays a powerful role in creating new companies, jobs, and fortunes. The allure of venture capital is simple—it works. Apollo, Apple, Cray, Compaq, Data General, Prime, and Sun became significant computer companies overnight. Adobe, Ashton Tate, Lotus, Microsoft, Oracle, and Sybase became standards in computer software, forcing giants like IBM and Digital Equipment to accept their existence. Amgen, CalBio, Centocor, Cetus, Chiron, Genentech, and Hybritech created businesses out of the wonder of Watson's double helix and formed a new industry called biotechnology. Advanced Micro Devices, Cypress, Intel, National Semiconductor, Texas Instruments, and VLI are some of the important companies that turned transistor technology into those magical semiconductor silicon chips.

Over the past 40 years, tens of thousands of companies have been created by the venture capital process and the big winners already account for more than 10 percent of the companies listed in the *Fortune* 500. This astonishing success is unique to America, and venture capital continues to be an important catalyst in bringing it about.

The Birth of Venture Capital

Prior to 1950, entrepreneurs were often inventors who got the money to start their businesses from relatives, friends, neighbors, and occasionally, wealthy benefactors. Some entrepreneurs were also clever promoters who raised money with inflated promises. It's never been easy to tell the difference between substance and puff. Raising money to create a new company was entirely opportunistic because no formal way existed to get risk capital for good ideas. It was all by chance.

Fledgling companies face start-up expenses and operating losses. Personnel, space, furniture, equipment, machines, and laboratories all require capital during the early years until the company generates enough sales to cover these costs. Banks and other financial institutions were not an answer to the growing demand for cash to create companies. The old canard that banks loan money only when it isn't needed applies absolutely to emerging companies because the inability to repay a loan means bankruptcy. The mere whisper of the word "bankrupt" scared all the bankers away. Baby companies had no collateral, were losing money, and seldom if ever qualified for a bank loan.

Bankers' natural aversion to high risk was one important factor in the creation of venture capital. The rapid economic expansion of the post-World War II era was another. In addition, expanding corporations created a work environment that was institutionalized and layered with hierarchy. Many bright people submerged in the organizational depths believed their employers managed by fiat. Rapid economic expansion also created a hearty appetite for new products based on amazing new technologies and discoveries—atom smashing, the transistor effect, lasers, jet engineering, digital switching, the electromagnetic spectrum, antibiotics, cryogenics, solid-state physics, and polymers. Established corporations did begin to create new technology-based products in earnest but some of the most talented and visionary people quit their stifling jobs at General Electric, General Motors, or IBM to start their own companies. The corporations were not overly concerned. Those people were considered misfits, anyway.

During this period universities and research institutes were also developing new technology at a geometric pace. Traditionally these developments were licensed to corporations in exchange for royalties. The Boston and San Francisco areas became important exceptions. Some university scientists from Harvard, MIT, Berkeley, and Stanford began to use technology developments to start their own companies. These professors often brought their best students with them to the exciting world of entrepreneurship. Some bright students copied their teachers and started up companies on their own.

This entrepreneurial yearning to start new businesses created an enormous appetite for risk capital. In response, during the early 1950s, funds dedicated to risk capital were created by financial visionaries who believed they could double the returns over traditional investments. These early investment managers shrewdly called themselves venture capitalists. It had a nice ring, so nice that I've heard half a dozen men claim they coined the name.

From the 1950s through the 1970s venture capitalists managed and invested money that came principally from wealthy individuals, a handful of corporations (Firmenich, the Swiss-based international perfume company, put up $500,000 and eventually increased its money by 25 times), and a surprisingly large number of British and European "fund of fund" managers. These foreign money managers raised cash from wealthy clients and were always on the lookout for new investment opportunities, including investing in someone else's fund (hence the "fund of funds" name). This practice is not permitted in the United States because investors wind up paying management two fees, one for the fund they are in and one to the manager of the second fund. Investing foreign money in U.S. venture capital paid off handsomely and, as a bonus, enabled investors to avoid capital gains taxes on profits because they were allowed to run their investment through tax havens such as the Channel Islands or the Dutch Antilles.

The money available as venture capital in the 1960s and 1970s, ranging between $100 to $300 million per year, fell far short of the demand, and was far less than the individual developmental budgets of large technology corporations such as IBM or GE. Consequently, only those companies deemed the most promising were financed by venture capital. Even then, these baby companies had to make do with meager or insufficient funds. Some new businesses literally started in a garage. The scarcity of venture capital was a very tough investment screen. Only the very best people and most exciting ideas needed apply.

The formal venture process in those years used a simple formula—hard working, undercapitalized entrepreneurs, especially those creating businesses out of new technology, could outperform corporations. Baby companies succeeded by working twice as fast and at half the cost of any corporation. Working almost fanatically, entrepreneurs beat corporations to the punch in new concepts in computers, high performance semiconductors, applications software, and the commercial use of lasers.

Silicon Valley was born and named as former employees of corporations like AT&T, IBM, and Lockheed spawned Intel, Siliconex, and Monolithic Memories. New computer industries sprang up near Boston—Cray, Data General, and Prime.

Corporate America had created a bureaucracy that was a perfect counterpoint to the entrepreneur's dream. There were important, painfully obvious defects in the corporate system. Some very bright corporate employees asked what would motivate me to work 70 hours a week—a pat on the back, a 10 percent raise, a fancy title, a pension plan? Not likely. Why did the big bosses always take at least six months to make important decisions like building a new factory or launching a research program, then turn around and delay introducing a new product because it might compete with an already profitable existing product? Why were executives so distanced from what was happening? Why was there such resistance to new ideas?

These questions become entirely irrelevant in an entrepreneurial setting. There isn't the time, the money, or the surplus of people to think them up, let alone give them serious consideration. While GE interminably debated the merits of discrete versus integrated circuits, Intel became a giant semiconductor company. Mighty DuPont and Union Carbide vigorously promoted cheap plastic films for wrapping fresh meats, while Cryovac became the world leader by selling an expensive "shrink" wrap that prolonged shelf life and was literally created in a garage. IBM stood pat on big mainframe computers while Apple and Compaq built multibillion-dollar businesses in personal computers. A baby company called Raychem, not GE or Westinghouse, created the industry standard for an electrical wire harness, a simple-to-use plastic device to connect the bundles of wires in telephone gear, appliances, autos, and electronics. Raychem's technology was even based on research discarded by GE.

Companies formed by entrepreneurs have either to succeed or be obliterated. There is no other possible outcome. It's not surprising that succeeding becomes an obsession. Most corporations, on the other hand, have enough critical mass that they don't fail. Their employees may fail (and often get fired for so doing). Entrepreneurs take gambles in order to succeed. To avoid failing corporate employees don't gamble.

During the venture capital pioneer years, colleagues, friends, and neighbors believed the person who quit IBM or MIT to start up a "garage" operation was nuts. Corporations, they thought, may be slow and stodgy but at least their employees had job security.

These attitudes changed dramatically during the 1970s when the venture-backed, successful entrepreneurs of the 1950s and 1960s started becoming visible millionaires with their faces even popping up on the covers of *Fortune* magazine. Then, as the 1980s approached, venerable corporations such as GM, Westinghouse, and Union Carbide started mass layoffs of long-time employees. As a result attitudes changed and many now believe that if smart, creative people don't quit IBM and start their own company, they are either nuts or don't have what it takes. During this time, the growing allure of venture capital to both entrepreneurs and investors was that it worked and made many of them rich.

Venture capital works because it brings cash, hungry entrepreneurs, and new technology together. Through the 1970s, nearly 75 percent of the venture capital activity clustered on the West Coast and in the Northeast. Success fed on itself as new start-up companies headed by entrepreneurs who had firsthand experience with building a new business spun off from venture-backed successes.

Universities in the Northeast and on the West Coast played an important role in the clustering of venture capital. Stanford, Berkeley, MIT, Caltech, and Harvard allowed and even encouraged their science faculty to participate in the formation of new companies. MIT put endowment money directly into venture investments. Stanford created incubators to move certain discoveries from the laboratory to determine commercial feasibility.

Cooperation with the venture process by these prestigious universities came in recognition of the fact that some of their top scientific faculty was being lured away to help create new companies. The universities also realized they weren't making much money from merely licensing their patents. In practice, universities seldom made money from licensing their patents to corporations. Often their technology was so fundamental that it took years to become commercially useful, so long that the patents expired before earning any royalties. The corporate insiders' joke was, "You could always tell the expiration date on a patent. It was the day before we made our first product sale." Secondary patents covering developments for the commercial use of a university's technology were owned by the corporate licensee. No royalties flowed to the universities from these improvements.

Neither the university nor the faculty inventor was making much money out of their discoveries except for consulting work. Scientific faculty were very underpaid in comparison to the research staffs of corporations. Faculty were permitted to augment their income by consulting for corporations, which could earn them as much as $500 per day, but generally there were few psychic and only minimal financial rewards in consulting. Good advice was often ignored without explanation by corporate clients. When a suggestion was used and made a pile of money for the company the consultant still got only a fixed fee. "Not invented here" (NIH) is a widely practiced form of technology chauvinism. This credo blandly states that the opinions of outsiders have no merit but are collected to create a drawer full of proof that "no stone was left unturned" before the company pursued its own course.

The universities eventually learned they could license technology for royalties and equity, the latter remaining valuable regardless of when the patents expired. Rather than leaving, faculty could work part-time for a venture-backed company in exchange for a salary and equity. This participation became an acceptable compromise for important West Coast and Northeast universities, a way of keeping faculty happy and making more money on their technical discoveries and intellectual properties.

Another factor that stimulated venture capital on the West Coast and in the Northeast was the existence there of new divisions or subsidiaries of technology corporations such as IBM, TRW, GE, Motorola, Raytheon, and Lockheed. These corporate enterprises spawned entrepreneurs and, most important, became hiring halls for baby companies. This subculture encouraged many people to leave the job security of a GE, IBM, or Eastman Kodak to take a risky position with Prime or Intel. Some talented people made the move because they got cheap stock as well as a thrilling day's work.

There were restless geniuses working in corporate research and engineering centers who, though well paid, watched with dissatisfaction as millionaires in the making emerged from the universities to form new companies. These corporate technologists knew they would never become millionaires working for DuPont or IBM. In those years they got paid one dollar for each of their patents, a gold watch on their twenty-fifth anniversary with the company, and a brass plaque if their patent made their corporate employer tens of millions of dollars in profits. Gene Amdahl quit an important research job at IBM to form his own computer company, as did Seymour Cray when he left Control Data. Corporations later acted to change these inequities but it was too late. The venture process was here to stay.

1980—Venture Capital Comes of Age

The biggest turning point in the short history of the venture capital business came about without fanfare in the early 1980s. Pension, insurance, and endowment funds were allowed, by a change in the security laws, to invest up to 10 percent of their billion-dollar pools of money in risk capital. These funds had been legally restricted to qualified investments, those that were liquid or had substantial tangible worth.

This action released an avalanche of capital from U.S. financial institutions eager to find new ways to beat the averages. The $100 to $300 million per year flowing into venture funds during the 1960s and 1970s rose overnight to billions in the early 1980s and has remained at the $2.5 to $5 billion per year level ever since.

What an explosive change! There was an order of magnitude increase in cash. A whole new group of players sprang up—lawyers who wrote contracts for peanuts and then watched their venture capital clients get rich, investment bankers who helped raise money for venture-backed companies, corporate executives who were keen observers of the venture scene, stock market analysts, an author of a technology newsletter, publicists, successful entrepreneurs, and money managers from the same financial institutions who made money available for expansion. Newcomers, all untrained and without any venture performance record, suddenly began to manage millions of dollars of venture capital investments. From 1981 to 1984, more than 300 new funds were formed. Since it takes six years on average for a venture investment in a start-up company to return a profit to investors, a smooth talker could make any portfolio loser that hadn't already gone bankrupt look like a winner. The institutional investor would not know the truth for six years.

These pension, insurance, and endowment fund managers gave blank checks to novice venture capitalists oblivious of the fact that they didn't know the likelihood of success. All they actually knew was that they were investing in risk capital. They just didn't know all the risks.

The billions of dollars flowing into venture capital dramatically changed the rules for entrepreneurs. With all the capital now available there was a far greater chance for an entrepreneur to get funded and this encouraged many more people, some marginal, to start new businesses. Because of the laws of supply and demand, more money meant higher stock prices at all stages of venture investing, a better deal for founders, but a lower return for investors. A big deal in 1970 was $500,000. In the 1980s that jumped to $5 million for the same percentage of ownership in the company. The number of new companies financed, as well as the average investment per company, exploded. Eventually this caused two gigantic fundamental problems.

The availability of dollars outpaced the number of good ideas. In the 1980s ten baby companies formed around one good idea, whereas in the 1970s there would have been only one or two. All these companies were potential competitors so the market became overcrowded even as it was being created. Eighty disk-drive companies were formed when there was room for six; 300 biotech companies, when only a handful could make it; 150 software companies when only a dozen could possibly become a $100 million business. In addition, because of the nature of the personalities involved, there was an insidious and cruel irony: Each individual company and its backers believed it alone was special and the best.

The second effect of the rush of capital is that entrepreneurs don't start companies in garages anymore. Even start-ups have enough cash to have flashy facilities with glistening laboratories, boardrooms, and atriums. Many entrepreneurs now believe glitz gives their companies the look of success, a hot deal, when in truth it is self-indulgence and a waste of money. Worse, it's an icon of flabbiness, a throwback to the excesses of corporate trappings. It's not a healthy trend.

Venture capitalists now buried under billions of new cash were under tremendous pressure to invest this flood of money.

The high returns promised investors would not be made on deposits sitting in a bank. The result was too much money invested per company at too high a price and too many companies being financed.

No one noticed the irony that the huge venture capital successes—Apple, Compaq, Genentech, Lotus—were built during the lean years of the 1970s and that increasing the velocity of venture capital tenfold, in cash as well as in geographic dispersion, could only increase the risks for everyone, investor, venture capitalist, and entrepreneur.

This surge of U.S. venture capital gave rise to substantial interest worldwide. Every country from Albania to New Zealand wanted to start a venture capital industry. Everyone, however, overlooked the vital factor that gave U.S. venture capital a big boost—the new issues market or the availability of a public stock market for emerging companies. A venture capital investment is unusual because of its illiquidity. While the company is private, there is no way to sell stock except at huge discounts.

The U.S. over-the-counter stock market provides an "exit" strategy or way to cash in on these investments. The public can buy into the company. In the 1960s and early 1970s the system was very inefficient. Wall Street paid little attention to emerging companies and penny-stock markets were too sleazy for most buyers. There was little or no research on the quality of emerging companies and no market maker to inventory stock or arrange trades. The sale of stock remained so thin that quoted prices were meaningless, rendering the public stock de facto illiquid.

Wall Street brokerages and underwriters shied away from involvement because these new issues were simply too small to attract their interest and the companies too fragile and obscure to be readily understood by traditional financial analysts. Worst of all, the transaction fees were lousy.

Hambrecht & Quist of San Francisco, Alex Brown of Baltimore, and a few other small firms pioneered the organized underwriting of worthy emerging companies. These companies placed special emphasis on technology, provided market research, and became market makers for small, public companies. By the early 1980s initial public offerings (IPOs) became the war cry of the venture capital community. It sounded something like "I'm rich!"

Now there was a clear path to liquidity. Selling the companies to the public became possible because a real market had been created for these stocks. Analysts issued quarterly research reports. Institutions could regularly buy and sell through the efficient system provided by NASDAQ, the national over-the-counter market. Retail stock sales to private individuals became an important companion market. There was demand for these stocks internationally. These small market cap (the number of shares outstanding times price equals market capitalization) stocks were believed to be truly liquid.

Major-bracket Wall Street firms did not want to be left out. Paine Webber, Morgan Stanley, First Boston, Merrill Lynch, and Salomon Brothers learned to successfully comanage initial public offerings, joining with an investment banking specialist in emerging companies, such as Hambrecht & Quist. (Morgan Stanley underwrote Apple, Paine Webber Genentech.) Wall Street brought its cash, credibility, and customer lists; Hambrecht & Quist et al. brought their track record and expertise.

Between 1980 and 1984 more than $20 billion of venture-backed new issues were processed. This was truly the golden age of venture capital. Venture capitalists and entrepreneurs became megamillionaires. They even became media personalities. Art Rock, the enigmatic superstar of venture capital, was on the cover of *Time* magazine. Steven Jobs was ten times more recognizable than Roger Smith. Jobs also made ten times more money than the chief executive officer of General Motors. (He also deserved ten times more.)

Investment bankers earned revenues well over $1.5 billion from both the underwritings and in the market from commissions on trades and gains on the increased share price of inventories of stock. In public markets, emerging growth stocks underwritten during this period soared by 600 percent. Everyone made money, at least on paper.

Corporations wishing to buy these baby companies now had some real competition. The market capitalization established the basis for the purchase price. On average, corporations paid one and a half to two times the market cap as a premium to buy a company. This often meant paying 10 to 100 times book value or net worth. Venture investors were no longer prisoners of illiquid investments; they were financial wizards beating the averages by a mile.

By the mid-1980s, however, most of these new issues had failed to live up to inflated expectations. Stock prices for technology took a 50 percent market haircut in 1985, recovered halfway by early 1987, then took another 50 percent haircut in the October crash of 1987. The market for new issues today is orderly, less volatile, and more predictable. IPOs remain an excellent exit strategy for venture-backed portfolio companies. The IPO serves as a basis to price companies for sale to corporations. Though now muffled, the venture capitalist's war cry remains the IPO and distinguishes the United States as the world leader in venture capital.

Silicon Valley on the Road

Mighty efforts have been under way in Europe and Japan to establish venture capital. They don't work as well as expected. The cultural tradition of working for one corporation for life remains a strong pull outside the United States. Other than in the United Kingdom, universities don't spawn entrepreneurs. Doctoral students don't have the same opportunities to develop technology as their American counterparts. In a foreign university setting there's no incentive to perfect research to a point worthy of commercial development. Since governments pay all the university's bills, royalty income or contract research is not needed to provide cash for salaries or laboratories.

Large corporations such as Siemens, Hoechst, Rhone-Poulenc, and Fiat dominate middle-class culture, providing jobs for life and real rewards for scientific achievement that result in profits. Unlike their American counterparts, European corporate scientists get a substantial royalty for inventions made while working for their employers. Corporations also offer perks to employees—housing, cars, travel—which offset high income taxes and discourage walking out to build a new company.

In Britain, despite more than one billion pounds for new businesses made available over the past decade by the government and the private sector, very few of the companies formed have the $100 million potential of their American counterparts. Nevertheless, investors, including the government, paid higher than American prices for the stock they bought. It was not uncommon for a raw start-up to be valued at $20 to $30 million instead of the $2 to $5 million it would have fetched in the United States.

British venture capital became an example of desire far exceeding potential. Also, as I am always warned by Brits, "We could do it but nobody wants to work hard, certainly not the 70-hour week and then there's those bastard unions." I helped form a London-based venture capital operation in 1984 and assigned one of my best people to help get the program started. The quality of the business proposals and of the companies that received venture capital and the pace of development were underwhelming and it will take decades to catch up to the United States.

In Japan, legal and cultural barriers exist that may be so insuperable that U.S.-style venture capital can never succeed. Equity investments are severely limited by law. The government wants low-interest debt to be the backbone of capitalization. Venture capitalists are legally prevented from serving on boards of directors. The Japanese financial mentality, with failing entrepreneurs contemplating hara-kiri, is completely alien to the business climate in the United States.

I formed a venture capital operation in Tokyo in 1983 with four leading financial institutions as my partners—Orient Leasing, a worldwide leader in lease financing; Daiichi Life Insurance, Japan's largest life insurance company; the Sanwa Bank; and Diawa Securities, the second largest investment banker in Japan. It was a privilege to be a part of such an illustrious group.

Our local venture organization was comprised of people "seconded" by each partner. This meant we borrowed our partners' employees for an unspecified time period. I visited our venture six times each year hoping to provide guidance in the "how to" of venture investing, and invited each employee to the States for a month of training. After one year their largest investment, $500,000, was in Diachi Kange, a late-stage private company specializing in robotics for automobile production. On one of my visits I asked how often anyone visited this company. I was astounded when I heard the answer "never." After catching my breath I sprang into action. I piled four of my "venture capitalists" into a car and drove off toward Mt. Fuji to visit the company. We were greeted by a production foreman and toured the factory and laboratories. The layout was attractive, the inventories were massive, but there was something very strange. No one was working and the place was nearly deserted.

A few months later the company went bankrupt. My biggest shock was learning that one of our partners, the Sanwa Bank who introduced us to Diachi Kange, seized our $500,000 soon after it was invested, calling in a past-due loan they made to the company just before it went belly up.

Another disappointment came when I learned that our "seconded" employees were in two categories: The first group was eager to learn everything they could about venture capital so they could return to their parent companies and start a competing fund. They were at least enthusiastic and far more tolerable than the second group who were in our venture business as a form of Japanese Siberia, exiled for mistakes in previous jobs. They couldn't wait to complete their penance and return to their former jobs. I sense that the venture capital process in Japan will suffer from enormous start-up problems. Anyone with partners like mine will certainly be doomed.

The main reason that venture capital doesn't succeed in foreign countries, however, is the lack of a new issues public market. One exists in theory in England, Japan, Germany, and France, but only a handful of companies have actually been underwritten. Without an IPO exit strategy, investors and entrepreneurs are financial prisoners holding illiquid stock. Investors don't make any money and entrepreneurs aren't rewarded for their risks and personal sacrifice.

Within the United States geographic dispersion has been very slow going. Despite mighty efforts by local politicians, the availability of money from state pension funds, and baby-company incubators sponsored by eager universities, the vast majority of venture capital-backed companies still appears on the West Coast or in the Northeast. Maybe it's something in the drinking water. There has been a gradual spreading of activity from Boston to lower New England, New York, and Pennsylvania. On the West Coast venture capital has migrated south to San Diego, north to Seattle, and east to Denver and Salt Lake City. Austin, Texas, is an important new area for venture capital as are the environs of the Washington, D.C., Beltway. People who want venture capital in their area must keep in mind it took 20 years to make Silicon Valley and Route 128 and the key ingredients are still necessary—money, an environment that encourages entrepreneurship, technology corporations, and venture capitalists.

Today in Venture Capital

Venture capitalists create investment funds or pools of money ranging in size from $25 to $100 million with each individual investor putting up $1 to $5 million. The venture fund is designed to exist for 10 or 12 years, after which the remaining money and stock in companies is returned to the investors.

A $100 million fund would have investments in 25 to 50 companies in its portfolio. The period for a first investment in new companies usually lasts three to five years after which the remaining funds are used for subsequent financing for those companies which survive. The fund manager, another name for a venture capitalist, alone decides where to invest and how to participate in the ongoing development of each portfolio company. The investor has no role in this activity. When the stock liquefies, the money is distributed back to the investors. If the fund is profitable, 20 to 25 percent of the profits, called an override or carried interest, go to the venture capitalist.

Investors want at least a 15 percent net return on their money. Without an expectation of this high return, they would not take the risk. Venture capitalists therefore need a 20 percent return before being paid their override in order to provide a net 15 percent return to investors. The fund must thus triple in value over its life.

Each successful entrepreneur usually owns 3 to 10 percent of his company when it becomes liquid. Therefore, he personally earns $2 to $50 million.

Since the majority of companies don't return a profit to investors, a few companies, perhaps only one per portfolio, make all the profit. I've heard investors complain countless times that I made all my money in one lucky investment. What they don't understand is that I make investments in at least ten companies in order to get that "lucky" one. Naturally we all want to invest only in the lucky ones and not in the losers, or to put more money in the winners and less in the losers. But who knows which is which? Each company looked like a winner on day one or I wouldn't have invested. It takes about six months for the warts to show up and years before there is any certainty of success. In the beginning there's no way to predict the outcome.

This low success ratio is the reason why investors need to be in a portfolio of companies to make a profit. Investing in one or two companies, no matter how attractive they appear, is a sure way to get wiped out.

All venture capitalists, therefore, bet on a gaggle of companies, not just one or two good lookers.

The entrepreneurs, bless their hearts, are innocent victims of venture capital statistics. Despite working 80 hours a week on a very good idea, the odds are they won't get rich. Why do they do it? Simple. They believe in themselves and in the dream of being their own boss; and the expectation of being one of the few to make it drives them. Besides, it's still a better alternative than working for Westinghouse for life.

All venture capitalists believe they personally add value and help their portfolio companies become successful. Investors in venture funds are also convinced of this or they wouldn't pay such high management fees. Entrepreneurs, without any other source of money, are more wary than open minded and hope venture capitalists will help, or at least not harm, their company. It's understandable. Imagine the frustration of being a scientist trying to explain the human genome or plasma etch or vector processing to a young, omnipotent Harvard MBA with an undergraduate degree in philosophy?

Venture capital is and always will be an imperfect market. Investments aren't fungible. If an investor wants to put $1 million in GE bonds, there are two dozen investment bankers who'll execute the order with identical results and fees. It's like buying gasoline from Exxon or Shell. It's all the same stuff.

Pension funds, over a ten-year period, all have more or less the same return plus or minus two percentage points. This is not so with a venture capital investment. The venture capital funds range in performance from outright losses to 50 percent compounded returns over a ten-year period.

Venture capitalists can't put money to work at will. Sometimes they can't get in on the investment they want or can only get half of what they hoped for. Pricing is intangible and unpredictable and, in hindsight, always either too high or too low. In other words, the person who said the venture capital business was one of managing risks was absolutely right. Cynically he could add, "To be successful at venture capital, there are three crucial rules. The only problem is no one knows what they are."

The venture process is exciting and rewarding as well as a catalyst for creating important new businesses. Investors who pick the right venture capitalists make a pile of money; entrepreneurs who succeed have a right to be enormously proud of their unique accomplishment; and venture capitalists get both rewards. If they are any good they make a pile of money and share in the thrill of helping create companies. It's no wonder so many talented people wish they were venture capitalists.

2

Taking the Plunge—The Investment Decision

Bill Hambrecht, my first partner, is one of a handful of venture capital superstars. He once wryly observed that, "You need to be a little stupid to be any good at making an investment decision." He's right. I've seen countless superbright analysts never make a decision to invest because they know all the reasons why the business in question will fail. The smarter they are, the longer their list.

Very bright, analytical people overlook or disregard good luck as a necessary part of the success equation. I know would-be venture capitalists who pride themselves on their unblemished record of never making an investment mistake. They also never make any money because they never make any investments.

Ironically, Murphy's Law doesn't always apply to venture capital. Fragile, venture-backed companies succeed only if *everything* does not go wrong. When *everything* that can go wrong does, these little companies crater. In the beginning they are all a high-wire act and need timing, nerve, and luck to survive. The last is an important part of the venture capital bet, getting a break or two.

Deal Flow

The decision to invest is the culmination of a process that begins with a detailed examination of an attractive business proposal. Such proposals are, in reality, nothing more than an elaborate request for money. Deal flow, or the access to quality investment opportunities, is a vital part of the venture process. Venture funds fail when the venture capitalist who manages them doesn't see enough quality proposals.

Most business proposals come in over the transom. It's a phenomenon similar to the piles of unsolicited manuscripts that flood literary agents. Over the past ten years would-be inventors, corporate employees who want out, and other people with snappy ideas have sent me thousands of proposals. Each one is read, logged, and answered. The vast majority of them are interesting and very good ideas and yet I have never invested in a single over-the-transom idea for the simple reason that none of them has met my investment standards.

The Four Hows

My investment standards boil down to the right answers to these questions: "How big?," "How fast?," "How much?," and "How can do?" Asking the questions is very simple. Getting the right answers is very difficult.

"How big" means the size of the market multiplied by the market penetration the proposed company is likely to achieve. Market size first means the United States, then Europe and the Far East. Market penetration must factor in competition, market trends, and the potential for a family of products flowing out of the proposed company's original offering. Family means enhancements or generations of the first product as well as companion products. For example, a 32-bit computer workstation is an enhancement or second generation of a 16-bit computer. A would-be company that proposes a diagnostic kit for Crohn's disease for sale to doctors would have a perfect companion idea by developing a drug that cures Crohn's disease.

Getting "how big" right requires knowledge, skill, experience, and guesswork as well as the ability to conduct and evaluate interviews with industry experts. The final conclusion is always imperfect and should be expressed as a range, not an absolute number.

I find it amusing to see business plan forecasts five years out expressed in absolute numbers, for example, 4,257 rather than a range of 3,750 to 4,500 or 3,000 to 5,000 or 1,000 to 6,000. Knowing the range is more useful than any precise number in assessing the most likely future event. Sometimes "how big" is self-evident and no work is required. A cure for AIDS is by definition big enough. On the other hand, a plan featuring a custom-designed gate array or plug for a silicon-chip microprocessor would require months of research and analysis to answer the "how big" question.

"How fast" means the time it takes to design, prototype, and develop the product; detail the manufacturing process; install and operate production equipment; test, evaluate, and modify; obtain regulatory approval; and sample customers with the product for approval and orders.

This cycle can be as long as ten years for a new drug or as short as one year for an instrument to measure water purity. Mistakes; false starts; procurement delays for raw materials, equipment, or assembly components; and quality problems all contribute to delays. Customers always take longer to evaluate a new product than expected. One or more of these problems will always occur, mandating that a venture capitalist factor slippage into assessing "how fast." Slippage costs money and enables competition to steal a march. Estimating slippage, its cost, then determining if delay might be fatal, is a very difficult but vitally important task. "How fast" is never self-evident.

"How much" means estimating the total capital required before a company achieves cash-flow break-even or the point where the bleeding stops. Financial forecasting is only useful when based on brick-by-brick details. This includes the precise number of people required at quarterly intervals throughout the forecast period as well as items such as equipment lists, space, revenues, and working capital. What it all costs is determined from these details plus the money for slippage. The next question is where will the money come from—venture capital, banks, lessors, corporations, landlords, research contracts, public markets, or government grants and subsidies. A lack of sufficient capital is usually the single most important cause of failure; therefore a venture capitalist must know not only "how much" will be needed but also whence and when the money will come.

"Can do" is sizing up the entrepreneurs, the toughest but also the most important question to answer. Countless characteristics must be discovered and evaluated such as dedication, intelligence, decisiveness, common sense, focus, leadership, and flexibility—and there is no script, no foolproof model. Entrepreneurs begin to reveal themselves only after hours of interviews, meetings, and casual conversations. They begin to take form after carefully checking references, understanding their records, watching their interactions with colleagues. There are few rules and even they are flawed or paradoxical. For example, experience is vital, but not necessary! Apple Computer's Steve Jobs and Genentech's Bob Swanson were winners without any relevant experience.

In practice, my investment screen filters out 99 percent of the business plans submitted to me.

I usually invest only in companies

- that can reach $100 million in revenues in five to ten years
- that can break even in three to five years or
- that can demonstrate the importance of their technology for less than $3 million
- that are differentiated from competition by something that is clearly unique
- that need less than $20 million in total equity capital to break even and
- whose original employee founders are high achievers, expert in their field and have proven functional skills such as engineering, marketing, or research

Absent from this list is a "great idea." Virtually every plan I see is based on a great idea. The popular fantasy is that all it takes is a great idea. That's untrue and results in bitter disappointments and failures. The toughest axiom for the novice venture capitalist to accept is that great ideas are only 10 to 20 percent of what it takes to succeed. Timely execution, market acceptance, and reliability are far more crucial factors. Hollywood-style success stories always focus on great ideas. Most people believe that a great idea is magic. Believe me, every company that fails had a great idea. Building the business step-by-step is what is required for real success.

Not all the business plans I see are good ideas, but even the bad ones can be good for a laugh.

- a semiconductor chip which, if it failed, would alternatively be a great guitar pick
- a truth detector used to quiz a potential spouse to determine compatibility
- a method of extracting gold from seawater developed by an inmate in an Ohio penitentiary
- high-tech knee pads for Catholics (endorsed by Rome) with a side market—gardeners
- a car that could change into a plane or boat and needed only $20 million for the prototype
- a high-energy, new age pyramid to be constructed on the roofs of all office buildings so employers would get more work out of their employees

So where do I find acceptable proposals? Viable business proposals come to me almost entirely from referrals. These referrals come from a venture capital network of people who understand the venture process, experienced lawyers, public accountants, university gurus, investors, and successful entrepreneurs. From experience they understand the venture capital investment standard and what it takes to succeed. These people source deals from their professional contacts and by hearsay. They pass on quality proposals to me and to other venture capitalists in return for getting the legal or accounting work, or for a board of directors seat or the chance to buy cheap stock.

This networking process is itself an informal investment screen.

Networking that operates most effectively for start-up companies represents the vast majority of business proposals that are venture financed.

The worst source for business proposals is brokers. Armed only with fee letters from their clients—the companies trying to raise money—brokers provide no quality screen whatever. They get paid when the company raises money regardless of the merits of the investment. They simply pass the name of the company along to all the financing sources in their Rolodex.

The other viable conduit for business plans comes from other venture capitalists who source these deals from their network. Most financing involves a syndicate of two or more venture groups, providing more capital availability for current and follow-on cash needs. Syndication also spreads the risk and brings together more expertise and support. These benefits pertain only to start-up financing requiring the venture capitalist's first investment decision. There are different strategies and motivations for syndication in follow-on financing.

Typical venture financing occurs in stages and there is informal agreement on the nomenclature:

- *Start-up* (first round) $1 to $3 million, devoted to creating a prototype and proving that the technology works
- *Development* (second round) $2 to $5 additional million, for customer-testing of products and readying for manufacturing in quantity
- *Expansion* (third round) $5 to $10 million, for working capital required to support sales and expanded manufacturing capacity
- *Mezzanine* (last money prior to going public, not always necessary) $5 million, most often used to "pretty up" the balance sheet; this term comes from the metaphor of building a mezzanine as the last structure put in place *before* the company opens its doors for business

Most second- and third-round financing is principally supported by the original venture groups who invested in earlier rounds. Along with new players they invest at a higher stock price. The stock is more expensive because there is less risk and more is known about the potential of the company. Some venture capitalists invest only in these later-stage situations. They are uncomfortable with the higher risk and long development time of earlier-stage investments or they lack the experience and credibility to add value to early-stage financing. Others, who have no network to connect them with early-stage deal flow, have no alternative to later-stage investments.

I avoid coinvesting in any start-up with novice venture groups. I've discovered it's best in the long run to syndicate only with experienced venture capitalists. New companies need help and there's no advantage or added value in accepting funds from someone who plans to be passive. Historically, many venture capitalists became wealthy by making passive investments and staying out of the way, hoping that others would build the company. Today passive investors have great difficulty finding investment opportunities in quality deals. More venture capitalists share my view that an investor in a start-up (first round) should bring more than money to the table. He must also bring hands-on business acumen. (The exceptions are a few egomaniac venture capitalists who want only passive investors so no one will second-guess their decisions.)

During the first 6 to 12 months of operation, no start-up company has a complete organization. Typically missing are a chief financial officer, employee relations, purchasing, sales (there's nothing to sell), manufacturing, security, maintenance, and a host of other functional jobs to be filled as needed. I expect the other venture capitalists who have invested in my portfolio companies to help fill in the holes in the organization chart. We become *partners* with the entrepreneur to build the company by helping prepare financial statements, budgets, sign checks, call on potential customers, expedite the delivery of important equipment, pick the computer system, design the office, look at the plant layout, talk to the FDA or EPA, interview job candidates, and make the coffee. I stress the word penses, profits (losses), and cash requirements. Entrepreneurs are usually shrewd enough to package financial forecasts that meet venture investment standards. There are a variety of periodicals and books that tell entrepreneurs what venture capitalists want to hear. "If the book says they want $100 million in sales, then they get $100 million," say entrepreneurs as they concoct business forecasts tailored to what they believe is the venture capitalists' taste.

Venture capitalists must have the skill to determine the most likely numbers. They must be able to draw on experience and judgment to bring realism to forecasts and budgets furnished by founders.

However, there are many novice venture capitalists who think that doing a bang-up job in math equals understanding the dynamics of a business. I analyzed 25 companies financed by Hambrecht & Quist from 1982 through 1984 and compared the original business plan forecasts with current reality. Eighty percent of these companies fell *more than a year* behind their projections! They needed more time and a lot more cash. Remarkably, despite these delays, only one-third failed.

I never invest until I have made my own estimate of the cash required to get to break-even, the point at which the company won't need any new money. A company no longer needs money when the cash from profits plus depreciation on buildings and equipment exceeds cash needs for inventories, equipment purchase, and interest on debt and taxes, plus money owed by customers. This is my magic goal line of success, where my portfolio company becomes financially independent and even banks are willing to loan it money. Cash-flow positive companies have the luxury of waiting for the right moment to go public or be acquired by a corporation. They don't need to sell out prematurely but can wait for the top of the market.

Once I estimate how much cash is required, I add another 25 to 50 percent. (Sometimes, in retrospect, I have wished I had multiplied that answer by two or three.) Then I figure out where the money is going to come from, other venture capitalists, other investors, leases, bank loans, corporate contracts, public offerings. Then I decide which sources can be counted on, which are spongy, and what the alternatives are. I always count on the other venture capitalists for their pro rata share of the money. Part of the venture capital unwritten code is to stand by a portfolio company whose progress warrants continued support.

Friends or relatives are not reliable. Banks loan only to companies with product sales and profits around the corner. Corporations are an excellent source but can take two years to decide to invest. Leasing companies, especially those granted equity kickers, are decisive and quick. With lessors, however, I read the fine print carefully to understand all the rules so the company won't be surprised if a truck rolls up one day to take away leased equipment for nonpayment or to make sure the security deposit doesn't tie up nearly as much cash as buying the machine outright.

A public market will support a promising company but, because of market cycles, predicting the availability of public equity is very difficult. The IPO source is always a timing puzzle. Mezzanine investors or fund managers willing to participate heavily in late-stage financing have the same unreliability as the IPO market since their exit strategy is based on quickly selling to the public.

In order to understand capital requirements versus sources, I created a financing matrix as shown in Table 2.1.

Most of the big money comes from the least reliable source and no reputable venture capital syndication would be willing to back up all that capital. Therefore, the business opportunity has to be spectacular to the venture capital investors to warrant financing the will-the-money-be-there-when-needed risk, and the dilution required to raise all the money.

If this cash-sources exercise doesn't make me feel warm and happy, I never invest! I now invest only in companies that reach cash independence on less than $10 million (venture capitalists plus lessors) or where corporations are likely to buy the company and pay for all the expansion costs. If the right

TABLE 2.1 ***Capital Requirements and Possible Sources***

Capital Source	Reliability (%)	*Start-Up*		*Second Round*		*Third Round*		*Mezzanine*		*IPO*		*Total*	
		$	%	$	%	$	%	$	%	$	%	$	%
Ven Cap	95	2.0	80	5.0	83	1.0	12.5					8.0	14.0
Lease	80	0.2	8	1.0	17	1.0	12.5					2.2	4.0
Bank	50					1.0	12.5	1.0				2.0	3.5
Other (Friends)	Nil	0.3	12									0.3	Nil
Fund Managers	20							10.0	67			10.0	17.5
Corporations	80					5.0	62.5	5.0	33			10.0	17.5
Public Market	20									25.0	100	25.0	43.5
TOTAL		2.5	100.0	6.0	100	8.0	100	16.0	100	25.0	100	57.5	100.0

Note: Dollar amounts in millions.

amount of money isn't available when needed, the company will either crater or wither.

Once the numbers part is satisfied, we progress to the other vital questions. Finding the answers here is even more difficult. I try to evaluate the complex and unique factors that drive the business. What's special about the product? How strong are the patents? Why would anyone buy it? How long will it take to produce it? Are there stringent quality requirements? How big is the market? How fast will the business ramp-up? How realistic are the hiring plans? How formidable is the competition? What's the product's life cycle? How much technical risk? What are the market trends? Who are the customers? How do you reach them? What about foreign markets? What's the unfair advantage? What's the regulatory situation?

These are a few of the hundreds of questions that must be answered. And when I have the answers I recognize that they are all imperfect because they all require judgments.

It's a truism that a new entry in any business won't succeed with merely more of the same. There must be something special that many customers want and are willing to pay for. One of the most overused venture capital buzz words is "niche," a company's little corner of the market, too small to interest others so there's no competition and products can be pricey. In theory, a niche is capitalism's nirvana.

Cray found the supercomputer niche; Intel the microprocessor; Polaroid the instant picture; Michigan Chemical bromine-based fire retardants; Byrd the blood oxygenator; VLI the contraceptive sponge; Chiron the hepatitis B diagnostic; Measurex the paper machine controller; and Adobe the bitmapping for graphic and office publication.

But beware of niches. They can be deceptive. They're usually too small to be worth the effort. Or six other venture-backed start-up companies have targeted the same area. Or the niche exists only as a fantasy in the mind of the founder. Venture capitalists need *independently* to study markets, evaluate competition, and judge the merit of the product. The checklist goes on and on.

Due diligence also includes consulting with experts, talking to potential customers, even buying market research on the company's area of expertise. After a positive conclusion from the due diligence process, the investment must be legally structured. This is usually accomplished with a one-page term sheet detailing the equity split between cash investors, founders, and other employees. Lawyers then turn the agreed-on structure into hundreds of pages of nearly incomprehensible language. These legal documents must be reviewed, explained, and readied for signing. The legal process must be well thought out by competent lawyers and experienced venture capitalists. Mistakes in the first-financing documents can haunt the company forever.

One common flaw in the contract is the failure to issue preferred stock to cash investors. This oversight means that founders and employees control key decisions regarding liquidation and refinancing which can unfairly reward noncash shareholders at the expense of investors. For example, if investors put up $1 million for 40 percent of the company, founders and employees in theory could instantly accept $1.5 million to sell the company and quickly cash in, making a profit of $900,000 (60 percent times $1.5 million) while the investors would receive only $600,000. Founders could also later refinance the company with entirely new investors and dilute out the original investors.

The contract should also allow investors to require vesting of founder's stock. The contract should require the entrepreneur to work at least four years before he "earns" his stock. Otherwise, he can quit or be fired on day one and walk out with potentially valuable shares without any new shares for a replacement and dilution would be needed to grant equity to new employees hired to take his place.

Provisions on how to "fire" key employees must be made that cover issues such as severance pay, vesting, and noncompete. These prenuptial agreements are far easier to negotiate as part of the original financing than during a bitter divorce down the road.

Company bylaws governing reorganization, refinancing, mergers, board of directors, and delegation of authority must be carefully written to be fair to all shareholders. Management must be free to run the business but not without clear boundaries to its authority. A rogue-elephant president inevitably harms the company and shareholders. A representative board must be in control of important decisions such as capital expenditures over $10,000 or firing anyone who reports directly to the president.

Given the history of most venture-backed companies—the appetite for capital, hiring the wrong people and replacing key employees—legal contracts for the initial financing must be carefully and thoughtfully prepared to handle the future. Using inexperienced lawyers plus negligence in studying and understanding documents can and does result in acrimony and litigation.

The investment decision, the wellhead of the venture capital process, is that heart-stopping moment when I sign the first check. Until that moment, everything has been posturing—huffing and puffing. Putting the money up is when the risk begins. This is when the venture capitalist shifts from cautious optimism to all-out advocacy. He no longer has any alternative but to succeed.

Decision making is a chronic problem for many who want to be venture capitalists. The worst people to deal with are the flip-floppers who suffer from terminal equivocation. They go home at night believing the investment they're about to make will be a colossal success. They wake up in the morning knowing with certainty the company will fail. By lunch they admit to confusion. By day's end they know with equal certainty that they should invest. I've seen this go on for weeks without a clue as to what the final decision will be.

Some venture capitalists waver based on the last person met. It goes like this: The venture capitalist spends hours bumping bellies with the president of the company seeking money. He leaves the scene slobbering over the blockbuster return he'll get, until he discusses it with a knowledgeable colleague. During this encounter he's readily convinced the company in question is fatally flawed for what are obvious, logical, and important reasons. This insight fades when he meets with his consultant who persuades him that the company will overcome all obstacles and has unprecedented potential. This flavor lasts until he interviews someone from a competing company who, with perfect clarity, proves there is no chance for a new company to enter the market. Besides, he's told, the company being evaluated has worn-out technology and incompetent management who were fired from their last job.

Everyone has put a different spin on the same ball. Anyone making an investment decision is constantly buffeted between powerful arguments for and against the company. Guard against buying the last opinion heard. Recognize the irony that strong opinions and advice come from people who don't equivocate. Most entrepreneurs, consultants, and confidantes take black or white, win or lose, positions. Every issue is good or bad, doomed or destined for greatness. Sifting through these strong, conflicting declarations is confusing but cannot be translated into permanent indecision. Otherwise no investment will ever be made.

Another classic impediment to making quality investment decisions is the "white coat" syndrome—scientists who look as if they know what they're talking about and engineers who speak in equations well beyond the grasp of any venture capitalist I know, especially me. There is an illusion that "white coat" concepts are sacred because most venture capitalists don't have the ability to judge their merits.

Nonscientists easily miss the reality that no matter how brilliant they are, scientists are imperfect, can be narrow-minded, egocentric, opinionated, and jealous just like the rest of us. I find in most cases that the three leading scientific experts on *any* subject always disagree. Determining who is right is impossible. The venture capitalist winds up betting that his man and his company are right, then hoping for the best.

Reference checking—reliable reference checking—is another crucial element in making good investment decisions. The quality of any reference depends on the thoughtfulness of the questions asked and the willingness of the reference giver to be honest and candid.

Most people I call for a reference try to present the person in question in the most positive light possible. It's human nature to give pals a helping hand, if for no other reason than that someday you may need the same help. On the other hand, where the reference giver bears a grudge against the person or is jealous, his reference will be unfairly negative. Neither report is useful.

The best reference checks come from people who have had direct experience with the person in question, not secondhand knowledge. I divide reference checks into three categories of bosses, subordinates, and peers, sampling from each category. I also check marketing executives with customers and competitors, researchers with their faculty advisors, chief financial officers with the public accounting firms they worked with. The most important element of reference checking is specific questions. Avoid generalities like "What did you think of him?" and always get examples to back up any comment. Reference checks need a preamble explaining why you are calling, the nature of the proposed job, the importance to everyone, including the candidate, of getting the best information.

The most difficult reference check concerns a person who wants to protect his current job and needs to maintain his confidentiality. In this situation, I check people who are safe but always reserve the right to check current employers after disclosure. I keep open the possibility of reneging on the job offer if I get bad references. While far from perfect, the threat of turning up serious problems in reference checks is helpful and sometimes necessary to keep candidates from misrepresentation.

Always remember that high-achieving people will, without exception, leave a trail of those who bear them ill will and another trail of those who idolize them. Venture capitalists have to talk to enough people to get a balanced view. These days fear of litigation makes reference checking even more shallow and unreliable.

Other avenues must be pursued such as talking to potential customers to find out if they will want the new product. What are these customers willing to pay? How long will they take to decide? If a venture capitalist calls up and asks, "Would you buy product X if it did these things?" he will most likely get a "yes" unless he gets someone on a bad day. Why shouldn't a potential customer say yes? He has nothing to lose. Encouraging someone to build a better mousetrap can only be to the buyer's advantage. After all, it's not his money at risk. He has no obligation whatever to buy it. He'll make that decision when and if. There's even a perversity among some to encourage others to break their picks whether or not they have an interest in what is produced.

The due diligence process, though of great importance, is truly Byzantine. It's imperfect at best and can be dangerously misleading. To get any value out of the process, *the person making the investment decision must be directly involved* in the actual interviews and analyses and cannot rely on another's interpretation. Beware of relying exclusively on consultants: They are paid a fee for their services and have no economic interest in the consequences of their advice. Ironically, I find the magnitude of the consulting fee usually inversely proportional to the quality of the recommendations. The venture capitalist's best consultants come from his or her network. Opinions from people interested in the subject and calibrated to the venture capitalist by past experience usually give the best advice—and it's free.

Don't overthink an investment decision! I bet on people who I believe can execute their great idea in a timely manner. I check enough to satisfy myself that the company meets my investment criteria. (I try to imagine the alternatives the company might have when things go wrong to see if there are reasonable safety nets.) I avoid being overly intuitive. It's a common and grandiose mistake to invest solely on "gut feelings."

After the Decision

Venture capitalists usually feel euphoria after they decide to invest: It is the greatest investment ever made! Mindless advocacy sets in. This obsession can be a fatal flaw or it can be the single reason a company succeeds. They won't know whether or not they have made the right investment decision for five to seven years, the time it takes to liquefy a successful investment. (The bad investments go wrong much sooner than that, usually within a year.) They must not doubt, however. Second-guessing the decision to invest is a total waste of energy. Besides there are always plenty of people around to second guess any investment decision. Once the money is in, all that matters is doing everything possible to help the company succeed.

Each subsequent financing requires another investment decision. The rules and rituals for these decisions are drastically different. The company, the people, the pluses and minuses are better known.

Very few companies develop in a more promising way than expected. This often causes panic among investors who are prone to make fatal mistakes because they are unable to admit failure. One common trap is to delay a write-off, using new money to keep a failing company from going under. It is inevitable that many investments won't work, but a venture capitalist's ego often prompts a decision to invest new money rather than admit the original investment was a mistake.

The worst later-stage investment decision is to dribble in just enough money to keep the company's doors open but not enough to accomplish what's needed to succeed. Unfortunately, it's done all the time. Sometimes new money is invested in the form of a "bridge loan" which is converted to equity if and when new investors are found. This enables the venture capitalist to duck the question of the price of shares and valuation of the company. Many of these loans become protracted bridges to a painful write-off.

No wonder the investment decision is a heart-stopping moment. What follows always ends in success or failure and no one knows in advance which it will be. Many venture capitalists, as a matter of good mental hygiene, deny the possibility of failure. Deep down, however, all venture capitalists know failure as a constant companion.

3

The Players

To build value in a new company and make it successful, quixotic people with vastly differing backgrounds must unite. That requires entrepreneurs and venture capitalists to work together, interacting effectively. Often both groups have entirely different styles, strategies, and objectives but they are bound to each other by one common theme—making money.

Entrepreneurs

What are the characteristics of successful entrepreneurs? Almost to a person they are daring, single-minded, egocentric, disenchanted with the status quo, impatient, and obsessive. Many are also brilliant, innovative, charismatic workaholics. Some are jealous, greedy, angry, grandiose, messianic, hateful, and sociopathic. The single quality every successful entrepreneur shares is the ability to endure an all-or-nothing world.

For entrepreneurs, there is no alternative to success except failure. Unfortunately, the odds are against them. Despite working hard, being smart, and having great ideas, entrepreneurs often do not succeed. Failure is very visible and entrepreneurs have nowhere to hide when it happens. They might blame a thousand external events, but to the venture capital community, the entrepreneur is the sole owner of his failure.

Between the start of a company and its ultimate success or failure there is nothing but uncertainty with an underpinning of bravado. The uncertainty is the product of stress, problems, delays, and disappointments, partially offset by progress and promise. Adding to uncertainty is the fear of being fired, running out of money, litigation, regulatory problems, technology failure, secrets being stolen, or competition getting the lead. With all that angst to look forward to, why does anyone want the life of an entrepreneur? That's one of the first questions I ask every entrepreneur looking to me for money.

Few entrepreneurs ever state the obvious, "To become rich and famous." When I prompt them with that answer they nod, grin, and blush a bit. A few entrepreneurs actually tell me they aren't in it for the money. I always assume that means money is all they want. I haven't been surprised yet. Given the high failure rate, being a little nuts helps entrepreneurs believe they will be one of the minority to succeed. A few believe they are doing God's work. Others desperately want to control their destiny, ignoring the fact that the company's board of directors will retain the right to control the company. Other entrepreneurs are motivated by hatred of the corporate environment—too inhuman, bureaucratic, political, hierarchal, risk adverse, punitive, and complacent.

Where do entrepreneurs come from? Many are former corporate employees—salespeople, engineers, or scientists who believed they were underpaid or unappreciated and who disagreed with corporate decisions. Usually they held line jobs, making products, selling them, or creating new ones. I have never known anyone quit a corporate staff job such as personnel or strategic planning to become an entrepreneur.

I know entrepreneurs who fled corporate life because of capricious acts by their bosses. Their projects were canceled, their new ideas trashed or stolen, and *no one* listened or cared. Some become entrepreneurs simply because of onerous rules—coming to work on time, wearing proper attire, having an acceptable hair length, or being forced to work on religious holidays. Others left when passed over for a promotion or when they came to believe they weren't being paid what they are worth. Unless they have an underlying motivation to make a lot of money and be in control of their destiny, I generally doubt they have the durability it takes to get the job done.

One big lure for corporate entrepreneurs-in-waiting is witnessing the success of colleagues and business acquaintances. There's nothing like someone else's victory to stir the entrepreneurial spirit. When Gene Amdahl, one of IBM's brightest, left to form his own successful computer company he motivated hundreds of others to follow his lead.

Coming from corporate life, the entrepreneur suffers an immediate shock. In his baby company there is no infrastructure. He has to do everything himself. There's no one to take care of payroll, insurance, purchasing, reports, cleaning the johns, paying the bills, or even answering the telephone. The entrepreneur must immediately create a spartan infrastructure to get this work done on a very austere budget. This usually means that the company presidents do most of the little jobs personally.

Ex-corporate entrepreneurs also must learn to live without trappings. They often say they revile and denounce trappings, but many wind up wistfully remembering them and hoping for a renewal of at least some pampering. The flood of cash from venture capitalists during the second half of the 1980s made flying first class, carpeted corner offices, lavish dinners, private secretaries, and country club memberships of renewed importance to a growing number of entrepreneurs. The ascetic life of the 1970s has lost its allure for many venture capitalists who, hungry for deals, are busily backing new companies, at least until the money runs out. Nobody starts a business in a garage anymore or so it seems. I expect this trend will reverse itself. Less money will flow into venture capital and more companies will fail as more entrepreneurs develop an appetite for trappings.

These ex-corporate entrepreneurs are not to be mistaken

for the professional managers recruited from corporations to work in the baby companies created by the entrepreneurs. Professional managers are hired by the board, usually with the help of a headhunter, to build a company because the entrepreneur can't do it. The majority of the original founder presidents are fired and replaced by experienced managers from corporations in the company's area of business. Professional managers are lured into becoming presidents by high salaries plus 5 percent of the stock of the company.

Another source of entrepreneurs are those people who have a congenital aversion to working for a corporation. They go right from school to join baby companies. Some take these jobs because they did poorly in college and no corporation will hire them, or they wanted to work on the West Coast and there were no other jobs. Sometimes they even found their own companies. They know little or nothing about corporate culture or mores. More often than not they know little or nothing about running a business but have "on the job" business training. They don't have any bad corporate habits, but they also don't have any of the good ones such as structure, discipline, and planning.

For the most part I believe people with direct experience in an entrepreneurial setting in a lesser role, not as part of management, adapt very well to creating their own company. They know what it's like to worry about meeting payrolls and how to operate without a staff. The manic-depressive atmosphere is no surprise to them.

Other entrepreneurs come from academia—doctors and researchers with new technology and wondrous dreams. They are always brilliant, but seldom sensible. Scientists can be unfocused, irascible, and unrealistic. They don't know what it takes to establish, then operate a profitable business. They also can be the single reason their company succeeds. Without their vision and creative genius, there would be no company. Differentiating between the scientists who are builders and those who are destroyers is very difficult. The answer is so illusive that the only safeguard is a mechanism built into the company's bylaws by which boards of directors can easily replace counterproductive scientist/founders.

The question becomes can the company survive without its founder? Without a positive answer, I'll take an irascible genius over a smiling plodder any day. Who wouldn't? Betting on idiosyncratic people is just another risk that must be taken even though it may ultimately be fatal to the company. Time and time again, I've seen boards of directors fire geniuses and hire caretakers to make life simpler and more predictable. These companies quickly become well run but plodding, take few chances, and are doomed to fail but without acrimony. My key barometer of a caretaker-run company is the volume of reports issued to explain why plans are falling behind schedule in contrast to the mad dog genius who not only doesn't write reports, but fails to tell anyone that he's behind schedule.

Venture Capitalists

The other human ingredient in building a company is the venture capitalist. There are not many of them. Probably no more than 500 in the United States are fund general managers and make the final investment decisions, and are, therefore, genuine venture capitalists.

There are presently two distinct groups of venture capitalists. One group has been around since before the expansion days of the 1980s, long enough to ascertain whether or not they are successful venture capitalists, that is, do they make money. Almost all of these veterans have made money. The second and much larger group of venture capitalists hasn't been around long enough to know if they will be successful. They are the "too-soon-to-tell" crowd. The poor returns reported on investments by venture funds created since the mid-1980s, however, herald dismal results for the rookie segment. Even some successful veterans are experiencing terrible returns on funds started after 1984.

The truly successful veteran venture capitalists in the

United States number no more than 50. They are easily identifiable. (They let you know who they are.) A Silicon Valley gag is that you would need Kezar Stadium for a meeting of successful venture capitalists to accommodate their collective egos. These are the men (I know of no women) who invested in the big winner companies, making fortunes for themselves and their investors. They are the deans of the venture capital business today, the men with the Midas touch who have multiple mansions (one even owns a castle). Charles Waite of Greylock Management; Reid Dennis of Institutional Venture Partners; Art Rock; Fred Adler of Adler & Company; Tom Perkins of Kleiner Perkins Caufield & Byers; the late and much admired Tom Davis of the Mayfield Fund; Benno Schmidt of J. H. Whitney & Co. (father of Yale's current president); Phil Greer of Weiss, Peck & Greer Venture Partners; Don Valentine of Sequoia Capital; Dave Marquardt of Technology Venture Investors; and Paul Wythes of Sutter Hill Ventures are some of these men.

The not-so-successful veterans' list includes another 50 people who were colleagues, partners, or associates of the superstars and who were astute enough to coinvest with them. Many in this group believe they were instrumental in the success of the investments that made them money. Few actually were, but many used the connection to raise their own venture funds during the mid-1980s. To date, few of these funds look as if they will be profitable.

The too-soon-to-tell, or rookies, group joined existing partnerships or formed new ones during the 1983 to 1987 venture capital expansion period. Some of these novice venture capitalists can materially help the companies in which they are invested, but many can't. They perceive venture capital as an easy, fast way to make a personal fortune. The veterans, successful or not, know venture capital is a tough, frustrating, and long-term process. After the 1987 market crash, raising a new fund without a proven record of success has become nearly impossible.

There are three ways to become a venture capitalist. The largest number of venture capitalist hopefuls seek entry by joining an existing partnership as an associate, a lofty name for an apprentice. Thousands of outstanding candidates apply for the dozen or so new openings each year. As a result, partnerships are able to hire incredibly bright, gifted people from top MBA programs with outstanding academic credentials including lawyers, M.D.s, and Ph.D. scientists.

Most associates receive little or no partnership interests which means there is no financial reward for them if and when a venture portfolio makes money. Associates work very hard. They perform detailed due diligence checks, screen business proposals, attend portfolio company board meetings, read complex legal documents, attend industry meetings, and listen to war stories colorfully recounted and edited by senior venture capital partners.

The life of the associate is akin to playing house. Since associates never make the actual investment decision, they are automatically distanced from any responsibility for the economic outcome of a portfolio company. Since associates don't sign checks, entrepreneurs treat them with benign disdain. Most associates never held noteworthy jobs before joining venture partnerships, so many entrepreneurs view them as smartass kids in three-piece suits.

One common and not surprising phenomenon among associates I have known is that they continually shift position on the healthiness of portfolio companies. They fret unduly over the initial investment decision. They become very pessimistic as companies run into trouble. (All companies run into trouble.) They exhibit wild euphoria when milestones are met or exceeded. Then they turn around and criticize and second-guess company management for everything that goes wrong. They are the first to be pallbearers for companies that fail, and if a company succeeds, they are the first to identify themselves with its success. One out of 20 associates has an uncanny knack of sniffing out winners and can materially contribute to a company's success. Dave Strohm of Greylock Management, for one, is a former associate on the verge of becoming a superstar.

These observations are not meant to be criticisms. Associates have tough jobs. They work very hard but seldom *contribute* by adding value. Worst of all, it's impossible to tell whether or not they'll be successful venture capitalists if and when they get the chance. They learn the technical aspects of the work—structuring deals, calculating cash flows, forming syndications, experiencing public offerings, and understanding documentation—but they lack the expertise and knowledge skills necessary either to pick a promising company and help that company build its business or to make a difference in the crucial effort of raising the additional money needed for a company's success. Only a handful of associates will ever become venture capital superstars. That's also true of any other rookie venture capitalist.

The associates who break out of the pack and become successful venture capitalists have learned what it takes to make a reasonable investment decision and to plunge in head first to help make a company succeed. They waste little time second-guessing decisions or analyzing mistakes, recognizing that there are only two alternatives—success or failure. They become partners with the entrepreneurs and other venture capitalists, taking action within their experiential limits rather than just talking about taking action. Associates who make it identify with a company in its totality, the melange of progress and disappointments, but always take a back seat to management when it comes time to take credit for success. Venture capital rewards come on payday, not in trophies along the way.

Associates who don't make partner often hang around as legmen or become investment bankers or join a venture-backed company. Some believe they had bad luck and live to try it again. Others recognize that they don't have what it takes to succeed and pursue other careers.

Successful corporate executives are the second source of new venture capitalists. Many have great stature in the industries they serve, with expertise in marketing, technology, or finance. All of them who have become venture capitalists participated in building businesses within the corporate system in which they worked.

Venture capital superstars such as Tom Perkins of Kleiner Perkins Caufield & Byers and his partners, John Doerr, Frank Caufield, and Brook Byers, all came from executive positions in corporations, as did Don Valentine of Sequoia Capital and his partners, Gordon Russell and Pierre Lamond. Rookie venture capitalist Jess Belser of Rothschild Ventures was an executive at International Paper, Robert Domenico was a former IBM executive, and Dick Power of Essex Ventures came from Bristol Meyers.

Ex-corporate venture capitalists are self-assured, well paid, decisive, and accustomed to command and the exercise of authority. They are also accustomed to having people pay attention to them. Some even enjoy being feared. *All* of them have a closet full of disappointments such as being squeezed out of a job by early retirement, or not rising high enough in their corporation's hierarchy, or not being backed on their pet projects. They all became weary and disdainful of corporate bureaucracy. These executives usually become venture capitalists by serendipity, not design.

I came to venture capital from a 15-year career as a corporate executive at both GE and W. R. Grace & Co. and by the sheer serendipity of being a childhood friend of venture capital superstar, Bill Hambrecht. We became reacquainted in 1978 at our twenty-fifth high school reunion which led to my appointment as managing partner of Hambrecht & Quist Venture Partners. Harry Rein, the manager of Canaan Venture Partners, was an executive at GE reassigned from the light bulb division to Gevenco, the GE venture capital operation, at just the moment GE decided to get out of venture capital. GE sold the business, now called Canaan Ventures, to Rein and his partners.

Though mysterious to most would-be venture capitalists, the notion of venture capital is universally believed to be an easy way to make a killing. This expectation is heightened when corporate executives meet people already in the profession. They find that venture capitalists look like bankers and seem to know a little about a lot of things but have no real depth or expertise. Unlike many established venture capitalists, corporate executives have the contacts and experience to help build portfolio companies from day one. They know a good plan when they see one. They are bullshit proof. They see through overoptimism. Alas, few of them are any good as venture capitalists.

Why? Because many ex-corporate venture capitalists have a low tolerance for entrepreneurs who often appear to them to be goofballs. They fail to recognize that their role is helper or partner, not boss, and that the entrepreneur left a corporation to get away from people like them. Entrepreneurs make mistakes, a lot of mistakes. Ex-corporate venture capitalists, brainwashed by a career-long punitive environment, don't tolerate mistakes.

It gets worse. The ex-corporate venture capitalists are accustomed to armies of staff people and a bountiful checkbook. In the corporate world, when a project fails or falters, there are usually unlimited human and financial resources to fix it. If it's not worth fixing, corporate executives are expert at "disappearing" the project. They shut it down, transfer it to another division, or merge it into an existing business.

Venture capital portfolio companies don't have these options or resources. Money is always scarce and, therefore, a severe limitation to rapid growth. Corporate executives are used to building billion-dollar businesses backed by an unlimited checkbook. No baby company can afford staff support or high-priced consultants. Entrepreneurs must use what limited resources they have available to them to become successful. There is no other alternative except failure. Ex-corporate venture capitalists either quickly adapt to the new rules or they become destructive.

Another insidious problem is the ex-corporate venture capitalist who is accustomed to trappings—limousines, first class travel, and squads of toadies. In a venture partnership, it's demoralizing for the venture capitalists to show up in a limo when the entrepreneur is worried about meeting payroll. I've seen ex-corporate venture capitalists riding in the front of the plane while entrepreneurs smolder in the back. The venture capitalists must view the entrepreneur as an equal, a partner, and realize that their mutual success is based on his or her ability to help the company achieve its goals.

It's a sad moment for the ex-corporate venture capitalist when he learns how little he is able to influence others. A lot of his business "friends" disappear. They were not his "friends," but friends of his former corporation. Without the corporate banner, he finds that people no longer leap at his voice. It's hard for these people to accept that a distinguished corporate career is merely a ticket on the venture capital ride, always starting out tabula rasa. Picking, then helping, companies to succeed is the only thing that matters, past glories don't count.

The third source of venture capitalists are successful entrepreneurs who sold their companies or whose companies went public and they cashed in, or who were eased out of their jobs. On balance, former entrepreneur venture capitalists have the highest success ratio of all. From their past success, they are wealthy, automatically respected, and have credibility. Phil Young of Concord Partners was an entrepreneur at Oximetrex, Irwin Federman of U.S. Ventures was from Monolithic Memories, Bob Morrill at Hambrecht & Quist came from Prime Computer.

On the other hand, they usually carry a heavy load of baggage from their former companies and thus are overly sympathetic to the entrepreneurs with whom they work. They often disdain other venture capitalists and investment bankers and have unrealistic expectations about how hard the entrepreneurs in their venture portfolio should work or how little money they should spend. It's like the lore of parents—stories often told of the miles they walked to school through deep snow or the meager size of their allowances. Their personal war stories, which they repeat often, make some of these venture capitalists overbearing or overly paternalistic.

The Venture Capital Scorecard

The success ratio among venture capitalists is very low. At best, one out of ten will make 15 to 25 percent average annual return for his investors. One out of 50 will become a superstar. The natural selection process is brutal because the results of each investment are so obvious. No one can hide from them. There are no winners based on showmanship or bullshit. There is *no* acceptable excuse for failure, not even adverse events entirely beyond the venture capitalist's control. Bad luck doesn't earn any money or real sympathy. If a venture capitalist makes a huge profit, it doesn't matter if he is stupid, obnoxious, or just lucky since only results count. He's a superstar! He will be able to raise new money. No one pays attention to critics or gossip. They are written off as petty or jealous.

One apocryphal aspect of the venture business is the attitude of entrepreneurs toward venture capitalists. A 1989 poll of entrepreneurs financed with venture capital revealed that less than 20 percent believed the venture capitalist helped build the company (I assume this omits the value of the money invested). The poll also revealed that entrepreneurs seek (trust) venture capitalists' advice less than that of bankers, lawyers, clergymen, family members, neighbors, and friends. See Table 3.1 for the sad truth.

I'm glad they didn't include gypsy fortune-tellers and Ann Landers. I'm not sure our egos could take still coming in last.

This negative attitude comes in part from the fact that the venture capitalist usually fires or demotes the entrepreneur company president. Naturally the entrepreneur almost never agrees with this decision. The entrepreneur may also believe he was screwed by excessive dilution from the various financings and that the investors conspired to keep the valuation low. Most venture capitalists dismiss these charges as groundless bitching.

I think we need to listen to these complaints carefully and work harder to educate, encourage, support, and treat fairly

TABLE 3.1 ***Small Business Profile 1989***
Who Is Your Most Trusted Business Advisor?

Advisor	Times Consulted (Percent)
Banker	5
Lawyer	18
Accountant	38
Venture Capitalist	2
Family Member	17
Other	20

Source: Arthur Andersen & Co.

our entrepreneurs. They have the ideas and fanatically perform the work necessary for their companies to succeed. Venture capitalists must be clear, fair, and consistent in their dealings with entrepreneurs and not rely solely on writing checks to win acceptance. Without the entrepreneur's idea and willingness to work tirelessly, the venture capitalist's money is worthless.

During the 1980s I hired 17 venture capital partners. They included seven recent MBAs, eight former corporate executives, and two former entrepreneurs. Of these, only two made any money for our investors. The most successful, Theo Heinrichs, former president of Miles Laboratories, was also the most controversial. Many of my partners originally felt he was too opinionated and would be unable to make the transition from life as an executive to that of a venture capitalist. The rest of the organization lost millions of dollars. Even in hindsight I realize there was no way to determine in advance which of the 17 would make it. In fact the most promising man of the 17 lost the most money.

I draw no further conclusions from this experience than that success is random. I've never been able to find a "red thread" to give me any clue as to who will succeed. In the world of venture capital, I have learned that past performance is no indication of future success. Brilliant work in a former job or school just doesn't translate into success as a venture capitalist.

Investors Always Reward Success

New money flows from investors to the venture capitalists with the best records who then become buried in money and are under tremendous pressure to put this capital to work. Inevitably these cash-laden venture capitalists invest too much money in too many companies and some become fallen angels to be replaced by the next crop of winners.

Venture capitalists who first lost money may make a fortune in the next investment cycle if they are lucky enough to keep their jobs. Those who made money in the past may bomb out. There are many examples of both.

I've given up trying to predict with any certainty who will be successful. Most venture capitalists or entrepreneurs fail the first time around, some succeed when they try again, others, given the chance, fail time and time again. Those that succeed the first time may fail catastrophically the second time. Go figure.

Venture capitalists and entrepreneurs both want to make lots of money and, despite the statistics, they always believe they will. Otherwise, they would never aspire to be part of such a chaotic world.

How to Become a Venture Capitalist

Young people with a burning desire to become venture capitalists need an MBA from a first-tier business school and the persistence to pester venture capital fund managers for an apprentice job. There are only 25 apprentice jobs available in a good year and thousands of applicants. Of the 15 people accepted (the other 10 jobs go unfilled), only one will ever be any good at venture capital. It's about the same odds as becoming a rock star.

Rather than waiting in the wings (sometimes for years) to break out of the apprentice role, I think these ambitious folk should consider working for a baby company to experience what it's like. This firsthand reality will not only give them invaluable experience, it will also provide them with a salary to live on and some equity while waiting.

The young, would-be venture capitalist should scour the area to find and join a venture-backed start-up, and then hope it succeeds. He should work like a madman to learn every aspect of the business from accounting to sales promotion. If he still wants to be a venture capitalist five years later he will have credibility. While he's working in the start-up he'll meet and be known by the venture capitalists who backed the company. Working in a significant company that succeeds is the best way to impress venture capitalists.

Another pathway to venture capital for recent graduates is via product development in a leading edge technology with a corporation. Learning about semiconductors or parallel processing computers back in the early 1980s got venture capital jobs for several young people. The same was true for people who learned about drug delivery systems and biotechnology. In the 1990s, superconductors, gallium arsenide, artificial intelligence, neurological science, or virology are hot areas. The product-development background may also lure the bright venture capitalist hopeful into becoming an entrepreneur based on knowledge and insights gleaned from corporate experience.

Young women have the opportunity of becoming venture capitalists and a few dozen have made it to partner but most only in the past five years. Women who are becoming prominent venture capitalists include Ann Lamont of OAK Partners, Janet Hickey of Sprout, and Pat Calausen of Patricoff. The venture capital industry, still dominated by elitist men, has largely ignored the concept of affirmative action. Several large partnerships remain exclusively male and show no sign of change.

However, as the availability of qualified women interested in venture capital increases, men will wake up to this potential resulting in more opportunities for females. I have seen women entrepreneurs play an ever increasing role in management in venture-backed companies. Inevitably women who work twice as hard as their male coworkers will become a new breed of venture capitalist.

The largest source of new entrants is corporate executives who are able to join venture funds directly as partner or consultant. The odds of finding an opening with the right fit are poor, however. Not more than ten people a year become venture capitalists by this route. The odds of being hired are much better if the corporate executive brings $5 million with him from his former corporation. I personally know of two such examples and there are many more. Corporations are interested in the venture capital process but they want benefits, like direct access to new products and technology, in addition to making money. Having their own man on the team helps and they can offer the lure of an early retirement package.

Raise your own fund! This may sound absurd but it is the easiest way to get started. What's necessary is expertise in some important business area such as health care or computers and a partner with complementary skills like marketing and finance. Another requirement is a novel fund strategy such as investing only in second-round financing led by first-tier venture capitalists, or an "Earth Day" fund, or a specialty materials fund. Add to this mix tons of persistence and stir in enough cash to pay travel and legal expenses while fund-raising. Then count on one to two years to get the new fund together. These days I see 5 to 10 new funds per year started by people with no venture capital experience, down from the 25 to 50 formed annually during 1982 to 1986.

All this adds up to: Even with outstanding credentials, it's damn difficult to become a venture capitalist without luck. Persistence, great talent, skill, and experience are just part of what it takes. The rest is some cosmic blend of being lucky and wanting it badly enough. It is, after all, the most exciting and interesting job in the world—just ask any successful venture capitalist.

4

Payday—The Exit Strategy

There are countless psychic rewards for participants in the venture capital process, but payday—huge profits—remains everyone's universal goal. The glow of success cures all the pain and anxiety endured along the way.

The moment the investor's check clears, his venture capital investment becomes illiquid. There's no obvious way to get any money back. Likewise, the equity or stock granted to entrepreneurs and other employees is also illiquid. There is no organized way to sell the shares. In fact, the very fact that a shareholder might want to sell shares at this stage would make a potential buyer wary.

Payday is ultimately dependent on the sale of the shares when they become liquid. The process of becoming liquid or to liquefy the stock requires careful planning and a large measure of luck. This planning is called the exit strategy.

On average, five to seven years elapse between creation of a company and liquefaction, or cashing in. During that time, the investors and management must constantly consider and revise plans to liquefy their stock. These same people also have to make a living during that time.

Making a Living While Waiting to Make a Killing

Traditionally, a top money manager earns three-quarters to one percent on investor capital under his management. That's his entire direct income. A venture capitalist makes his living from management fees, usually 2 to 2½ percent of the total capital under his management, charged annually but paid in quarterly installments. Traditional money managers earn less than half this fee amount. Venture capitalists earn this extra vigorish as compensation for the time and hands-on expertise they bring to intimate supervision of the investments.

They also get the extra dollars because they shrewdly call themselves by the upscale title of venture capitalists instead of money managers. Don't remind investors that venture capitalist is a synonym for fund managers.

The fog rolls in when cash is invested and it becomes illiquid. What's an illiquid investment worth? It's worth whatever the venture capitalist says it's worth. There's no way to prove or disprove the value a venture capitalist places on the stock, no way of determining its true worth until it's sold and the buyer establishes the price. The industry practice is to take the venture capitalist's word on valuations.

There are a few rules of thumb. Illiquid investments are carried at cost. For example, if a venture capitalist pays one dollar per share for a portfolio company, the investment is carried at that value on its books. If a venture capitalist starts out with $10 million in cash from investors, then invests $1 million at a dollar per share, he now has $9 million in cash and $1 million in stock. For valuation purposes, the fund still has $10 million under management. The venture capitalist gets paid 2½ percent, or $250,000 a year, to manage that money.

Valuations shift in the second round of financing. In the present example the venture capitalist invests $2 million in the same company but this time at two dollars per share because he believes the company has increased in value. The stock acquired in the second round and the original stock are now automatically valued at two dollars per share. The venture capitalist has $7 million remaining in cash, one million shares purchased at a dollar but now worth two dollars per share, and one million shares he purchased for two dollars per share. The total money under management now is declared to be $11 million even though $4 million is illiquid. His management fee becomes $275,000 or 2½ percent of $11 million.

Guess what? The venture capitalist makes more money by writing up the valuation of illiquid investments even though they have no realizable value. The venture capitalist obviously makes less money if portfolio companies are written off. If the company in this illustration goes bankrupt, as many do, the venture capitalist must write off $4 million from his earlier valuation of the shares. Now he manages only the $7 million of cash and his fee drops to $175,000 or 2½ percent of $7 million.

It's not a big surprise to discover that some venture capitalists try to write up the valuations of their portfolio companies and avoid write-offs until it becomes absolutely necessary. I've seen many examples where companies are fed new money merely to keep them solvent enough to avoid write-offs.

I've seen low-ball financing, offers to refinance companies at a lower price than paid by the original venture capitalists, rejected outright to avoid write-offs even though the company might succeed if it had the new cash. It works like this:

Newco Financing			
Venture Round A	$1 million @ $1.00/share		
Venture Round B	$2 million @ $2.00/share		
	$3 million @ $2.00/share	=	2 million shares carried at a $4 million valuation

The company does poorly but remains promising. Another venture capitalist likes the company and offers to put up badly needed money. Let's say he offers $2 million but at ten cents per share. (This is called "down and dirty," a phrase borrowed from stud poker but in this business it means slashing the price and diluting, or washing out, the earlier shareholders.) If the offer is accepted by the board of directors, 20 million shares would be owned by the new venture capitalist while the original venture investor would own two million shares, which he would have to write down from two dollars per share to ten cents. If the board of directors determines the only way to get $2 million is to price the company's equity at ten cents, a good venture capitalist will swallow hard and encourage the board to take the money, then write off most of his $4 million. This venture capitalist might even invest new money at ten cents. Some venture capitalists, however, desperate for a management fee, will actually put up the minimal amount of new money to keep the company going at two dollars a share just to avoid the write-off.

Who protects investors from unrealistic valuation? No one! Public accountants haven't a clue as to how to value a venture portfolio company. They rely on the integrity of the venture capitalist. Valuation committees comprised of financial consultants have been formed to address this problem, but they don't have any better insights than accountants with which to judge the value of illiquid investments. They usually wind up rubber-stamping the venture capitalist's decisions.

I know one corporation which ran its own venture fund. They "kept score" by keeping everything at cost until the stock liquefied. For a while, the company believed it was doing great because it cashed in the winners but kept the losers in the portfolio at cost. Then there came a day of reckoning when they discovered there were big write-offs lurking in their portfolio. This corporation is no longer in the venture capital business.

The investors who pay the management fees not only depend on the venture capitalist for valuations, they sometimes also become accomplices. One of the biggest surprises in my venture capital career was the reaction of one of my investors to my valuations.

I have always prided myself on maintaining a conservative, realistic valuation policy for the money under my management.

As a matter of policy, I carry all my investments at cost unless the company falls behind its plan at which point I write it down or off. I don't write valuations up unless there is an extraordinary development such as a new investor buying at a higher price at least as much stock as I hold. Even then I keep my investment at cost if the new investor has another discernible motive such as acquiring the marketing rights to products.

Several years ago, on a visit to a giant insurance company that invested in dozens of venture funds including many of my own, I learned that it compared valuations of portfolio companies common to more than one fund. Beaming, I saw case after case where my valuation was the lowest (often half that of others).

To my utter dismay, rather than being praised I was castigated for being overly conservative. By the insurance company's rules, their other investments had to be written down to the lowest level, totally disregarding the valuations reported by the other venture capitalists. Because of my candor, therefore, the man in charge had much lower results on paper on his total venture capital investment which made him look bad. I was no hero for being responsible. On the contrary, he encouraged me to submit the highest possible valuation. In an investment pool the size of the one he ran, that meant a $50 million swing which would make him look good. I would get a higher management fee. Everyone would be happier. I never changed policy and the insurance company has stopped investing in venture capital because of disappointment with the ultimate write-offs, the illiquidity, and poor returns. They characterized their experience in the venture business as "high risk, low reward."

Entrepreneurs make a living from salaries and bonuses. Though still not comparable to a corporate executive's income, the compensation of an entrepreneur is no longer a slave wage. The equity or stock, however, is still the real, or should be the real, reward. Not counting bonuses, chief executive officers of venture capital-backed companies usually earn $75,000 to $150,000 annually. Research and development, marketing, and manufacturing directors make $60,000 to $125,000. These salary numbers have doubled over the last ten years reflecting the availability of more cash and a shortage of worthy entrepreneurs. The magic of venture capital hasn't repealed the laws of supply and demand.

Entrepreneurs make a living as long as they don't get fired or as long as their company avoids bankruptcy. This means they're good for two to three years before the balloon goes up and they become unemployed. Venture capitalists have much more security. They earn management fees for the life of the fund, usually ten years, and seldom get fired.

Time to Celebrate

The big payday comes when investments become liquid. This occurs when the company "goes public" or is bought by a corporation (at a high price).

The initial public offering (IPO) is the dream, if not the obsession, of most entrepreneurs. Typically, they get stock or options to buy stock at pennies per share. On average, entrepreneurs own 5 to 25 percent of the company when it goes public. A typical venture-backed public offering underwritten by a major bracket investment banker is sold at a market capitalization of $50 to $200 million. On paper, successful entrepreneurs quickly become very wealthy.

The catch is the difficulty in selling their stock. Since 1983, the average IPO issued has been under water or below the IPO share issue price. Underwriters, along with security laws, make it difficult for entrepreneurs to sell much of their stock. Unless there is a hot public market, the very act of selling trashes the share price. Stockbrokers, even the market makers of thinly traded stock, simply can't find buyers unless they drastically lower the price. (The reciprocal is true if a buyer wants to buy a great deal of stock other than through an organized block trade. The price spikes or goes up like a rocket until sellers are found to drive it back down.) In a down market, many horrified entrepreneurs watch the paper value of their stock plummet to a point where it doesn't seem worth selling. They hang on, hoping for the best, and hope to continue to make a living from salaries and bonuses. Many stocks never recover as buyers have long memories and don't easily forgive companies that get in trouble.

Entrepreneurs who head truly successful companies where earnings and revenues continue to grow are able to cash in gradually. Entrepreneurs in these increasingly rare cases are supported by investors.

Venture capital investments are often caught in the same trap. It's hard to sell thinly traded stock without crunching the price. One irony is the more a venture capitalist owns of a successful company, the harder it is for him to get out. In other words, investing big in winners may injure his ability to cash in because he has too much stock to sell without deflating its value. There is cold comfort for venture capitalists, however, in the fact that they still make a living off management fees based on valuations now set by a public market.

All venture-backed companies have or should have an exit strategy, whether it be a merger or an IPO. Companies planning on a successful IPO must create excitement and promise. People who buy stock in an IPO expect to make a big profit. That's why they accept the risk of buying into an emerging company which may still fail. Since 1983 the wreckage of under-water IPO has made institutional investors a very wary group. They need lots of convincing and cajoling. Before the October 17, 1987, market crash, the rule of thumb among underwriters was that the public would pay two and a half times more than the last private investor paid for stock in a company. If the last private financing was at $10 a share, the IPO would be priced at $25 a share. Some cynics have said this pricing was set because the public is two and a half times stupider than private company investors.

There was also a rule of thumb among merger and acquisition investment bankers that corporations would pay one and a half times the quoted public price to acquire a publicly traded company. Their theory was based on the incentive needed to induce the public to sell. I don't recall any comment on the stupidity of corporations.

Except for a few "hot" companies, these merger rules are no longer valid. New investors in IPOs now pay little more than the price of the last round. Corporations buy companies before they go public or buy public companies at, or sometimes even below, market price. A corporate merger remains the only sure way for everyone to cash in.

Since the 1987 crash, cash has been king because on that day investors learned that in a crisis, small cap stocks couldn't be sold at any price and that the ultimate liquidity of large holdings in an emerging company's public stock is always in doubt. In those days, corporations could bottom fish, buying good companies for cheap prices.

This softness in pricing is the direct result of the 1982 to 1984 market excesses with simply too many venture capital-backed companies in the IPO quay. Many underwriters believed "when the ducks quack, feed them," so there were hundreds of new issues. When the pace slowed in 1985, underwriters waited for the next wave. It never came and the bitter disappointment of institutions after the October 1987 market crash ended the cycle of high-flying IPOs, as it had in 1968 when it took 14 years for the market to recover.

The Roller Coaster World of IPOs

The IPO celebration began in 1980 with the amazing success of Apple Computer and Genentech. Both of these companies set a new standard for the amount of capital raised and revealed the voracious demand for new companies among institutional investors. The case of Genentech also demonstrated an eagerness by investors to buy stock in a company with no product sales, technical risks so formidable that no investor could assess the likelihood of success of the science, and great uncertainty about patent rights, so murky that I doubt any investor even knew there was a potential problem.

Pricing IPOs is as subjective as pricing venture capital private financing. Underwriters want to get the stock issue sold to earn their 7.2 percent fee on the total capital raised; the existing shareholders want the highest possible price to minimize their dilution; the new investors want the lowest possible price. As usual the lawyers don't care, they make their $250,000 fee regardless of what happens.

In the case of Genentech, the underwriter tells an amusing tale of how the deal was priced. He took the share price of the last round of private financing in which a corporation paid $10 per share. Using the golden rule that the public is two and a half times more stupid than corporations, he figured the IPO price should be $25 per share. Judging by the tremendous attendance and the unusual length of question-and-answer periods, however, the road show (a dog and pony show designed to travel from place to place to whip up investor enthusiasm) generated great interest among buyers. Counting on that "feel" of interest, the underwriter edged the proposed price up to $30 per share. The underwriter claims he felt so great when he got out of bed on the morning of the actual sale of stock that he edged the price up further to $35 per share.

The day the company went public, the market went into a frenzy. The stock shot up to $85 per share, hit tilt and fell back to close at $35, the original offering price which was based mostly on the underwriter's whimsy. (Wall Street calls this a spike—investors who bought above $35 probably remember it as a shaft.) The IPO sold one million shares at $35 per share which translates into a public market capitalizatin or valuation of $250 million.

Genentech was formed in 1976 by Bob Swanson, then 28 years old with no business experience, and Herb Boyer, a world-famous genetic engineering scientist. These two men believed that billions of dollars of pharmaceutical sales would come from their new biotechnology by 1990, more than ten years after this public offering.

Genentech was originally backed by venture capitalists who bet on the vision of Swanson and Boyer and the novel promise of biotechnology. As the company went public, its board of directors represented the majority of the company's ownership.

Bob Swanson, President and CEO	14.3%
Herb Boyer, Stanford Faculty, Research Advisor	14.3%
Tom Perkins, Managing Partner, Kleiner Perkins	14.5%
Don Murfin, Lubrizol Ventures	24.0%

Tom Perkins, one of the few venture capitalist superstars, syndicated the original venture financing among a short list of lucky venture capitalists.

Lubrizol, a corporation, believed in its own genius after the tremendous success of Genentech and later invested heavily in other venture-backed companies none of which has equaled Genentech.

Through the years that followed Genentech's stock rose to a $6 billion market capitalization, then fell back to $1.7 billion. In 1990, 14 years after its formation, the company sold 60 percent of its stock to the Swiss pharmaceutical giant, Hoffman-LaRoche, at a value of $3.5 billion. The original venture investors made about 500 times on their money, a world record, their only disappointment that they didn't own more.

Apple Computer, founded in 1977, also went public in 1980, but with a vastly different profile than Genentech's. The company created the concept of a user friendly personal computer. There were no significant technical risks or patent problems. Apple's sales rate at the time of the IPO was $120 million; $100 million was raised in their IPO at a share price of $20.70 which translated into a market capitalization of $1.1 billion or nine times sales. Apple was profitable, with net income of $11 million or a price/earnings ratio of about 100. The Dow-Jones average price/earnings ratio in 1980 was about eight.

Institutions gobbled up the Apple IPO and wanted more as the price, unlike Genentech's, surged in the after market. No investor had to worry about spikes or shafts during the first year. The public market was willing to bet that Apple Computer and its team of boy geniuses (Steve Jobs was then 25 years old) could not only survive competition from Big Blue (IBM), but could prevail in the consumer PC market. This investor belief was an incredible leap of faith! No one had ever beaten Big Blue before, not even tough guys like GE and Honeywell. There was no established consumer market and who had ever heard of PCs anyhow? And where would all the application software come from?

Whether investors were visionaries or just plain lucky, Apple rewarded the faithful through the decade of the 1980s, reaching a market cap high of $7.5 billion. They kicked the shit out of IBM.

The Apple board of directors, prior to going public, was dominated by:

Steve Jobs, Vice Chairman	15.0%
Mike Scott, CEO	5.6%
Peter Crisp, Venrock	15.2%
Arthur Rock, Private Investor	2.3%
Henry Schlien, Macy's California	0.2%
Henry Singleton, CEO Teledyne	2.4%

Peter Crisp, the managing partner of Venrock, the Rockefeller venture capital arm, and Arthur Rock are good friends and are both venture capital superstars. In Apple, they led a syndication of venture capitalists who made more than 100 times on their start-up financing.

In 1983 Lotus, a company founded by Mitch Kapor in 1980, went public at $16.75 per share, raising $50 million in an IPO at a market capitalization of $355 million. This incredible value built by Lotus in such a short time was based on application software for accounting systems for personal computers, originally suitable for use only with IBM PCs. Lotus had the incredible vision to bet on the growth of the PC market, and even more important, to bet that IBM wouldn't do what they had done with all their other series of computers—dominate the application software market with their own products. Before Lotus, IBM was infamous for delaying the introduction of new hardware to complete a full line of application software. Lotus also had to fight off corporate systems engineers who were paid to develop in-house software for use with megabuck hardware. Lotus 1,2,3 was so useful, however, that it quickly became an industry standard, outperforming both Big Blue and the armies of systems engineers.

At the time of the IPO Lotus had a revenue rate of $25 million with $5.7 million in net income. The company's book value was only forty-eight cents a share when it went public at $16.75, a price of 35 times book value at a time when the average Dow-Jones stock was selling at one and a half times book value and there were plenty of companies selling well below book.

One financial attraction of application software is that only a small amount of capital is needed, $1 to $5 million to enable a company to become profitable if the product is a hit (a big IF). The manufacturing cost of software is negligible and the software itself can be copyrighted. The risks are: Will anyone buy it and coping with theft and pirating. These are very formidable risks.

Lotus's board of directors, prior to going public, was dominated by:

Mitch Kapor, CEO Founder	23.6%
Alex d'Arbeloff, CEO Teradyne, a test equipment company	negligible
Ben Rosen, Sevin Rosen	26.6%
Chester Suida, Crown Partners	7.2%

Rosen became an immensely successful venture capitalist because of the Lotus investment (400 times on his money and another million in Compaq Computer). It didn't matter that the other 100 companies his partnership invested in didn't turn out so well. His fund was enormously successful.

Today Lotus continues to be an industry standard with a market capitalization in excess of $1 billion. A side effect of the Lotus success was that hundreds of venture-backed application software companies were started. Only a handful, such as Oracle and Adobe, succeeded to the level of Lotus. The vast majority failed.

The Genentech success launched hundreds of venture-backed biotech companies but few real successes emerged. One of the exceptions was Centocor, a company founded in 1979 that went public in 1982. Centocor focused on products for therapeutics and diagnostics centered on bioengineered monoclonal antibodies. These substances are similar to the antibodies or disease fighters humans develop to cure illness or to provide immunity against them.

As in the case of Genentech, Centocor faced formidable technical problems, years of expensive clinical trials, patent disputes, and no product revenues for many years. Despite these risks the public market gobbled up $20 million of stock in the IPO at $14 a share which translated into a market capitalization of $100 million, though the book value was a paltry $5 million with no sales and huge operating losses. The board of directors at that time was dominated by:

Mike Wall, Chairman and CEO	17.3%
Hilary Koprowski, Wistar Institute	15.0%
Carlo Croce, Wistar Institute	3.3%
Hubert Schoemaker, CFO	1.3%
Tony Evnin, Venrock	12.5%
Mike Jaugey, Paribas	20.0%

Like Genentech, the company was founded by a visionary businessman, Mike Wall, and extraordinary scientists from the world famous Wistar Institute. Tony Evnin led the venture investor syndicate and established himself with Centocor and a half dozen other brilliant successes as the guru of biotechnology venture capital. A decade later Centocor continues to reward investors with a market capitalization as high as $1.5 billion, surviving the decade it needed for clinical trials to develop profitable product sales.

Between 1980 and 1984 public technology stocks soared.

The widely recognized bellwether, the H&Q Technology Index, rose from 400 to 1400. The balloon went up in 1985 as the index fell back to 600. It recovered to 880 in 1986 only to collapse back to 450 in the market crash of October 1987, which meant that an original 1980 investor took a round trip.

Two long awaited and much heralded IPOs were issued in the month of March 1986 and, since he had invested in both of them, Dave Marquardt was automatically inducted into the venture capital hall of fame.

Sun Microsystems was the more modest of the two companies. Founded in 1982, Sun was based on phenomenally powerful semiconductor chip-set microprocessors used to build powerful engineering workstations that could run alone, or be networked to communicate with siblings, or connected to interact with a high capacity computer mainframe. By 1986, 4 years after its founding, the company had generated $150,000 million in sales and a $5.2 million profit. The IPO raised $15 million at $15 per share, a market capitalization of $500 million, less than half of Apple's IPO though sales were a third higher. By 1986 the public market had become "gun shy" according to underwriters, "realistic" according to institutions.

At the IPO, the board of directors was dominated by:

Scott Nealy, CEO	4.8%
Bob Sackman, U.S. Ventures	14.6%
John Doerr, Kleiner Perkins	5.9%
Dave Marquardt, Technology Ventures	5.5%
Doug Broyles, Glenwood Management	5.0%

All the outside directors were venture capitalists and all regretted not owning more stock. Every investor was rewarded, however, by making 40 times on his original investment.

The other 1986 IPO jewel was MicroSoft, founded in 1979 by Bill Gates. MicroSoft developed the industry standard PC operating software, MS-DOS, still in use more than a decade later by all IBM compatible systems. The company raised $55 million at $19.50 per share which translated into a $500 million market capitalization. With sales of $170 million and $35 million in profit, MicroSoft was in a much more cautious market. With sales and profits six times those of Lotus at their IPO, MicroSoft had a market cap only 50 percent greater than Lotus's.

The board of directors of MicroSoft was dominated by:

Bill Gates, Founder	49.2%
Dave Marquardt, Technology Ventures	6.2%
Portia Isaacson, a consultant	negligible

Marquardt made his partnership, managed by TVI, $30 million or 60 times on their investment. It was an unforgettable month for TVI investors and for Dave Marquardt.

The IPO exit for venture capitalists has been an extraordinarily profitable vehicle by which to cash in. Despite the cyclicity of public markets, litigation, and restricted stock obstacles, most venture capitalists prefer IPOs.

Management doesn't always survive an IPO for very long. Huge successes make management rich and provide them many more options for their lives than continuing with their companies. In this group of 1980s IPO wonders, the management that entered the decade of the 1990s is as shown in Table 4.1.

One factor seemingly overlooked in the IPO exit strategy is fairness to the new investors. The vast majority of stock sold by venture-backed IPOs in the first half of the 1980s remains

TABLE 4.1 ***Management in 1990 of 1980s IPO Wonders***

Company	Founder	Current Status
Genentech	Swanson	Still obsessed with running the show
Centocor	Wall	Remains on board of directors but resigned as CEO and became a gadfly investor
Lotus	Kapor	Resigned, started new software company
Apple	Jobs	Fired, started a new company
MicroSoft	Gates	Going strong, still runs show
Sun	Nealy	Resigned, still on board of directors

under water, gives no dividends, and, in some cases, suffers the dilution caused by secondary stock offerings and senior convertible debt instruments or bankruptcy. The public was especially battered in these stocks in the October 1987 crash. The opposite is true of the other three parties to the IPO exit, the company, the venture capitalist, and the underwriter. These three groups earned fortunes as a result of the IPO process.

Between 1980 and 1985 venture capital investments earned a lion's share of the $20 billion raised in IPOs. These venture investors owned 30 percent of the companies for which they paid $1 billion and now owned stock worth $6 billion, a profit of $5 billion. Their 20 percent carried interest meant that the venture capitalists earned $1 billion if they sold their stock. The denominator in that equation was less than 300, the number of venture partners cashing in at that time.

The underwriters earned 7.2 percent of $20 billion (plus 7.2 percent of secondaries, dilutive or not) or $1.4 billion with very little variable expense which meant most of their fees were pure gross profit to be paid out to employees or put into deferred profit sharing plans. Underwriters sensing the shark feeding frenzy began investing in mezzanine rounds of baby companies that had the promise of a near-term IPO. This investment activity had nothing whatever to do with the possibility of making a capital gain. That event, if it were to happen, would be frosting on the cake. Their real incentive was gaining the inside track in the underwriting business solely for the purpose of collecting the 7.2 percent IPO transaction fees. There was little or no due diligence by the underwriter, no investment screen whatever, no determination of value but tremendous hocus-pocus on the appearance or perception of value.

A typical road show to sell stock was a forum to present sales and earnings forecasts by management as interpreted by the underwriter. The technique was pure sophistry. The road show forum was a perfect place to verbally exaggerate the company's prospects because SEC rules forbid written market forecasts in the selling prospectus. For example:

"Newco grew in revenues to $50 million per year in just four years. Therefore, even if it conservatively grew 30 percent per year during the next five years, sales would still reach $175 million. Profits of high-tech stocks are 20 percent of sales or, in this case, $35 million. The market will pay 20 times earnings for a future market capitalization of $700 million. Therefore, buying the stock at the IPO at today's market cap of $150 million enables the investor to look forward to making four and a half times on the investment."

In reality, technology IPOs grew on average only 5 percent per year after 1984, not 30 percent, with many a cyclical drought along the way into the 1990s. Profits were more like 10 percent of sales. Even though the market did pay 20 times on those earnings, what happened was:

1984 IPO "Forecast" for 1989		1989 Results
Sales	$175 million	$ 65 million
Earnings	$35 million	$6.5 million
Market Cap	$700 million	$130 million
IPO Market Cap	$150 million	$150 million
Percent Gain/(Loss)	450	(13.5)

An insidious part of the role of the underwriter is market making or the willingness to organize the after market or the buying and selling of stock. This activity necessitates inventorying stock to facilitate these buy-sell transactions. Therefore, underwriters invest their capital in the stocks they underwrite. Part of the market making service includes quarterly research reports on the company, a built-in conflict of interest.

In the after market, the underwriters make money if the stock goes up and lose money if it goes down (as well as making public investors mad as hell). Conflicts of interest abound especially when researchers own the stock personally. No investor is very sympathetic when underwriters suffer losses, but they are remarkably placid about the hype underwriters generate to send the stock price soaring in the first place, thereby sowing the seeds for a crash.

The companies benefit by receiving millions of dollars of their IPO proceeds (about $18 billion of the $20 billion raised in the first half of the 1980s). Some companies spent all this money covering operating losses or to expand manufacturing capacity. A few of these companies had disappointing results, no money left, and no credibility to raise more and failed either through bankruptcy or a fire-sale merger.

Some profitable companies didn't spend the new cash, then had disappointing results, watched the stock price plummet, and either lived happily ever after, or bought their own stock back at bargain prices with the cash brought in at inflated prices.

Therefore, though the IPO investor on average lost money, not all companies with disappointing results failed. Many had the good life and joined the ranks of selling venture capitalists and underwriters in praise of free market capitalism.

A few fallen angels that paint a grim picture are listed in Table 4.2.

Then there are those companies that are listed under real tombstones, RIP. See Table 4.3.

Imagine a room full of public market investors in the IPOs of Apple, Genentech, Sun, MicroSoft, Centocor, and Lotus. They should be smiling, smug, and rich. Why aren't they beaming? Most of them, alas, also invested in the likes of Miniscribe, Storage Technologies, IPRI, Magnuson, Eagle, Hanna Bio, MoGen, Diasonics, and Mass Comp. Investors in emerging company IPOs are in a tough business. No wonder they no longer laugh at jokes told during road show presentations!

TABLE 4.2 ***Fallen Angels***

Company	$ Raised IPO	IPO Profit to Underwriter	Est. VC Profit	Cash Remaining	*Stock Price* IPO	High	1990
Mol. Gen	$ 20	$ 1.4	$ 1.0	$12	$25	$37	$ 3
Hanna Bio	20	1.4	2.0	13	25	50	1
Symbolics	15	1.0	1.0	0	15	15	1
Diasonics	100	7.0	20.0	0	10	30	2.5
Alliant Comp	20	1.4	2.0	15	10	24	2

Note: Dollar amounts in millions.

TABLE 4.3 ***Requiescat in Pace***

Company	$ Raised IPO	IPO Profit to Underwriter	Est. VC Profit	Stock Price IPO	Stock Price High	Current Status
Miniscribe	$100	$7.0	$20.0	$15	$25	Bankrupt
Storage Tech	50	3.5	20.0	20	40	Bankrupt
IPRI	20	1.2	3.0	25	35	Bankrupt
Magnuson	25	1.5	1.5	20	40	Bankrupt
Margaux	25	2.1	3.0	15	30	Bankrupt
Eagle Comp	50	3.5	5.0	20	80	Bankrupt

Note: Dollar amounts in millions.

But nothing has really changed. The market, as it has always been, is still cyclical. At some point in the future the stock market will again lunge at IPO stocks and bid up their prices. Corporations seeking new opportunities and diversification will pay up. It's only a question of when, not if.

Mergers of baby companies into corporations have distinct advantages. Shareholders, venture capitalists, and entrepreneurs get cash or corporate stock easily converted to cash. Venture capitalists are instantly set free of any further involvement. And since corporations have their own people to run the newly merged company, entrepreneurs are usually set free in less than two years, especially since it's bad for morale to have an entrepreneur millionaire running around with more money than the president of the corporation might earn in a lifetime.

Besides the capital market cycle, there are other formidable obstacles to a successful exit strategy, including the selling of marketing rights. For example, some venture capital-backed companies trade marketing rights to their products for cash from corporate partners. Perhaps the emerging company can't afford to hire its own sales force to market its product or can't raise cash any other way. Selling marketing rights, however, seals the company off from most merger opportunities. No corporation will buy a baby company without the right to market its products.

A similar problem exists when a baby company sells its patented technology to one or more corporations. A common ploy to raise cash and the promise of a downstream royalty is granting to corporations exclusive rights to technology. Obviously, this severely limits any merger exit strategy. An IPO is more difficult to sell because the company has relied too heavily on royalties rather than its own product line profits. Royalties last only as long as patents are useful and no one can predict how long that might be.

For 20 years I've been on both sides of the merger business involving transactions worth billions of dollars. It's clear to me that corporations buy companies primarily for political, not strategic, reasons. The sponsor gets visibility, looks like a doer, a go-getter, a visionary. After the fact no one pays much attention to mergers gone bad. It is a long time before anyone knows and baby companies are easily buried or swallowed by a corporation's infrastructure.

Exiting by merger is a time-consuming, frustrating, and unpredictable task. There is an art form to it. To be successful the buyer must have within its organization a sponsor or advocate with clout and determination. The seller should have competitive alternatives to get the best price and to move the transaction along. It must continue to operate as if the merger won't take place. Management can be so preoccupied with selling the company that it shortchanges its own business, neglecting operations and destroying morale.

I tell everyone that the odds of a merger with a hot prospect are only one in five. No one wants to believe me but history says I'm an optimist. Buyers, because they write the check, have an inalienable right to be capricious and demanding and they can change their minds without warning. For example, the sponsor for the merger within the buyer's organization may not be able to sell the deal. His lack of clout is often not known by, or disclosed to, the seller until right before the scheduled closing aborts. There are countless situations where a buyer takes a right turn and changes his strategy. He decides at the eleventh hour that he no longer wants to diversify or enter into the seller's line of business. I've seen buyers scared away by lawyers worried about antitrust, patent infringement, or product liability questions. Sometimes buyers lose interest because of an internal reorganization or preoccupation with fighting off a hostile takeover or a giant product recall. Sometimes they just get cold feet. I have seen mountains of closing documents painstakingly drafted by squads of lawyers and businesspeople washed up on the beach from aborted mergers.

It takes at least four months from a handshake to a closing. It's often longer, seldom shorter. Experienced and competent lawyers should be involved right from day one. Deal breakers and the merger structure must be dealt with by the negotiators at the start of the process, not near the end. Better to stop there than months and millions later. One very important question must be asked and answered by the board of the seller, "How much damage will our company suffer if the merger aborts?" This means calculating the cost of the wasted time and resources, the secrets disclosed, the attacks in the marketplace by competition, the disappointment among personnel, and the subtle devaluation of your company.

The announced merger between Magnuson Computer and Storage Technologies caused a celebration among Magnuson investors which was premature. The deal cratered literally on the eve of the closing. A year later Magnuson went bankrupt. There was a black cloud over Magnuson from the moment the merger collapsed because the computer industry worried about what Storage had discovered in the last minutes. (I heard it was just cold feet.) Baby companies devalue because other potential buyers wonder what really caused the merger to fail. The question always lingers, "What did the buyer who walked learn that a new buyer hasn't yet figured out? There must be something wrong." Some years later Storage went bankrupt. Who knows, maybe the merger would have saved them.

Pricing a merger is the most difficult and challenging problem of all. A private company has no liquid value, so what's it worth? There are no standard financial formulas for pricing a baby company and few, if any, comparables that make sense. The selling prices can't be determined by multiples of earnings or revenues because the company is in a very early stage of development. Using internal rates of return on investment is very spongy because of the vast uncertainty of future cash flows.

Basically, corporate buyers think low; entrepreneurs think high; and investment bankers tell both of them what they want to hear. Venture capitalists must play a strong role in setting the price. The only real guideline is to set the price "high but not crazy." Many companies go for a song because the seller doesn't have the chutzpah to ask for a bigger pile of money. Many buyers are scared away by a back-breaking price. The technique I use is to decide the minimum I will take, then add 50 to 100 percent. Once I establish a price, I stick to it tenaciously.

I also try to make sure that there's a gaggle of buyers because that's when mergers work best. I avoid being turned down officially by a prospective buyer because I want to keep all the potential acquirors in the hunt. There is incredible importance to being pursued by a howling pack of suitors. This means I don't press for an answer from someone who appears unlikely to say yes. I would be duplicitous to say a potential buyer is in pursuit if he has said no. If he hasn't closed the door, who am I to speak for him?

I find there's great sophistry in the baby company merger game, but it works. A buyer willing to pay $50 million will also be willing to pay $55 million. Logically, the company's board would accept a $50 million offer but if they are real players, they'll hold out for $55 million. If a merger deal blows, it's never because of holding out for the extra $5 million.

One company president I know was asked what price he wanted for the business. The president, a very analytical engineer, had thought long and hard about the price and had decided on a low of $20 million and a high of $35 million with the most likely offer to be $25 million. Rather than answer the price question, however, he merely shrugged. The buyer, hot as a howling cat at midnight, blurted out, "How about $75 million?" Fortunately for the company president, he was able to pretend he was choking on his pipe long enough to compose himself to say yes. On the other extreme, a company president who had established a range of $40 to $60 million choked on his pipe long enough to avoid saying "fuck off" when the buyer offered $10 million.

I never worry about the buyer justifying the purchase price to his corporation. All corporations are expert at cosmetics. An eager buyer will create whatever business model it needs to justify the price it paid even if it requires liberal use of more sophistry. Don't try to do that work for them. I have found that each corporation has its own unique system or ritual. If it wants to acquire a company, the financial analysis rationalizing "doing the deal" is the easiest hurdle. The justification is merely a mathematical expression designed to memorialize a decision already taken.

Sometimes it's impossible to find a mutually acceptable purchase price for a merger. In order to establish a price, the company may have to go public. Corporate buyers sometimes feel more comfortable using public market prices to justify their offer. I call this a real red herring but there may be no other way.

All merger machinations are very complex and have a huge subjective component. There are no golden rules or all-inclusive checklists, just guidelines and the Braille method. The seller needs stamina and guts most of all.

Uglier Alternatives

There are far less attractive types of liquefactions. One is a "bucket shop" IPO, or a public offering retailed to sucker lists by underwriters with thick skins. This creates lots of problems for the company. The underwriters' fees are very high—10 percent plus warrants or options to buy cheap stock equal to at least another 10 percent. Warrants are valuable because they require no investment. The stock is overhyped and inevitably investors are greatly disappointed. The stock price often crashes and shareholder litigation is common. Limited amounts of money can be raised—$2 to $5 million—in these "bucket shop" IPOs but the company's original shareholders, venture capitalists, and management usually must agree to a five-year lock-up of their stock during which time their shares can't be sold. The stock is so thinly traded that the tiniest volume can push the price up or down dramatically. "Bucket shops" are a bad alternative and may be worse in the long run than letting the company go under.

These sleazy deals are an example of the peculiar way investment banking operates in general. The shakier the deal, the higher the fee and, therefore, the less net money for the company. There are few businesses in which people get paid more by buyers for an obviously inferior product.

Another unattractive liquefaction is selling off assets, real and intangible, for what anyone will pay. Companies unable to attract the capital necessary to build their business and become profitable, must liquidate (usually through bankruptcy) or sell off assets. Emerging companies have little to sell except for a nascent product or special technology.

This is a tough plan to execute especially with buzzards circling overhead or waiting in the trees. Potential buyers are quick to figure out that the company is terminal and they price their offers accordingly. Even worse, by the time a company gets to this stage, both venture capitalists and entrepreneurs have little stomach left and often put little effort into a sale. I believe this is the time when the venture capitalist should work hard at this unpleasant, unrewarding task. In the long run, an asset sale is in everyone's interest. Selling off assets avoids the horror of bankruptcy and enables the shareholders to get part or all of their bait back.

Payday Arrives

"Realizations" and "distributions" are venture capital words used to describe liquefactions or payday. For entrepreneurs and other common shareholders, this road to cash isn't entirely sanguine.

Entrepreneurs and employees either own or have options to own common stock at bargain prices. Options are used to enable employees to acquire stock without any up-front cash. Bargain price means that common stock is priced at ten cents per share while investors pay a dollar per share for preferred stock. Except in rare cases, all employees are granted some shares.

Most common shares are encumbered by a four-year vesting schedule which usually means that each employee receives annually one-quarter of the total shares granted. Vesting is designed as golden handcuffs as well as to justify the bargain price.

In an IPO, common shareholders are able to sell stock they have owned for two years. Furthermore, significant common shareholders such as the president and key executives are allowed to sell 10 percent of their holdings at the IPO regardless of the holding period. This stock lock-up restriction is an attempt to protect new investors, giving the public a fair deal by encouraging management to act in its self-interest.

Management can have a tough time selling the balance of its stock. Not only do insider trading regulations limit sales, the very act of management selling, except in dribbles, can trash the stock price. The argument is, If the company is so promising, why is management selling? That's compelling and unassailable. Besides, selling stock is dangerous to management's mental health. If the stock price declines during the months following a management sale, litigation inevitably follows. If the stock crashes, the management is sued regardless of its stock sales. There are ambulance chasers who sue when the stock goes up, claiming management held their shares because they had inside information.

The venture capitalist fares a lot better in an IPO. If he hides out from the underwriter, has owned the stock for two years, and doesn't own a significant portion of the company, the venture capitalist can sell his holding at the offering.

However, the underwriter usually forces the venture capitalist to hold his stock for up to 120 days after the IPO. This action is designed to minimize price volatility during the early trading.

It's very difficult for the venture capitalist to sell large holdings any time without crashing the stock. He can dribble sales out or wait for a hot market where new buyers will gladly snap up his stock.

Investors pay venture capitalists 20 to 30 percent of the net gain or profit in an investment. This means if $2 million is invested in stock costing one dollar per share and the stock is sold at $20 per share, there is a profit of $38 million. The venture capitalist receives 20 percent or $6.6 million not including management fees. (Not a bad payday! No wonder everyone wants to be a venture capitalist. The trick is to invest in a company whose stock becomes worth $20.) An alternative, practiced by some slick venture capitalists, is to distribute stock to their investors thereby handing them the sales problem. In this situation venture capitalists get their 20 percent cut of the distributed stock and if they move quickly enough, can sell some or all of it before their investors wake up. With luck the venture capitalist turns a handsome profit before the stock crashes from others trying to sell.

A merger is a much cleaner payday. In this case the venture capitalist gets bought out immediately. The common shareholders cash in all their vested stock. The only catch to a merger payday is the long-held belief (hope) that the public will pay more than a corporation. It's a circular argument since corporations are believed to pay more than the public to acquire a company. Both statements are true depending on the market cycle. Corporate mergers were best from 1970 to 1978 and 1985 to 1990 (and beyond). The stock market was best the rest of the time, as long as the stock was sold at or near the top.

Payday for a $100 million merger looks like this:

Shareholder	Original Cost	Percent Owned	Cash Realized	
Founders & Employees	Nil	25%	$25 million	President $12.5 Other Mgmt. $10.0 All Other $2.5
Venture Capital	$12 million	60%	$60 million	Investors $48 Ven. Cap. $12
Others	$8 million	15%	$15 million	

The others are the other people's money (OPM) groups. These consist of lease financing warrant holders, mezzanine investors, and camp followers who are wealthy private investors referred by retail brokers always looking for new ways to earn commissions.

However, if the same company sold for $50 million:

Shareholder	Original Cost	Percent Owned	Cash Realized	
Founders & Employees	Nil	25%	$12.5 million	
Venture Capital	$12 million	60%	$30.0 million	Investors $24 Ven. Cap. $6
Others	$8 million	15%	$7.5 million	

Picking the winners from the losers and observing the perils of being OPM are easy in hindsight. Most important, there is an equal chance to sell the same company for $50 million or for $100 million. The company is illiquid and has no value other than what someone will pay for it. On lucky days, it's $100 million, on bad days $50 million.

Venture capitalists don't automatically get 20 percent of the gain. They actually receive 20 percent of the gains minus the losses. Sometimes venture capitalists don't get a penny until the investors get all their original capital back. Most venture capitalists with good track records can avoid the wait for their payday by making more favorable arrangements with investors.

Venture capital, for both the entrepreneurs and the venture capitalists, is a cash-to-cash business. The venture capitalists put cash in. Entrepreneurs put sweat in. The stock they acquire is worthless until converted back to cash. This is true of exciting and promising companies as well as dull or failing ones.

There is one rare exception. If a company is profitable and the entrepreneur owns a controlling interest, management can sit back and pay itself exorbitant salaries and eventually dividends out of a tiny portion of the profits. In this instance, the venture capitalist is an absolute prisoner, able to sell stock only at a discount to a value warranted by profits. Entrepreneurs gloat over such cases. It's just reward, they say, for the venture capitalist who makes too much money for too little contribution.

In defense of the venture capitalist, let us say that few have made any money in the late 1980s or 1990 based on liquefactions or realizations, a situation that's not likely to change significantly before 1995. Some venture capitalists are content with earning their management fees. They shouldn't plan on a lifetime career in venture capital, however, because without realizations, they won't raise another fund.

When cash was flooding in, many venture partnerships had hundreds of millions of dollars to invest. Some venture capitalists used this huge increment in capital and the corresponding management fees to hire more partners. Other venture capitalists gobbled most of the fees up and paid themselves barrels of money instead of hiring new people. Neither technique worked well for the investors. Partnerships that expanded with newcomers suffered from inexperience and ineptness. Partnerships that didn't expand became overextended and overinvested and performance rapidly declined.

The venture capital process enriches participants who are successful. Individual entrepreneurs take the biggest risk. Investors in successful venture funds make a lot of money and never know the risks they are taking until payday.

The venture capitalist must understand the liquefaction alternatives before investing his first dollar. Exit strategies as an afterthought can and often do significantly decrease a company's value. The entrepreneur is usually so excited about his company that he is totally unrealistic about liquefaction. Time and time again I've heard entrepreneurs rave about hefty IPO prices before the company is even founded!

Paydays come years after the initial investment. Neither bravado nor despair changes the boundaries. This is why it takes so long to find out who is any good at venture capital or if the dream of the entrepreneur can become a reality or if the investor can really beat the market averages.

5

Making the Cut

Each year I seriously evaluate 25 business proposals but I only invest in two or three. Getting to the final cut is a wrenching experience both for me and for the entrepreneur. Each of the 25 proposals has met my overall investment criteria and seems worthy of funding. As a consequence, when I begin my detailed appraisal of one of these specific business opportunities, I always believe that I'll more likely be writing a check. The winnowing process from 25 to 2 is not a beauty contest, however. I step up to invest only when I firmly believe the company will not only succeed but also generate a substantial profit. Only one out of ten candidates make the grade.

The longer the final investigation drags on, the less likelihood the deal will be done. The basic flaws begin to surface and combined with the passage of time cool off the venture capitalist's initial ardor.

Making the final cut is an excruciatingly difficult process for the venture capitalist. His decision can often mean life or death for the entrepreneur's dream. Entrepreneurs who fail to get funded after this exhaustive process generally find themselves at the terminus of a slow ride from a premature celebration (most venture capitalists at the early stage behave as if they are ready to commit) to bitter disappointment and personal loss. Some entrepreneurs keep trying to find new investors with a flock of revised plans but only a few who are rejected after a serious look by a major venture capitalist ever get funded. No other investor wants to find out why the hard way.

What is wrong with proposals that start out looking so right? Here are some of the subjective judgments I use in making the final cut: The entrepreneur doesn't seem to have adequate leadership qualities. He's not pragmatic, focused, decisive, tough, or objective enough to execute the business plan on a timely basis. For a variety of reasons I become convinced that the key people won't be able to get the job done despite their total confidence. When I didn't follow my instincts and invested anyway, the entrepreneurs who failed also desperately fought against being replaced when they did.

A few years ago I reluctantly turned down investing in one of the most elegant concepts I've ever seen. Why? Because after I spent six months of study and thousands of dollars in legal fees, the founder/president in a moment of candor told me quite proudly that he was on a mission from God to save the world and would only hire His followers to work in his company. This is an extreme example, but a little megalomania lurks in the hearts of most founders. It's my job to subjectively judge how damaging or useful this craziness might become.

- On closer inspection, the technical risk outweighs the potential reward. Some venture capitalists duck this issue by assuming the technology will work and when it doesn't, blame the failed investment on bad luck. I deal with this issue by spending a lot of time listening to the widely diverse views of experts and then making a qualitative judgment as to the likelihood of success based on my own assessment. I usually invest only when the technical development can be broken up into discrete milestones, each of which can be funded sequentially. This minimizes the total financial risk if, along the way, the technology doesn't work. Sometimes the milestone approach isn't feasible because one penultimate experiment is required that takes years and millions of dollars to prepare. As much as $100 million might be needed to prove a theory. This was the sum invested to prove that human insulin can be mass produced using a bacteria commonly found in polluted water. In this example Genentech found the money to pay for the $100 million experiment and the gamble paid off. But more often than not, these expensive gambles don't pay off and I don't invest in such projects. Two that I passed on were speech recognition (the "talking typewriter") and the optical writing of memory. Both have so far lost their investors some $50 million. There are lots of bones on the beach based on these ideas but many companies are still being formed to keep on trying.

- Sometimes, I conclude that the company requires too much capital to build its structure. Many wonderful business concepts require $25 to $200 million to be successful. Like most other venture capitalists, I generally limit the total equity investment exposure in any one company to $15 to $20 million. The business plan assumes that additional financing will come from banks, corporate partners, or public markets (IPO). I find that these business plans nearly always underestimate the capital needed and the ease of raising it. Both aspects, the amount needed and where it will come from, are difficult to predict so I assume the worst and usually don't invest in capital intensive businesses. On the other hand, some very expensive concepts are so intriguing that they become seductive and, once in a while, even make my final cut. I've turned down investments in leading-edge computers, sophisticated capital equipment for semiconductors, seminal biochemistry for pharmaceuticals, and expensive medical instruments. I've watched other venture capitalists take a bath on deals I've been lucky enough to pass up. I've also watched a few, like Sequent Computer and Cypress Semiconductor, become quite successful after I turned them down.
- We are unable to negotiate mutually acceptable terms of the financing agreement. Failure to agree to terms can be an excuse to say "no" to a deal, but too often eager venture capitalists and entrepreneurs ignore "deal breakers" until the very end. They are not unlike people who refuse to go to a doctor when they are sick because they don't want to know they are dying. The

> entrepreneur's theory behind this mindless "deal breaker" strategy is the belief that by getting all the money men committed to the deal, the investors' enthusiasm will override their judgment and they will agree to onerous terms. I believe that's nonsense, derived mostly from people's natural aversion to openly discussing problems. I work hard to raise all the potential deal breakers at the beginning of any negotiation. This saves everyone time and (me especially) money.

The most common deal breaker is price. The entrepreneur wants the venture capitalist to pay five dollars a share valuing his company at $10 million while the venture capitalist wants to pay two dollars a share or a $4 million valuation. In part this bid/ask difference is a negotiation, but both sides need to agree on the price early on in the final cut process because it's likely neither side will budge. Avoiding the discussion and postponing the price decision until the end of the process won't make the dissonance go away.

Many venture capitalists and entrepreneurs don't understand the term sheet, especially the implications of matters such as shareholder rights, dilution, preferred stock liquidation, and voting classes. Both sides need competent lawyers to explain the deal structure right up front, not at the final hour.

Every financing agreement contains representations and warranties made by the founder to "guarantee" that what he promises about his business plan is correct and true "to the best of his knowledge." Representations cover matters such as the legitimacy of patent rights, undisclosed liabilities, pending litigation, disputes with former employers over trade secrets, and anything else lawyers can think of to prevent surprises later on. The entrepreneur must understand that part of the stock granted to employees by cash investors is based on his representations and warranties (the other part of his stock share is "sweat equity").

I have had the very unhappy experience of walking away from an investment because of a dispute over the terms of the financing agreement. When this cut occurs after weeks and months of analysis and evaluation, everyone's disappointment really stings (except for the lawyers; they get paid regardless of the outcome of the deal and relish drawn-out arcane contracts). Despite the time wasted and the disappointment, the disagreements over the terms and conditions that cause an investment to abort are at the heart of a venture capitalist's ability to measure an entrepreneur. Regardless of fault, the inability to come to terms is a convincing argument that tells me we'd be unable to work together effectively later. Venture capitalists should never "sell" (or con) an entrepreneur into accepting something unpalatable or unfair and entrepreneurs should never agree to terms they believe to be unfair. Inevitably this will lead to mistrust and anger. It is far better to part company early on than to smash a deal together. Both the venture capitalist and the entrepreneur must find a way to match expectations within the structure of the term sheet or be prepared to waste time and money on acrimony in the future.

Three That Didn't Make the Final Cut

Three business proposals that really grabbed me but failed to make my final cut illustrate most of the roadblocks I look for. When you read about them you'll understand why I've disguised the names and some of the details of the businesses.

In 1987, I became intensely interested in investing in a promising concept for a new medical device for treating human blood. The proposed system, called blood perfusion, consisted of a cartridge about the size and shape of a banana filled with tiny microspheres, each the size of a grain of sand, each capable of being designed to absorb very specific chemicals from the blood. For example, microspheres had been created to absorb a drug called digoxin, a heart stimulant so potent that it is often overdosed causing death. In concept if a patient overdosed, his life could be saved by connecting the perfusion cartridge to a primary vein. This sounds drastic but is actually easy to do. The entire blood system could be completely cleansed of digoxin. The microspheres in the cartridge would readily absorb all the digoxin and have no other effect whatever on the blood—no damage or change in blood cells, platelets, nutrients, gases, or other blood chemistry. The most attractive part of this miracle of the microsphere technology was that it worked and was not just a theory. A prototype system had been used successfully on a dozen digoxin-overdosed patients and all the evidence showed it had saved their lives.

Further study revealed the likelihood that other forms of microspheres could be created to remove overdoses of a wide range of narcotics, poisons, toxins, and alcohol as well as specific poisons caused by bacterial or viral attacks such as toxic shock. The perfusion system had the potential not only to radically improve the effectiveness of detox centers but also to lower emergency care costs.

Even more important potential applications were suggested in my discussions with medical experts as part of the verification or sanity test of this concept. What a pleasant surprise. These due diligence sessions usually raise doubts rather than possibilities. In theory, the experts felt that microspheres could be designed for slow release of certain potent drugs that are difficult, dangerous, or impossible to administer orally or intravenously. Some chemotherapy drugs and immune system therapies, for example, are not effective or even used because researchers are baffled by how to get them into the blood stream.

My conclusion was that though the market for digoxin overdose was small, using the digoxin model as a demonstration project to prove the concept seemed perfect. Digoxin's chemistry was well known and understood. Human blood entered the perfusion cartridge loaded with digoxin and left a second later completely clean. The whole blood system could be cleaned in 20 minutes.

The system was an *ex corporeal* device (outside the body); living, or in vivo, blood was to be shunted through the device and put back into the body. I knew that the Food and Drug Administration (FDA) would require extensive trials with animals before permitting extensive trials with humans. The original human work done with digoxin had taken place in Israel. The results were promising, but massive work would be required by the FDA in the United States before clearance could be granted to market this unique device. I believed clinical tests to obtain FDA approval would cost between $7 and $10 million for digoxin and another $5 million for one other important poison such as amphetamine.

Proving that the drug or poison was removed would be easy. Proving that the blood was unharmed and could safely be returned to the body was the tough part. Normally, the technical risk would have been too great for me to justify the huge infusion of cash for clinical trials. Considering the Israel tests, however, I felt the technology of the blood perfusion device was so powerful that it could be a sound basis on which to build an important and very valuable company.

There were three separate constituencies involved in the enterprise—Dr. Black and his colleagues who had formed a research and development project in Israel to make the microspheres and the cartridges; Yeda, the Israeli government agency that licensed the patents owned and developed by the University of Tel Aviv to Dr. Black; and Mr. White who headed up a group of Israeli investors who had put up $200,000 in seed money to support Dr. Black's research effort. By the time I was introduced to BP, Yeda had already legally granted Dr. Black's company, Blood Perfusion, Inc. (BP), the exclusive right to all the relevant patents.

Mr. Grey, an Israeli deal broker, gave Dr. Black a long list of U.S. venture capitalists—my name was one of the dozens provided—to fund BP U.S.A. Mr. Grey never spoke to me directly. In fact we had never met. I heard nothing from him. He sent me no papers and made no calls.

Right from the beginning I made sure that the terms of the deal were straightforward and clear:

- I would invest $2 million for 40 percent of the U.S. company thereby valuing that company at $5 million. This was a generous offer, designed to provide sufficient stock to fairly compensate the University for the patents, the Israeli investors, and Dr. Black's group.

- Yeda would cancel the patent assignment to BP Israel and reassign all the patents to BP U.S.A. BP Israel would cease to exist. I didn't want any involvement in a foreign company.
- Dr. Black and his colleagues would move to the United States immediately to conduct their research and to manage the business of BP U.S.A. A search would begin at once for an American CEO and management personnel including people with commercial experience in blood-related devices.

Trouble began with tiny footsteps. Mr. White reported that Yeda preferred the patent licenses to remain with an Israeli company. This presented no problem, he said, "because BP U.S.A. would own 100 percent of BP Israel." I didn't like the concept because it meant I would need to evaluate the liabilities of the Israeli company. Naturally, I was assured there were none, but words are not enough especially when a foreign country is involved. Reluctantly I agreed to accept Mr. White's proposal and asked for extensive financial and legal data on BP Israel.

I also asked for copies of the original patent license agreement. They finally arrived in my office after a month and a dozen reminders. At this point I had spent three months evaluating this business proposal.

While I was studying the license agreement, Mr. White phoned to ask, on behalf of Yeda, if I would agree to an exclusive license for everywhere except Israel and one European country. He told me this was for political reasons. The Israeli government wanted its technology, invented in an Israeli university, to benefit the whole country, not just a few investors. I reluctantly gave in to this demand, but demanded in return absolute certainty that neither the European country (I chose Denmark) nor BP Israel would export its product or technology to anywhere else in the world. I didn't like the direction the deal was taking but I had growing confidence in the technology.

A month later Dr. Black and a lawyer representing Mr. White arrived in San Francisco to complete the contract negotiations, draw up documents, and close the deal. I was excited about the meeting, anxious to get BP U.S.A. started and to stop wasting so much time negotiating by fax and telephone. I cleared my calendar and with my lawyer started the drafting process.

During the first hour of the negotiations, I had a spirited discussion with Dr. Black who revealed that he had decided he and his people should stay at BP Israel because it would be faster, cheaper, and more efficient to keep research there and not move it to the United States. I patiently explained why the company had to be in the United States and why everyone had to be together. I got words of agreement but sensed lip service only with no real intention to do so.

By the end of the second day I had become very concerned because the documentation drafting was such slow going. The license agreement between Yeda and BP Israel was completely inadequate. The patents weren't cited, the territory was vague, the duration was too short, and the heart of the license, the definition of exclusivity, was fuzzy. I asked Mr. White's lawyer to draft new language to meet my needs. He produced another completely unacceptable proposal. Most annoying to me was his angry defense of what was obviously an unacceptable document.

When I read their proposed contract I took a careful look at the exhibits. There I discovered a $200,000 liability on BP Israel's balance sheet with no explanation.

After a heated exchange with BP Israel's lawyer, I learned that the $200,000 was a charge from Mr. Grey, the broker, as a finder's fee for finding me. I was especially infuriated because during the preceding two months I had written several letters to Mr. White stating that I would not pay a finder's fee to anyone, including Mr. Grey. Whatever the agreement with Mr. Grey, it was to be charged to Mr. White's personal account. The stock Mr. White would get in BP U.S.A. was in part to compensate for all his liabilities including Mr. Grey.

This balance sheet surprise was precisely why I was reluctant to have anything to do with the liabilities of BP Israel and pointed up why I'm always reluctant to become involved with a foreign country in a deal. It's just too hard to get all the facts.

I was so angry that I jumped all over Dr. Black and Mr. White's lawyer, and Mr. White himself (by telephone) who admitted that he had deliberately tried to slip the $200,000 by my nose. Why not, he felt, all's fair in business. The negotiation ended, everyone went home. I was ready to make the cut.

A week later Dr. Black and a mutual friend who interceded on his behalf asked for clemency and expressed a willingness on the part of all parties, Black, White, and Yeda, to go back to the letter of my original term sheet. I reluctantly agreed. Although I didn't trust anyone any more, I still loved the BP concept.

Everyone agreed that my lawyer would draft the license agreement and contract and that in light of what had happened, no other countries, including Israel, would be granted a patent license. BP Israel would be dissolved and not be part of the deal. Dr. Black would move to the United States.

The documents were drawn, everyone said that they were in agreement, and the closing was only days away when I received a telephone call from Mr. White who asked if I would, as a personal favor, grant Yeda a small face-saving sop, namely grant another country, even an unlikely country like Bulgaria, a separate license.

At that moment I could have crushed the telephone in my hand. Not very politely, I refused the request.

The BP review had begun in the spring of 1988. Now after six months of trying to put this deal together, a week after Mr. White's last telephone call, on the night before the scheduled closing I received a telex from Dr. Black saying that the contract had to be changed to provide for BP Israel to retain the patent rights which, in turn, would grant BP U.S.A. a nonexclusive sublicense. My lawyer and I fired back an expletive-deleted response that simply said the deal was off.

A day later, Dr. Black telephoned to say he had resigned

over the incident, that Mr. White had forced the board to send the telex asking for changes, knowing I would not agree. Later on that same day Mr. White, acting as if nothing was wrong, called and asked if I was willing to invest $500,000 in BP Israel. I declined with extreme prejudice.

Three months later Dr. Black and Mr. White visited a number of U.S. institutions trying to arrange for a BP IPO or private placement at a value somewhere around $20 million. My offer had been valued at $5 million. I found out about this financing proposal because potential investors called me to get my insights on BP. I demurred. I never did find out if Dr. Black's "resignation" was a sham or if he was talked into staying. The question no longer mattered.

During our early negotiations, there had been a run-up in the over-the-counter stock market in emerging medical product company valuations. Maybe BP believed it could raise money at a higher valuation without me. Maybe the BP people couldn't get Yeda to license the technology exclusively to an American company and never told me. I was never able to talk directly with Yeda and the ultimate deal breaker, nonexclusivity, didn't surface until the last minute. BP was a great idea, never got financed, and will probably never make anyone's cut. It failed with me because no one was willing to negotiate all the deal breakers so we could find a resolution. BP relied on an eleventh hour panic.

I wasted more than six months of investigations and spent $60,000 on my lawyer. I'd do it again for an investment that looked as good up front.

The moral is that great business proposals often don't make the final cut because of the terms of the contract. Sometimes real agreement can't be reached, but it's still worth the try.

A prominent law firm sent me a very credible business plan for a start-up company called Technical Materials (TM) seeking funding for state-of-the-art semiconductor production equipment. The technology was way over my head which made me feel both uncomfortable and vulnerable. Since I had considerable faith in the recommendations of the law firm, I arranged to spend a couple of days at MIT's materials laboratories and hired one of their distinguished faculty members as a consultant. The consultant was a perfect choice, having both intimate knowledge of current technology and (prior to MIT) work experience in a semiconductor factory. He was not a prisoner of the academic ivory tower. From the very first he was able to explain very esoteric physics to me so that I felt I understood at least the broad parameters. As part of my education, I even ran a few experimental laboratory machines and observed firsthand on a small scale exactly how these new semiconductor processes worked. The experience of rubbing shoulders with MIT geniuses made me feel pretty smart though I knew I was taking the "Classic Comics" approach to solid-state physics.

I have had a lot of professional experience with companies that produce specialty chemicals so I was quite knowledgeable about the techniques used to chemically etch circuits into semiconductor chips as well as the deposition of metals by electrolysis plating or reduction. In the late 1970s, several companies had been successfully formed utilizing a brand new solid-state physics technology to do an even better job than chemicals. They found that etching lines in a silicon chip for tiny circuits could be done by a plasma beam. The desired metals could be deposited on the surface of a chip by evaporating the metals in a vacuum chamber then allowing the metals to condense by reducing the temperature. Pure silicon and silicon oxide could be layered on a chip with new dry vacuum processes very quickly and with great accuracy.

Silicon chip technology was rapidly moving toward a process in which very complex tiny layers of metals and silicon and circuits were laid one to three microns apart rather than 10 to 20 microns apart as had been the practice in the recent past. This change in technology dramatically improved the power or density of the chip at very little increase in cost. The semiconductor industry was poised to enjoy a tenfold increase in productivity.

The new process made these new chips possible. Companies supplying reliable equipment to perform these tasks could readily achieve hundreds of millions in sales and be very profitable. In the early 1980s the silicon chip business was on the edge of rapid expansion, ready to serve new markets with new technology.

Armed with my new knowledge and my new MIT consultant, I began to study the TM business proposal in earnest. The principal founder and president of TM was Dr. Black, a middle-aged quiet man with a distinguished career in research at RCA. His plan was to build an electron milling machine for use in a semiconductor company research laboratory to create application-specific chip prototypes. Dr. Black believed every semiconductor producer would buy such a machine and ultimately adopt it for production. I talked to research people at three semiconductor companies and even spent a day visiting a pilot operation at Motorola. This investigation confirmed that an electron beam milling machine would be useful, but there was less certainty about the eventual use of the technique in production.

During that time, tiny lines for circuits were readily made by plasma etching and advanced techniques were being developed for even tinier lines, one micron or less. Research efforts in universities, semiconductor research laboratories, and several venture-backed start-up companies were under way on X-ray, laser, and electron beam etching. All these processes are part of what is called lithography (a term borrowed from printing), cutting a circuit into a chip from a precise, computer-derived pattern. A micron is one-ten-thousandth of an inch, smaller than a red blood cell and just as invisible to the human eye.

I spent months talking to experts on the subject of advanced lithography technique and found absolutely no consensus. Each method—electron beam, X-ray, and laser—had its expert advocates. As a further complication, there were many experts who believed the existing optical system using a plasma etch would be optimized and used for another ten years. (These experts proved to be right, at least at the start of the 1990s.)

Despite my MIT minicourse, I was confused by the conflicting opinions, but eventually concluded that though electron beam milling might be fine for laboratory work, it would never make it as a production machine. TM would therefore only sell a few dozen instruments to research laboratories rather than thousands for production.

Dr. Black argued, however, that this would get us into the door of all the top semiconductor companies in the free world so later we could sell them our second product, a patented electronic means of depositing layers of pure silicon to replace the currently used awkward process of making pure silicon by chemically reducing silicon tetrachloride.

Unlike electron milling, the silicon metal deposition process had yet to be developed and was, I believed, years and at least $10 million away from commercial reality. This time all the experts agreed that TM's idea was wonderful and would be adopted if it really worked. It was a tough call. Could Dr. Black provide the leadership to execute his plan? Could the money be raised to finance the whole project? How rapidly could TM develop the technology and commercialize the concept?

I talked to enough semiconductor companies to know that TM's silicon deposition machine would be a hit item, requiring no more than three months of testing before, if the system worked, there would be an avalanche of orders. Sketchy patents had been issued to TM, but I doubted they were strong enough to block a competitor's entry into the market. The winner in this business would be the company that developed the first reliable gear. Semiconductor companies don't like to change suppliers once a process is in place and works well. The question was: Could TM become that supplier? After two months of study I became convinced that TM could become an important company and, despite my doubts about the difficulty of building the company under Dr. Black's direction, I became very excited.

All my concerns added up to my judgment of Dr. Black's

ability to build the business, developing a detailed product plan, and hiring the best people to manufacture, sell, and service the product.

Dr. Black was an accomplished researcher on paper, but he had only managed a few laboratory technicians and a secretary. He had been a product manager and twice successfully transformed technical theories into successful commercial products. All his work had been done with RCA's checkbook and infrastructure, however. The availability of a corporate infrastructure meant that if Black needed special equipment, someone researched the problem and bought it for him; if a fixture needed to be machined, the head of the machine shop took care of it; if he needed a micrograph, the analytical laboratory made one; if his telephone broke, someone fixed it.

TM would have no infrastructure. Dr. Black would have to take care of almost everything himself, from getting the permits to work in the building to locking up at night. I visited Black in the small building he rented to get TM started. The space was way too big for the present and way too small for the future, if there was a future. Three people had been hired, a secretary whom he had brought with him from RCA, a maintenance machine shop man hired from the local community, and an electrical engineer fresh out of a local university.

The secretary was prepared for and expecting to type reports, answer the telephone, and arrange for Black's travel. The maintenance man was ready to build prototypes. Black planned to set up a laboratory, to direct the electrical engineer, and to hire a technician to do the work. He set up a mechanical drawing table and computer workstation in his office and was working 18-hour days producing designs and sketches. Part of the facility was strewn with components for incompleted electron milling machines. When they got an order for a machine, Black and the maintenance guy slapped it together and shipped it out. They had shipped five in the last three months but had been paid for only three. The nonpayers were considering shipping the machines back because they weren't being used.

The business concept I had created in my mind before

watching the TM team in action was pure fantasy. The business wasn't going to work the way I imagined it or the way it was supposed to work according to the business plan. I had talked to Dr. Black countless times at lunch or dinner or in my office, but never in his lair. I knew him only on paper by his résumé and reference checks, not the man in action. With familiarity, my enthusiasm waned, my excitement diminished. When I asked him about his people and dealing with the tasks at hand, and the plans to sell milling machines while rapidly developing the deposition machine, Black dismissed my concerns with a wave of his hand. He had done this type of work before, he said. He had created an electron milling machine that worked, and left alone, he would build a deposition machine in six months. No, thank you, he didn't need to hire any hotshot engineers (or marketing people), he needed people who would do what he wanted when he wanted it, nothing more, nothing less. Implicit in his comments was the observation that I had never built, and knew nothing about building, semiconductor capital goods. He was right and his disdain fed right into my own feelings of inadequacy.

I didn't invest in TM because I came to believe Dr. Black couldn't get the job done. He managed to raise enough money to keep going for a few years. The investors eventually fired him as president but kept him on as head of engineering, a job that entailed extensive travel, visiting semiconductor companies to talk up his new, but not quite ready, machine.

TM went bankrupt in 1985 followed by the explosive news that Black had been indicted by the Department of Justice for selling semiconductor technology secrets to the Russians. I don't know if spying was always on Dr. Black's agenda or if, faced with bankruptcy, he used desperate measures to raise money. In any case, he had managed to get into most semiconductor company plants within the United States and to see their secrets.

Regardless of the bizarre ending of Dr. Black's entrepreneurial experience, TM was a great idea and people could have been found early on to build the concept into an important and valuable business. They weren't; TM didn't; and I avoided a painful loss.

In March 1988, the Sunrise investment group introduced me to three distinguished scientists who had a brilliant concept for an entirely new medical pharmaceutical treatment therapy. The man who aspired to be president of the company was Dr. Black, an associate professor of genetics at Prestigious University whose specialized area of interest was the biochemistry of genetics. He was articulate, gracious, accommodating, ever patient, and not patronizing when I asked amateurish technical questions. His colleague, Dr. White, was a renowned biochemist and research investigator at Sloan-Kettering whose specialty was RNA. In contrast to Dr. Black, Dr. White was introspective and expressionless, a person who obviously didn't laugh without good reason. The third man, Dr. Grey, a research investigator and assistant professor at the university, specialized in virology, the study of viruses. He was big and hearty and ready to argue about any subject.

These three men believed that RNA, the most fundamental structure in the process of life, could be used to combat disease caused by infection or genetic defect. RNA, in their opinion, could be made to kill viruses or bacteria, or add to or subtract genes from the human genetic structure, or change the hematopoietic balance (the blood system) by altering the blood cell production of bone marrow.

One feature of their theoretical concept was the ability of RNA to stimulate certain human cells in the bone marrow to produce their bioengineered therapeutic RNA for as long as it was needed and useful, then to turn off the cell or shut down its production. This meant that the person under treatment would literally produce his own pharmaceutical. Dr. White had vast experience tinkering with plant RNA or antisense. He had discovered a way to force tomatoes to grow with more solids and less water. There was every reason to believe that human RNA (or antisense) could also be altered to do a number of things including produce certain drugs to combat diseases such as AIDS and hepatitis.

Another aspect of their concept had to do with the recent discovery of a new class of pathogens or infectious disease agents called viroids which may be the tiniest living organisms, even smaller and more primitive than a virus. A viroid is believed to cause Crohn's disease, a nasty flare-up in the bowel which often requires surgery to remove the infected area. President Eisenhower suffered an attack of Crohn's while in office and underwent highly publicized surgery to relieve his symptoms.

The three scientists wanted to name the company Newco Therapies (NT). They were particularly interested in treating viroid diseases because viroids are virtually a pure RNA fragment. They believed NT could develop a perfect therapy against viroids, one that could be rapidly developed. Crohn's disease is rare, but viroids are believed by some to play a triggering role in hepatitis B, causing it to turn lethal. Dr. Black believed they likely existed undetected in the autologous or donor blood supply, that every unit of blood plasma could carry these potentially deadly viroids. Before 1988, no one had heard of viroids.

I left our first meeting with my head spinning. I was unusually euphoric. The NT concept was potentially a blockbuster investment having all the tickets for a big success, including top scientists and world-famous institutions—a univerisity known for spectacular research, and Sloan-Kettering, one of the most famous medical research facilities in the world. The science was timely, important, revolutionary, patentable, and feasible. The market potential was enormous.

My only niggling doubt came from the breath of potential uses of NT's technology. There would have to be strict discipline to avoid taking on too many projects at once. I had a vision of Dr. Black running down the street trying to carry 25 volleyballs, dropping one, then two, then all the rest.

The NT saga never had a brighter day than that first one.

My second meeting one month later centered on the overall plan—the staff, space, spending, timetable, and milestones. A week earlier, Dr. Black had sent me 50 pages of text and numbers thoughtfully portraying a grandiose plan.

Business plans almost always assume that everything will work perfectly in the shortest imaginable time. His plan called for $7.5 million and three years to create two materials, an antiviral and an antiviroid. After spending $7.5 million, they would be able to produce these altered RNA materials in their laboratory and make them available for preliminary animal tests. When I factored in what I thought would be a more realistic timetable, the time became five years and the $7.5 million became $12 to $15 million—way too rich for my pocketbook.

Their plan included an elaborate laboratory costing lots of time and money, to be constructed in a renovated building on the Upper East Side of New York. Dr. Black had contacted the Mayor's office and met with great enthusiasm, encouragement, and the hint that maybe seed money might be available from the City of New York. Listening to him, I could tell that Dr. Black was already dreaming of his picture on page one of the *New York Times* embracing Mayor Koch as they jointly announced this landmark project for the city. As an added benefit, the laboratory would be so located that Dr. Black could easily walk to work. Half the plan's budget was earmarked for this laboratory, the construction of which would additionally cost at least a one-year delay.

Whenever I get a grandiose plan in support of an elegant idea, I restrain my natural inclination to laugh or just say no. I listen patiently instead and through persuasion alone attempt to convince the founders to be reasonable. I'd probably save a lot of time and money by laughing.

It took several more meetings to convince Drs. Black, White, and Grey to scale back spending, hire just enough people to do the work, and compress milestones. I also persuaded Dr. Black to forget Mayor Koch and walking to work, and to find a low-cost laboratory already built somewhere near New

York City. There are many such facilities in Westchester County and New Jersey built as incubators for research projects or abandoned by failed start-up companies whose investors were now looking for a way to salvage a dime.

The next sticking point in our negotiations was Dr. Black's insistence that he be president of NT now and forevermore. I told him I would give him a chance, but history suggested the odds were low that he would make it. I said those words clearly and often but, as it turned out, he didn't hear me.

We finally constructed a plan to get NT into animal testing in two years with an antiviral agent and a viroid diagnostic, no new laboratory, and ten employees, at a cost of $5 million. Even at this reduced level, I needed to syndicate a financing and began the process of showing NT to other venture capitalists able and interested in this area. The investors would get two-thirds of the company, valuing NT at about $8 million. The founders argued for a higher stake but finally agreed to the financial terms.

As other venture capitalists, including the Sunrise group that had introduced me to the company, began to evaluate the investment, a West Coast group sought financing for a vaguely similar technical approach. Sunrise stunned us all by agreeing to invest in the West Coast company and summarily dropped all interest in NT because it was a "potential" conflict of interest.

This action by Sunrise triggered a "what do they know that we don't" reaction among all the venture capitalists looking at NT. Most of them ran for cover, never to be seen again.

Horizons, a venture capital group with particular technical expertise, remained interested in NT believing the West Coast group had inferior technology. But they also had serious concerns about Dr. Black. On several occasions Horizons' venture capitalist, Mr. Blue, urged me to check Dr. Black's references carefully, but steadfastly refused to tell me anything about his own checks. I had already conducted extensive checks on Dr. Black with mixed, though generally favorable, responses. There was nothing to warrant the mystery of Mr. Blue's oblique warning. More curious than concerned, I did some research on Mr. Blue and discovered that both he and his wife were professional colleagues of Dr. Black and that Mr. Blue's wife served on a civic board of trustees with Dr. Grey. Their unexpected relationship and experience explained Mr. Blue's wariness of Dr. Black as well as his reticence to discuss him with me. Actually this extra checking confirmed my conclusions that Dr. Black was personable, honest, and even tempered. He was also single-minded, tedious, adversarial, elitist, and circumspect. These traits are common among brilliant scientists and as they did with most creators, would one day disqualify Dr. Black as president of NT. I was not overly concerned about this; I was more concerned about an entirely different problem. What did Dr. Black bring to NT? The company would not pursue his specialty, gene therapy, for years to come, if ever. Gene manipulation would take five to ten years to develop and of all the potentials of NT's technology would be the most costly to pursue. Dr. Black would be frustrated that the company could not pursue his area of expertise and he could not, other than administratively, contribute anything to the success of the company. Since Dr. Black had no experience whatever as a manager and administrator, I sensed a problem justifying his participation. Dr. Black had organized the plan for the company, however, and Drs. White and Grey pledged their loyal support to his stewardship. There could be no NT without those two men.

By year-end 1989, it was obvious I was not going to be able to raise $5 million to finance the NT plan. The West Coast competitor and the time it was taking to complete the financing were making investors wary. I formally withdrew my support and suggested to Dr. Black that he and his colleagues consider alternatives and that we meet again after the New Year. During this time, Dr. Black desperately sought financing from corporations, foreign institutions, and a few New York fund managers. As is usually the case, a few said no, no one said yes, most said maybe, we'll get back to you on it. I knew there was very little chance anything would come of this activity but Dr. Black was hopeful, if not confident.

At our next meeting, I proposed that NT become a research

project created solely to prove, in existing laboratories at the university and Sloan, that viroids could be detected and destroyed in a test tube. If viroid detection and therapy worked, financing NT would be simpler from both venture capital and pharmaceutical companies.

I stipulated one important caveat, the absolute requirement that once the project started we (I and the three founders) would search for a president with the experience and credibility to build the company and help with subsequent financing. I told Dr. Black we could not raise money around him and said again that he had to accept a lesser role in NT's hierarchy as director of research, not as president. His mouth said he understood and agreed but once again I doubted he meant the words.

The valuation I proposed, half the company for $1 million, met stiff opposition from all three founders. They pointed out that I was willing to take 60 percent for $5 million, so how could I justify 50 percent for $1 million? My answer was, "That was then, this is now." A research project with only $1 million in funding is far riskier than a fully funded company. I expected to be paid for the risk and, if anything, believed my offer to be overly generous. The meeting ended on reasonably friendly terms and with the promise of a quick answer. My last words were that the offer was nonnegotiable and they had one week to decide. The time had come to get going or forget the whole idea. By this time NT was rapidly becoming three-day-old fish.

Two things went wrong before the sun set. Dr. Black asked his lawyer, a man totally ignorant of venture financing, to draft a counteroffer. Dr. Black also contacted several potential investors to say I was in for $1 million, how about you? It might even have been set to Cole Porter's music.

What turned out to be our last meeting occurred a month later. By that time I had received a counteroffer which not only ignored my proposal but asked for a valuation twice that of my offer, a board of directors that gave the founders a voting majority, antidilution for the founders on the next financing, and an absolute veto over any candidate I proposed for president.

I also received telephone calls from two other potential investors who wanted my due diligence reports to assist them in making an investment decision as to putting money alongside my $1 million. Both of them were unsophisticated investors with regard to venture financing and actually planned to syndicate their investment in Europe among a group of wealthy families.

The meeting with Dr. Black was brief and to the point but without acrimony, though I was very angry and disappointed. I withdrew my offer, rejected outright without comment the counteroffer, and related my conversations with NT's potential investors. I reminded Dr. Black that I had warned him my offer was nonnegotiable and wished him luck.

A week later Dr. Black telephoned to say he wanted another "negotiating" meeting and couldn't understand why I was so inflexible. We never met again. Six months later I learned that he was still pursuing capital from foreign sources and including a few corporations. The project was never financed. NT never came into being. Several other companies have been formed to explore this new area including the West Coast operation.

NT was an excellent concept, but failed to get started because the entrepreneurs could not agree to terms and conditions. They had heard the war stories about companies that succeeded such as Genentech and Centocor. They forgot about the hundreds of biotech companies that failed because there wasn't enough time and money to enable them to succeed.

Since 1981, I have refused, after months of careful scrutiny, to invest in hundreds of business proposals. During that same time, I decided to invest in 22 companies and to personally play an active role in helping those companies succeed.

Seven of those companies have completed their venture capital cycle, some successfully though others have failed. Each company passed my investment screen and on the day it opened its doors was filled with great promise and hope. The following seven chapters present the odyssey of each company and some of the drama and dilemma that each faced.

6

Dreams Are Not Enough—Agrion

In the fall of 1981, Tony Frank, then a San Francisco banker (he later became Postmaster General), introduced me to a group of prominent scientists at the University of California at Berkeley. They were convinced that a laboratory curiosity could be converted into a profitable business. I recognized their pride in this discovery and their dream of becoming rich and famous. I know from experience these characteristics are vital to the success of any venture.

Compared to thousands of other scientists I had interviewed, their spokesman, Dr. Burton Dorman, was remarkably articulate. He walked me through their very esoteric discovery so that I could grasp its commercial significance. Without Dorman's vision, this scientific oddity might have remained merely a laboratory curiosity.

The Berkeley scientists had discovered that a substance called psoralen, occurring naturally in plants, was readily absorbed in a test tube by certain, if not all, viruses. This meant that when a tiny amount of psoralen was added to a virus culture, a few molecules of the substance quickly infiltrated every single virus. The viruses and the psoralen then coexisted peacefully until and unless they were activated by a beam of ultraviolet light. When that happened, the psoralen inside each virus instantly reacted with all the DNA or RNA present, cross-linking or coupling the strands together. As a result, the viruses no longer replicated. In biological terms the viruses became immobilized or sterile and thereby ceased living.

I was intrigued by two things, first by the simplicity of the process and second, that these cloistered university scientists recognized this phenomenon could be the basis for a successful business.

Vaccines had traditionally been made by taking living viruses and literally killing them with a noxious chemical called formaldehyde. The dead virus no longer causes sickness but its surface contains the chemical signals that trigger the production of antibodies to fight off the disease. For more than a century this technique had been used to produce vaccines against a wide range of viral and bacterial diseases infecting man and beast. Polio, tuberculosis, mumps, and cholera were conquered by this class of vaccine.

There are two deficiencies in killed live virus vaccines. First the killing agent, formaldehyde, destroys some of the virus's surface chemistry thereby reducing the efficiency of antibody formation after inoculation necessitating multiple vaccinations or perhaps imparting insufficient immunity to a specific disease. The second deficiency arises from formaldehyde's occasional failure to actually kill all the viruses. In this case, the vaccination introduces live, pathogenic viruses thereby causing the disease rather than preventing it. The wonder of psoralen-treated viruses is that they are killed with 100 percent certainty and without any damage to the surface chemistry of the virus.

Based on test-tube results Dorman and his group hypothesized that there would be a significantly greater antibody response to this form of vaccination. The vaccine would be more effective and would be safer.

Dorman proposed to establish a research company to develop a slate of psoralen vaccines against four very different viruses to prove the breadth of the technique. This would involve building a laboratory and hiring a half dozen highly skilled scientists to prove both the safety and efficacy of the psoralen vaccine technology. Dorman figured, and I agreed, that this proof of concept would cost $4.2 million.

The details of the budget were clear and thoughtful, including the scientific staff necessary to do the work, laboratory benches, materials and equipment, administrative costs, and rental of space. There is always clarity in defining a budget; the guesswork comes in deciding how long it will take to get results. A time line looked as shown in Table 6.1.

My investment decision was based on the bet that we could prove efficacy for one vaccine within 18 months, thus enabling me to raise money in a second round of venture capital. The spending, or burn, rate at that point would be $200,000 per month. Six months of slippage would run the company completely out of money.

Intuitively I believed this technology would be very valuable if it worked. I liked Dorman's business strategy—to develop the new vaccines then test them on farm animals. It would be much easier to obtain regulatory approval for vaccines for animals from the Department of Agriculture than from the FDA for use in humans. Time and money would be saved and the psoralen vaccines could be quickly brought to market. The early 1980s was a good time to raise money for biotechnology. The promise of this new technology had exploded on the investment scene because of the huge financial success of companies like Genentech, Biogen, and Cetus. Raising $4.2 million would be easy.

I spent the next two months in due diligence—confirming the quality of the science, the scientists, the markets, and the potential for patents. This included a literature search in scientific journals concerning vaccines, interviews with various Berkeley faculty about the men in question, checking on Dorman's time at Yale, getting an independent appraisal of the patent, asking for a scientific appraisal by biochemistry consultants, reviewing an Arthur D. Little report on animal health markets, reading relevant articles in agricultural trade magazines, and interviewing a marketing executive for a corporation selling therapeutics to the animal health industry. My conclu-

TABLE 6.1 *Time Line for the Development of Psoralen*

Time	Start	3 Months	6 Months	9 Months	12 Months	15 Months	18 Months	21 Months	24 Months
Milestones	Close financing	Lab completed	Staff hired	Virus cultured	First vaccine	• Animal testing • Second vaccine	• Third vaccine • Efficacy proved first vaccine • Refinance	• Fourth vaccine • Efficacy proved second vaccine	• Efficacy proved third vaccine
Remaining Cash	$4.2	$4.0	$3.8	$3.4	$3.0	$2.3	$1.6	$0.8	$0.0

Note: Dollar amounts are in millions.

sions were mostly positive. As always, there was the niggling anxiety that accompanies any venture investment decision, especially one that hinges on a scientific theory.

The probability of strong patents looked solid. Each psoralen vaccine was patentable individually. However, my patent lawyer and technical consultants pointed out that other chemicals might work as well or better. If and when they were discovered, these analogues, as they are called, might be outside the scope of our patents. These cautions were what I call "fear of phantoms," the unknown that jangles nerves when making an investment decision. The concern is always there. People who can't handle this acute anxiety should stay out of the venture game. They don't call it risk capital for nothing.

In my venture capital life, I have learned that building companies solely around brilliant scientists is always problematical. Academicians, without business experience, regularly become bogged down in the beauty and symmetry of the science rather than its application. Despite this, our plan did not include an experienced business person for some time to come, a decision based on the fact that there would be nothing for this person to do until we knew what we had. I would serve as the interim businessman. In retrospect this decision could have been a fatal flaw.

Further examinations revealed that the market for animal vaccines was actually surprisingly small, around $200 million. I had intuitively assumed from my casual exposure to the industry that the market would be over $1 billion. I found that the market for vaccines for farm animals, or large animals as they are called, had been saturated. For the past decade there had been no real growth and profit margins were meager. The small animal, or companion animal (dogs and cats) vaccine market was about $75 million for the producer. Though profitable, selling small animal vaccines required an extensive sales organization in order to detail veterinarians. Based on this information, we decided Agrion's initial work should focus on large animals, later on small animals, and ultimately, vaccines for humans.

Despite my niggling anxiety, I went about raising the $4.2 million while continuing my due diligence. Dorman's attorneys drew up the contracts and other documents required to form the company and to provide for the equity ownership of the investors. The $4.2 million cash came from my investors and a corporation. The three founders, a scientific advisory board, and future employees were also given shares in exchange for their psoralen technology and future work. These shares are the "sweat equity" for the people whose job it is to make the company succeed. The cash investors received only 40 percent of the company, which made it a very rich deal for the founders but consistent with the "hot market" that existed in biotechnology in 1981. (Under normal circumstances the investors would have received at least 60 percent for a start-up such as this.) With this financing the company was created and valued at a little over $10 million since the investors paid $4.2 million for 40 percent.

Three additional men, two key scientists and a CPA (Dorman's neighbor and a childhood friend), were hired. A board of directors was appointed consisting of Dorman, Tony Frank (who brought me the deal), me and, in what could be characterized as a moment of whimsy, Dorman's father, a retired businessman from southern California. It was with the Agrion investment that I learned conclusively what I should have already known—nepotism is unhealthy to the workings of a board of directors.

The financing closed on New Year's Eve 1981 and the company was launched. Our first board of directors meeting, held a month later, was little more than a celebration of our expected success. Our collective euphoria enabled each of us to transform individual dreams into an expectation of vast rewards. After the board meeting we had dinner at a nearby restaurant. I fell down a dimly lit staircase on the way to the men's room. Although unhurt, I should have recognized that incident as an omen.

It took four months to build the laboratory, acquire the equipment, and hire the right people. It was a thrill for me to visit our new company and tour rooms filled with shiny laboratory benches, awesome equipment, and instruments. The virus containment area was the highlight. It was built to avoid any danger from working with live, pathogenic viruses. Everyone visiting that area had to dress in a white hat, gown, and mask. This made me feel even more certain that we were doing important work. Much later I realized that the entry to the virus containment area looked just like the orgasmatron in Woody Allen's movie, *Sleeper*. That was always good for a laugh in the tough times that lay ahead.

We continued to have monthly board meetings though the laboratory was not finished and no work was under way. These meetings were a rehash of what we were *going* to do. Soon I began making weekly phone calls to Dorman for status reports. They were void of any scientific progress. This was Agrion's golden period of self-delusion. Though I realized nothing was happening, I kept setting myself up to be encouraged and excited. After all, I represented the interests of investors who put up $4.2 million solely on my say so.

Almost a year later Dorman informed the board that a vaccine produced by psoralen inactivation had worked in a challenged animal (an animal exposed to the virus). Unfortunately, the disease the vaccine prevented was very rare and there was little or no sales potential for it. By this time I had absorbed a lot of buzz words, including "challenged," that gave me comfort and the conviction that I knew what was going on. I learned about hoof-and-mouth disease, blue tongue, enteritis, and shipping fever. I called pigs "swine," bulls "bovine," and horses "equine." I learned about doses and adjuvants, serum titers and antigens. In reality, the biology was so esoteric I was, despite my new vocabulary, technologically illiterate.

In 1983 we heard about a major market opportunity based on a new cat disease called feline leukemia. This silent cat killer was caused by a virus, always fatal, and not a pretty death. The 75,000,000 cats kept as household pets and treated by veterinarians were obviously a big market. Agrion scientists believed they could develop a feline leukemia vaccine and quickly capture a market for at least a third of the 75,000,000 cats. We believed the vaccine would sell for $10 a dose to vets who would sell it to cat lovers for about $50 a dose. Our cost per dose would be about five cents. Multiplying that out, we saw that Agrion could become very profitable.

In our excitement we overlooked a few things: We had no idea if a psoralen inactivated vaccine for feline leukemia could be developed or, if developed, would work, or if it could be sold for $50 a dose, or if it could be manufactured in production quantities. A Ph.D. scientist mixing psoralen with a live virus in a test tube then shining a beam of ultraviolet light on it was one thing. Making 25,000,000 doses a year in production was quite another.

Then a number of important technical developments went wrong, any one of which could have been fatal to Agrion and my $4.2 million investment. This is the "pit-in-the-stomach" phase of venture investing. First, the feline leukemia vaccine Agrion developed did not work. When it was injected in cats some resisted the disease but most died and, worst of all, we weren't sure why.

Our initial cash would be depleted in a year. The development work necessary to produce vaccines was more than a year behind our original business plan. More money than anticipated was needed just as the promise of biotechnology was waning among investors.

Dorman's management style was intense, very deliberate, and painstakingly thorough. He was wearing down the organization. Dorman had a falling out with his principal scientific collaborator and this relationship of many years ended after bitter disagreements over scientific approaches. The two men no longer spoke to each other although neither told me about the problem for six months.

The original money was gone by the end of 1984, and I was unable to attract new capital to continue the development work. Based on my continued faith in the technology, I made a highly risky (in hindsight I prefer to call it gutsy or visionary) decision to put $2 million more of my investors' money into this company in the hope that the necessary technical breakthroughs were just around the corner. It would then be easy to attract new capital from new investors.

Meetings with the company became increasingly frustrating to everyone. There were always glib management explanations as to why our vaccines (such as the one for feline leukemia) hadn't worked but would work after the next modification, while our other vaccines that did work didn't have any market but were easy to make.

While Dorman was a brilliant scientist, by 1985 I concluded he was the wrong person to run the company. I made no secret of the fact that we desperately needed someone with commercial and management experience to take over. Dorman and all the other board members vigorously disagreed with my assessment. Over the next six months we had heated debates that always wound up with the usual bromide—"hope for the best." I had learned by then that hoping for a technological breakthrough is akin to praying for a miracle.

Despite our professional problems, my personal relationship with Dorman flourished. I respected his honesty, brilliance, and humanity. I became well acquainted with his family which was a wondrous experience in itself. His four children, then aged 6 to 12, are all prodigies and outgoing, loving, and interested in and knowledgeable of an incredible range of activities. Each child was an accomplished musician on one or more instruments, sang like a bird and spoke at least one other language. Each also had a specialty—ceramics, painting, dance, and one, the youngest, computer science.

Dorman, who doesn't believe in making things too easy, bought a PC for this child without any application software. It was the boy's job to create his own which he did with little parental assistance. Agrion later hired this son, then aged eight, to help sequence the genetic codes needed for our vaccine development. We paid him the minimum wage. (This time nepotism worked.) Dorman's wife, an artist, cook, and wonderful parent, was during this time illustrating a cookbook as well as keeping up with her progeny and perspicacious husband. I'll never forget the Dorman dinners I attended preceded by music and song, with gourmet food interrupted by stimulating conversation among children and adults alike.

Luckily for Agrion we did hire an experienced director of marketing. He was brilliant from a theoretical point of view. He understood the markets and the potential value of our technology. Working with Dorman, he put together very aggressive marketing plans that were to lead, inexorably, to a very large profitable business three years in the future. His plans counted on scientific progress but there was no consideration of how to mass produce the vaccines. With each passing business quarter, the three-year market forecast remained a constant. Management just pushed the numbers out to match delays in solving technical problems.

Agrion was in a shambles by the end of 1985. I was rapidly losing all hope that the project would ever work. I was, in fact, rapidly losing confidence in my own judgment. Was I wrong to believe the technology was useful and would be developed with additional time and money? I had put $2 million more of my venture funds into financing operating losses in the belief that the feline leukemia vaccine looked promising.

The biggest blow came early in 1986 when a competitor, the Norden division of SmithKline French, introduced their version of a feline leukemia vaccine and beat us to the market. We had been right. The vaccine was big and profitable—but not for us.

Agrion was bogged down in the worst possible black hole—no money, no products, and growing discontent within the company and between management and me. We were in a moment of utter despair. I was beginning to face the bleak prospect of having to write off over $6 million and wind up the company in bankruptcy.

Then a miracle happened. It began with a chance meeting with the senior management of the Pioneer Hi-Bred seed company of Des Moines, Iowa. This very successful and dominant producer of corn seed was looking for ways to diversify the company's activities. Novel vaccines for farm animals fit their strategy perfectly. There was immediate chemistry between Agrion and the executives from Pioneer.

At that same moment, Syntex, a billion-dollar pharmaceutical company, decided to unload its animal vaccine business. By a lucky coincidence it was also located in Des Moines, Iowa. The Syntex animal health business had never been profitable despite over $40 million invested in manufacturing facilities, laboratories, and offices. They wanted to sell this division for $25 million and, among a dozen buyers, including Pioneer (which is how we met), it was also offered to Agrion.

The offer was a joke since Agrion was nearly bankrupt. I judged, however, that Syntex would have difficulty finding a buyer willing to pay anything near $25 million for their losing business. I was right. Three months later their employees started to quit and three months after that Syntex dismissed its entire sales organization. Their company in Iowa was on the verge of total collapse. There were no buyers.

With great fear and trembling combined with a lot of moxie, we made an offer to buy out what remained for about $6.5 million. Syntex swallowed hard and agreed. We swallowed even harder since we had no idea of how to get $6.5 million. Banks might be reckless enough to loan us part of the money based on the asset value of the property and buildings, but there would be millions of dollars of shortfall to cover. Even worse, the losses incurred by Agrion would be added to those of Syntex. Neither business had any revenue as an offset.

Then the second half of the miracle happened. Tom Freeze, former president of Fort Dodge Pharmaceuticals, a division of American Home Products, indicated an interest in joining Agrion. He was widely recognized as a leader in animal health products. His requirement was the acquisition of the Syntex operation. He recognized we needed a facility to build a business. Freeze possessed a lifetime of relevant experience. His desire to join Agrion gave us the confidence to renew efforts to find the money to buy Syntex. With it we felt Agrion could instantly become a successful business. It would have an established name and a manufacturing facility to launch new psoralen products. Once again we all had that manic swing from utter depression to total excitement. Unfortunately I was totally unsuccessful in finding new money to invest in Agrion. Then unexpectedly Pioneer said they would invest. In record time (45 days) they put up $6 million in cash and cosigned a $12 million revenue bond issue that enabled Agrion to buy out the Syntex operation, fund near-term losses, and rebuild the facility to suit our new products.

This all took place so fast it is still hard for me to believe it happened. It was like being reprieved by an angel from certain ignominious death. Almost overnight Agrion went from the brink of bankruptcy to the opportunity to build a successful business. We were exhausted from slapping each other on the back. We boasted that none of our peers could take biotechnology out of the laboratory into a commercial success. We held a testimonial dinner in Des Moines with our new executive, Freeze, the gang from Pioneer all breathless from having just signed the checks, and me and Dorman looking mighty smug. That night I set aside any further thoughts of dumping Dorman.

I didn't fall down the stairs during that dinner, but I might as well have for our dream was utterly shattered three months later. Our losses in restarting the Des Moines business were far greater than we had imagined. We had underestimated the difficulties of manufacturing and bringing products to market. We also made a critical error in timing. We tried to launch the business just as the seasonal downturn in demand for large animal vaccines began. Why didn't we know this? We just hadn't asked the right persons the right questions. We certainly had the talent and experience on board to have foreseen this insuperable problem.

Two months later, in February 1987, five months into the new operation, we were once again at the brink of total disaster. The company was out of money and, even worse, late in paying its bills. Dorman was working 70-hour weeks trying to push the business to success. He continued to reassure both Pioneer and me that everything would be all right.

Huge internal problems developed. Dorman and Freeze were at loggerheads. Freeze completely disagreed with Dorman's direction and vision. Dorman continued to believe in overoptimistic forecasts and in his ability to get local bank financing to cover losses. Freeze disavowed Dorman's forecasts but took no initiative in developing plans and estimates he could support. He detached himself from the problem by blaming others, especially Dorman. Neither man trusted the other.

It became absolutely clear to me and to Pioneer that Dorman could no longer be the chief executive officer of the company. Aside from all the other problems, Dorman lived in California and the company was in Des Moines. During an emotional board meeting in early March of 1987, acting on behalf of the investor shareholders who owned the majority of the company, I fired Dorman from his position as chief executive officer and the three other board members, including Dorman's father, who continued to support him. This moment not only devastated Dorman and his constituency, but nearly devastated the company. Dorman was under such tremendous strain that it took him several months to accept his fate and the legal right of the majority shareholders to oust him from his job. I became acting chief executive officer. Pioneer and I each put in another $2 million bringing our total investment to $14 million in Agrion since inception. We felt, once again, that given proper financing and human resources we could set the company straight.

I became interim chief executive officer to smooth the transition from Dorman's leadership to the Des Moines-based leadership. Freeze was to become chief executive officer in a year.

The next nine months were a nightmare of missed forecasts, overspending, and such a poor accounting system that we didn't even know how we were losing our money. Furthermore, there was an economic disaster in United States farming that made sales of vaccines for large animals more dismal than ever.

Gradually, piece by piece, we began to solve the manufacturing problems, cost problems, and quality problems. The entire staff attacked the problems in parallel. The financial people developed, revised, and finally installed a cost accounting system that worked. This required immediate price increases in products we had thought profitable but that turned out to be big losers. We didn't lose a single customer.

Research and development people worked in the factory, teaching the new production workers how to work consistently, to control all the variables such as temperature and ingredients, and to measure precisely the passage of time. This research and development exposure to the factory had an additional benefit. Our scientists learned firsthand about production problems and were able to go back to their laboratories and improve the processes.

The biggest help to operating the business came from stabilizing or fixing the sales forecasting technique. The manufacturing cycle took two months from start to finish, so the vaccine-in-process couldn't be increased or decreased or changed to a different vaccine without discarding the entire batch. The salespeople, trying to grow territories and eager to please, had influenced the manufacturing people to change direction every week. We stopped what should have been an obvious stupid operating mode, developed a two-month forecast system, and stuck to it.

By mid-1987 we could produce products that were well accepted in the marketplace. Furthermore, the feline leukemia vaccine and the other important novel vaccines for the pet market started to look very promising. This was, again, just in the nick of time. The investor group was nearly at the end of its patience and courage.

I had always believed in my heart that Pioneer would eventually buy Agrion. Between direct cash infusions and cosigning the bond issue, they had invested a total of $20 million. In the fall of 1987 I began to negotiate with Pioneer executives about the purchase. Over the next six months, Pioneer went from enthusiasm to passing interest in a merger. The diversification strategy Pioneer had embarked on some years before had not proven to be successful. The Pioneer board was seriously divided over whether or not it was a good idea to do anything except be the best producer of corn seed in the world. The corporate climate within Pioneer about veterinary pharmaceuticals changed from bright, shiny optimism to cold indifference. Only one senior executive saw merit in an animal vaccine business and he was reluctant to impose his decision on the operating business management. There was nothing for me to do but hope enlightenment would strike the board. Meanwhile I began looking for another buyer.

Once again fate intervened. In late 1987 the multibillion-dollar Bayer Company of Leverkusen, Germany, contacted me and we started preliminary merger discussions. Bayer, already in the United States animal health business, quickly understood that novel vaccines could help them become dominant in the United States and in world markets. Biotechnology and research advances in infectious diseases combined with a growing concern over the use of antibiotics in food animals made vaccines a much more attractive alternative than they had been in the last 20 years. It was becoming clear to researchers in pharmaceutical companies that a new class of therapeutics could be developed based on vaccine technology. It had become possible to inoculate animals, including humans, with a therapeutic vaccine not only to prevent, but also to treat, disease.

Our first serious merger discussion with Bayer took place in Des Moines, Iowa, in February 1988. With Bayer's obvious interest, I felt we could consummate a merger by early summer. It turned out I had a better chance hoping for world peace.

Bayer was organizationally unable to come to a rapid decision, though it was clear they wanted to go ahead. I came up with an idea that eased our anxiety. In return for not shopping Agrion to other potential buyers, Bayer agreed to pay $5 million for an option to buy the company by February 15, 1989. Both sides expected that Bayer would complete the transaction by early December 1988 or, at the latest, by year-end.

Mergers are always very frustrating and debilitating. Since every Agrion employee was a shareholder, they all stood to make a lot of money. The initial rush of excitement over the potential merger carried both an economic and a psychic reward. There was relief that a large corporation was going to support Agrion and help it to become a major entity.

When negotiations bogged down, rumors of a collapse of the merger were rampant and dreams of rewards became nightmares. With the passage of time people's hopes waned and the majority began to believe the merger would fall through. The prospect was frightening. No one from senior management right down to the ranks was immune from fear. One key employee actually quit in December 1988 to take another job. By leaving at this crucial moment for our company, he walked away from hundreds of thousands of dollars of unvested stock. But who knew for sure that the merger would take place?

These anxieties and disappointments exist in every merger process and they are especially troublesome when the acquiring company is foreign. There is a built-in mistrust of people from another country. Equivocation or indecision is interpreted to mean the worst.

The white-knuckle wait for Bayer took an enormous toll. And there was another catastrophe. The minority shareholders, Dorman and his original coterie of shareholders, became increasingly frantic about the proposed merger transaction, believing that the dilution of stock that had taken place after they left the company was not fair. They also believed that Pioneer had, through the years, taken unfair advantage of their business relationship with Agrion. Consequently, Dorman hired a tough San Francisco law firm to raise troublesome legal issues in a most unfriendly and untimely way. Along with the legal documentation and negotiations surrounding the merger with Bayer, we were now forced to spend considerable time researching issues raised by minority shareholders. This, in fact, took more effort than the Bayer deal. After thousands of dollars were spent answering questions and examining documents, at my instruction my law firm told the minority shareholders they had no basis for any settlement or special treatment. That was my decision, not supported by my lawyers. It worked. Dorman and his group dropped their lawsuit.

As the merger transaction proceeded toward a closing date, the capricious gods of venture capital decided on a new form of torture. Agrion had submitted a series of vaccines for cats to the USDA. They included a feline leukemia vaccine which was finally approved in late 1988, two years later than originally forecast.

Agrion was notified by the USDA in January 1989, a month before the Bayer option deadline, that a combination dosage of vaccines for cats had failed clinical tests. We had immediately to notify Bayer. Naturally they became very concerned. A few weeks later the USDA informed us that their test procedure was invalid and the vaccine had not failed, but by federal regulations they still had to retest it completely. It hadn't failed the test, but it also hadn't passed. Though the USDA's admission that they had botched the test gave us a sense of relief, it also meant 90 days of additional testing before approval. A Bayer executive told me they would not complete the merger without the retest and asked for an extension of the purchase option from February 15 to May 15.

We had been negotiating for a year. Agrion morale was at an all time low. I realized that a further delay in completing the merger could demoralize the Agrion organization so badly that the whole enterprise might go under. After consultation with other board members, I told Bayer that we would not extend the option. They had to complete the merger by February 15 or we would pursue other alternatives. The risk to us was that Bayer would drop out and our other alternatives were bleak. We held our collective breaths for a week. Agrion management, headed by Freeze, threatened to quit if I didn't give in to Bayer's demands. I told Freeze to shove it. This was no time for ultimatums.

The very next day Bayer announced it would proceed with the merger. Our shareholders received payment a week later. The closing took less than three hours, a new world record, at least in my experience. The lawyers, with nothing better to do during the wait had whiled away their time by completing all the documents. They knew they'd get paid the same fee regardless of the outcome.

This was the only time in my venture capital career I have seen so many incredible, unpredictable problems, spanning so many years, conclude with a happy ending. When this many terrible problems occur, it is axiomatic that the company will fail soon thereafter. In this case, however, the conclusion united everyone with a great sense of accomplishment and well-being.

The happy ending was no accident. All of us worked very hard and had the courage to face adversity. We also had a lot of luck. What pulled me through my moments of utter despair was the conviction that Agrion had something special and important.

Bayer paid $65 million for Agrion—a company founded on a laboratory curiosity. Our investors earned four times on their money, the total cash reward among the highest they ever gained in a venture investment.

In a happy postscript, Dorman and I renewed our friendship and I am advising him in his new start-up company called Acrogen. He personally made over $4 million in the Agrion deal and believes he can do it again. This time, however, he knows that dreams are not enough.

7

They Built a Better Mousetrap—Visic

The most attractive and appealing venture capital opportunity I ever reviewed was in 1983, for a company called Visic. It was immediately obvious to me that the two founders had a business concept that was important and unique. Both had distinguished careers filled with notable accomplishments and their targeted business area, semiconductors, was a huge, accessible industry run by people eager for something new. It appeared that they were onto something revolutionary. I know of no other business where technology dominates profitability as it does in semiconductor companies. During the 1980s, new technology made a hundredfold increase possible in chip density or power. This productivity was achieved in volume production with virtually no increase in unit cost. I believed Visic had discovered a better way to further improve semiconductor performance.

My investment decision process began in mid-1983 when Jack Balletto, who had created a wonderfully successful semiconductor company called VTI, introduced me to Visic. Balletto brought Hambrecht & Quist new deals or investment ideas on a regular basis. We believed that he knew about every new semiconductor product hatched in Silicon Valley. Most of them seemed to emanate from the bar at Rickey's Hyatt, a hotel in Palo Alto, a hangout for entrepreneurs and their groupies.

Balletto was thrilled to be the self-appointed chairman of the world's most important venture capital network. He eagerly passed judgment on the merits of start-up companies, the quality of the people who worked at them, the importance of the technology employed, and the potential of their worldwide markets. He fashioned himself into a one-man fount of due diligence. Why not? Balletto was engaging, knowledgeable, shrewd, very funny, and he had already made millions founding VTI.

By the time Balletto introduced me to Joel Karp and John Reed, the two founders who wanted to create Visic, I was already well briefed about their backgrounds. They had worked together for 20 years designing semiconductor chips. They held dozens of patents. Most important, their chip designs were widely used by the world's leading semiconductor companies such as Intel and National Semiconductor. I was particularly intrigued by their extraordinary contacts and their personal insights into the current directions and global needs of the semiconductor industry.

They had been making a good living as consultants, but in 1983, when they invented a novel chip design that they believed would double or triple the speed of memory circuits with no increase in cost, they readily quit it all to create Visic. Their discovery meant that a computer could complete memory iterations twice as fast at current costs, or could maintain its old speed with half the chips and therefore half the cost. Chips cost three to five dollars. Computers use 5 to 25 chips. Both Visic alternatives were obviously attractive.

The two men had worked out the pecking order by the time we met. They decided that Karp would be president and chief executive officer while Reed would be executive vice president and technical director.

At that first meeting I asked one of my standard questions: "Why do nice guys like you want to tackle the horrendous task of starting up a company?" They both answered thoughtfully and in vivid detail. In summary, their reasons were:

- *To make megabucks*. They were both tired of watching second-rate guys like Balletto become multimillionaires while they settled for the nickels and dimes due consultants. At that, they were well paid, $1000 a day, and all the work they wanted.
- *To build a company with a heart and soul*. They believed they could create a company that would be humane, exciting, and challenging, void of the crippling bureaucracies that burdened all other semiconductor companies. Visic's culture would enable Karp and Reed to attract the best and brightest employees from anywhere in the world.

Both men substantiated these two goals with dozens of vivid, compelling, and credible examples. I didn't tell them that the majority of entrepreneurs I interview believe they will make megabucks and create paradise in the workplace.

The most powerful and lasting first impression I had of Joel Karp was that he was believable in a very charismatic way. He had a personal third reason to start Visic.

- *It was preordained to succeed*. Karp told me he planned to donate much of his financial reward to the Maharishi. I've heard these pledges before and wasn't put off by it. Besides, anything legal that would motivate Karp to work 80 hours a week was fine with me. Messianic sounded better than the grandiosity I usually encounter. Anyone wanting to start up a semiconductor company in 1983 had to be a little nuts—along with the venture capitalist who backed them.

Over the next 90 days, I met with Karp and Reed a dozen times to discuss business strategy and develop a financing plan. Meanwhile, I started checking on them as well as their concept for a company. I interviewed executives at Texas Instruments, Intel, Ricoh, GE, RCA, and VTI who had firsthand knowledge of Karp and Reed. Everyone agreed that these guys were among the best in their field. Their glowing endorsements were especially impressive because all of them had worked with them or successfully used their designs.

At one of our meetings I clearly told Karp that the odds he would successfully lead this company all the way through its climb to success were statistically low. I was willing to give him a fair chance, but he had to accept the fact that he might have to step down as president. I explained that Visic deserved the best possible chief executive officer and in the long run that might not be Karp. Right from the beginning, I tell every founder the same thing but few hear or believe the words.

Developing Visic's business strategy was very difficult and extremely important. Karp and Reed were vehement about two principles. They absolutely had to have their own foundry or production facility to make chips. They also demanded that Visic hire a process engineering staff right from the start to begin translating chip designs to a manufacturable process. Nothing else would do. They believed a foundry vital, a matter of life and death for Visic to be in control of the entire manufacturing process. They could see no other way to achieve the quality, cost, and yields necessary to make Visic successful.

A new state-of-the-art foundry costs $50 to $200 million depending on the capacity and level of automation. Japanese and Korean companies were building a half dozen of these new $200 million factories. The Japanese were determined to dominate the U.S. market by owning the lowest cost manufacturing capability, then dumping the selling price. Semiconductor production worldwide, however, was entering a slump and operating at less than half its capacity.

A $50-plus million foundry for Visic was a strategic and financial impossibility, too rich for venture capital. Since raising money by going public would be very difficult or impossible during this downward cycle in the semiconductor business, there was no possible way to borrow the money or lease-finance the facility.

Before I would invest, I told Visic, it had to find an alternative way to design, produce, and market chips without building a foundry. I discovered that the technology risk was formidable. The chip had to be designed and prototyped before we could be certain the Karp/Reed invention really worked. Karp zealously promoted a strategy to build a process engineering and marketing organization in parallel with the design effort. His fear was that the passage of time could be fatal. If

Visic didn't quickly commercialize this concept, another group with a fast chip would likely beat us to the market. We knew of no such company but semiconductor lore is filled with frightening "bones on the beach" stories about situations in which technology became obsolete overnight. Karp's plan called for $10 million to be spent before we knew what we had. I wouldn't take that gamble and insisted on a serial strategy: First, prove the technology works, then build process engineering, then build marketing capability. If they wanted me to write a check, they had to accede to my demands.

My challenge was to find alternatives that met my investment criteria that Karp and Reed could accept enthusiastically. Despite his reassurances I never felt that Karp supported anything except an all-out effort. The concept was so promising, however, that I was willing to take a chance on Karp.

My strategy was to create milestones that would have to be met before additional funds would be invested.

The first milestone was the development of a working prototype chip, financed through what was then a tax-advantaged R&D partnership. We would raise $4 million, the amount we believed adequate to fund the chip design. If it worked, we would find a way to finance the next milestone. If it didn't work the investors would at least get half their money back through tax credits.

Milestone One provided for hiring about 25 people, leasing space for laboratories, and purchasing a sophisticated computer design system to create the millions of precise details in the chip's circuit design. The $4 million would last for about 15 months. I made no promise to fund Visic beyond Milestone One. My offer was structured to give the investors 60 percent of the company, thereby valuing Visic at $6.7 million ($4 million divided by 60 percent). Karp, Reed, and the rest of the employees that would be hired would get stock worth $2.7 million, at least on paper.

The investors were granted three seats on the board of directors, the employees two. There was never any doubt that the investors controlled the board.

A key element of Visic's business strategy during Milestone

One was to find a corporate partner with surplus foundry capacity. The hope was that the corporate partner would produce "super" chips for which Visic would pay a reasonable cost, plus grant to this partner the right to use some of the technology in certain of its own products.

This scheme gave away a portion of Visic's birthright, but it also avoided spending $50 to $100 million to build and to hire dozens of production engineers and train hundreds of workers. As part of Milestone One, the investors demanded that the corporate partner be in place before the $4 million ran out. Milestone Two financing hinged on the chip working and having production capacity set aside for Visic.

In theory, at Milestone Two Visic would be able to "ramp-up and roll-out" their exciting new product quickly. This was Silicon Valley insiders' talk. It sounded to me like *Wagon Train* dialogue, but I was happy to be aboard on the way to Death Valley.

Karp and Reed tried hard to find a better alternative to my milestone financing proposal, with no luck. In the end they accepted, but not in their hearts.

The financing closed on New Year's Eve 1983. Greylock Management, one of the top venture capital groups in the world, joined me in the investment. One of their partners, Dave Strohm, was elected to the board of directors. Larry Sonsini, of Silicon Valley's leading law firm, Wilson, Sonsini, Goodrich & Rosati, agreed to be Visic's lawyer. As a newborn, Visic's pedigree was as good as it gets.

The company started business in surplus space at VTI, then the leading candidate for corporate partner. The first board meeting was also held there and, for the most part was a celebration of the birth of Visic, complete with Moët champagne paid for out of the $4 million in the bank.

During the first six months of operations, there were countless other reasons for celebration. Visic leased space in a prominent and trendy new building. It was perfectly sized to accommodate the administration, design, development, and engineering activities for the next 25 years. (As in all start-ups, the space was way too big unless the company was a big success. Then it would be way too small.) We celebrated the opening of the building. I remember thinking that the size of the signs and the elaborate security system were overdone. By this time I certainly knew Karp had champagne taste as well as some serious flaws in business judgment.

The first major dispute I had with Karp was over his candidate for sales manager who, it turned out, had already accepted the job. The board authorized hiring a marketing manager which Karp interpreted as including a sales manager. Visic had nothing to sell. The company badly needed a marketing manager to help with product planning and strategy. One venture capital rule is don't let engineers totally design a product for they will make what they think the market wants, seldom the same as what the majority of customers really want.

Out of courtesy but in shock, I interviewed the sales manager who turned out to have only two years of relevant experience as a distributor's representative, selling a broad product line of electronic components all out of a large catalogue. None of the products he handled were new entrees; they were all undifferentiated commodities. Prior to selling electronics, he had been a sales manager for consumer electronics (Walkmen and woofers) and a door-to-door vacuum cleaner sales representative. He was bright and successful at what he did but clearly not what Visic needed. I "unhired" the man immediately and attacked Karp sharply for his poor judgment and for acting without board authorization. He defended the man as someone he could work with, meaning, I believe, that he would do what he was told. Karp believed the product he was creating was so spectacular he didn't need quality marketing or salespeople, just a big stick to keep eager customers from storming the product warehouse.

Soon after this we hired Peter Bagnell as director of marketing. Though deferring hiring a marketing and sales organization until Milestone Two, we needed an experienced, credible marketing executive to help define precisely the products to be made. Bagnell, then a Motorola executive, was widely recognized as one of the top marketing people in the semiconductor industry. His reference checks were outstanding, including a wonderful commendation from the president of VTI. Heads turned and the perception of Visic materially improved when Bagnell signed on. He validated Visic's plans and products. Many people believed Visic must have something very special to attract Bagnell.

We all wanted him. The entire board of directors not only interviewed Bagnell but we put on a full-court press to enhance our chances of hiring him.

We had another celebration when we hired a half dozen outstanding chip designers. As I hoped, Karp's charisma and Reed's steadiness attracted the best people. It was another validation for Visic's exciting potential.

We celebrated when a leading specialty semiconductor company, Monolithic Memories, surfaced as an eager corporate partner. Now we had not only VTI but a second suitor competing for Visic's hand. Irwin Federman, Monolithic Memories' chief executive officer, eventually joined Visic's board of directors. This was the best stamp of approval. Federman was widely known as shrewd and having an excellent nose for the best deals. Visic had become the hottest little company around.

The board of directors met monthly. The initial meetings were well organized, the presentations were crisp, the attitudes were friendly, constructive, and harmonious. I visited the company weekly, usually without notice.

The warts started to appear six months into the operation. By this time the board of directors realized that too much space had been rented, not only wasting money but contributing to sloppiness. The company utilized empty areas with atriums, glamorous conference rooms, elaborate security systems, and a lavish reception area. Money was being spent on trappings.

Negotiations with VTI bogged down. An agreement on manufacturing capacity was crucial. VTI wanted too much money both for pilot development support and for future production. Karp spent valuable time trying to find ways to limit the technology going to VTI while making them believe they were getting what they wanted.

When I entered the negotiations as a facilitator, I sensed that the heart of the impasse was Karp's hatred and mistrust of the VTI people. In my judgment, this was completely unwarranted by any facts. It was a case of bad chemistry between Karp and the VTI people, coupled with a last desperate attempt to justify building a Visic foundry.

Negotiations proceeded well with Monolithic Memories and concluded with an excellent contract. Monolithic Memories, however, did not have any surplus manufacturing capacity. It would be at least two years before their plant expansion was completed. Visic needed VTI, not a contract with Monolithic Memories. I finally succeeded in bringing both sides to a compromise agreement.

VTI would produce chips for test and confirmation. Both companies would collaborate on the final production process which clearly would take everyone's collective skill because the chip design was so complicated. VTI would manufacture production quantities of chips at cost plus 40 percent on a "take or pay" basis. This meant that Visic had either to buy the finished chips or pay severe penalties. In return, VTI was allowed to use Visic technology in its ASIC designs but not as a direct chip competitor. This was a fair contract but Karp continued to believe that VTI would steal his technology and give it away to its customers, a worry that turned out to be groundless. The development work got under way at once.

Technical progress ran ahead of schedule. With each passing week, the results made Visic's future look more promising. In less than one year, the company was edging toward tangible proof that the "super" chips would operate twice as fast as any other chip ever made.

We got an unpleasant surprise when Karp told the board that he had bought an ELXSI computer which he believed to be the best for the mathematical calculations required to complete the chip design. ELXSI was itself a start-up computer company. The machine was expensive, had incomplete software, and was useless for routine computer work such as accounting and word processing. We had to buy another computer system for these purposes and struggled to use the

ELXSI system for the sophisticated number crunching. The board knew Visic would waste a lot of money performing computations.

When the Monolithic Memories agreement was in hand but not signed, Karp aligned himself with its chief, Federman, who became a director of Visic. He told me he believed Federman, a long-time semiconductor man, would be sympathetic and not a financial roustabout like me and the other outside directors. I learned later that Karp liked Federman because he had no technical training. He had come to be president of Monolithic Memories from being the chief financial officer. Karp felt more comfortable with nontechnical people because he absolutely could not stand anyone criticizing his scientific judgment. Karp then hired a Federman protégé as chief financial officer. Quickly there was an obvious polarization on the board. The relationship with Karp chilled the venture capitalists overnight.

After ten months in operation, major personnel problems erupted. I could hear a din of grumbling from everyone during my weekly visits. Visic's most talented designer quit after being forced to work during the Thanksgiving holiday. Then Reed and Karp had a verbal blowout in front of many employees complete with highly personal invectives. From that moment on, Karp was negative about everything Reed did or said. Reed was ultimately forced off the board. It was sad and worrisome to see a 20-year relationship disintegrate.

I never understood how these two men could work together so closely for all those years and then in the Visic setting come to hate each other. Unlike Karp, Reed was reserved, a good listener, patient, and quietly friendly. Karp's management style was that of a Prussian officer, Reed was a team player. Karp complained about everything, Reed tried to smooth problems over. The biggest difference was that Karp was far more aggressive and current about semiconductor technology. Reed, a conservative, became increasingly cynical about Karp's boasts of Visic's potential. Karp felt Reed was losing his nerve in the blistering pace of new technology. The situation went from bad to worse.

Ironically, Reed's last board meeting was Bagnell's first. Our new marketing guru was taking over Reed's board seat. After a long deliberation, the best ever, the board unanimously approved the final design version of the new Visic fast chip. The most important feature of the design was its nonstandard plug. It was a brilliant concept. It meant that potential competitors would be slowed down or thwarted in trying to copy Visic's product. No commodity chip produced in the Far East could knock off Visic without changing its standard-plug design. Everyone applauded this strategy.

It was time for another celebration. Bagnell had joined the board and the company, despite its problems, was moving ahead rapidly to develop superchips. The scene this time was a luau at Karp's home, a magnificent setting for a party. He had a huge house, giant swimming pool, and beautiful gardens. The company had expanded to the point that employees, friends, and directors were now a sizable group. Karp, his hand usually on a microphone, made speeches, emceed the entertainment, and kept the party in motion. He was a gracious host. Later that evening he invited me into his study where I got to see his fabulous jazz record collection, heard him play sweet music on a trumpet, and listened to tapes of a little Dixieland band he had organized. He was very impressive and in sharp contrast to John Reed's behavior that night—quiet and almost invisible.

Right on schedule, at the end of the first year, the development work to complete Milestone One was nearly complete. Several prototype chips had been made on an experimental line at VTI. They were not two but three times faster and met our most optimistic expectations.

It was time to raise money for Milestone Two. With Visic's progress and the quality of its people, we targeted raising $6 million at a price of $2.50 per share, two and a half times that of the first round. This would value the company at $20 million. We ended up taking $7.5 million and could have raised $5 million more. The current investors turned down the extra money partly in fear that Visic's management would waste the excess on pet projects and trappings.

The euphoria from the technical success and the happy

faces used to raise money did not obscure the obvious. Karp wasn't the person to run Visic. We needed a new chief executive officer. After spending only a few hours with Karp, the new investors all came to me with that conclusion.

Karp's passion to build Visic into a billion-dollar company unwittingly convinced the investors, old and new, that he was unfit to be chief executive officer. Given the chance to talk, he ranted about the venture capitalist board members' incompetence and the need for a "high road" strategy to build a $250 million production facility. Karp thus opposed the very heart of the business plan he was using to raise the second round of financing.

The two other investor board representatives and I met informally with Karp to discuss his future. It was at a Saturday morning breakfast designed to give Karp the rest of the weekend to think about our conclusions.

I began the conversation by reminding Karp of our first meeting in 1983 when I warned him that he might not make it as chief executive officer but I was willing to give him a chance. In what I believed was an objective, sympathetic, and well crafted portrayal of Karp's deficiencies as chief executive officer, I concluded by stating we wanted him to resign as chief executive officer and become chairman and chief technical officer. We then all asked for his support in helping Visic find the best possible chief executive officer. This was clearly in Karp's as well as the investors' best interest. I told him that this meeting was informal so he could embrace the idea by our next board meeting. His failure as CEO, if handled smoothly, would be invisible, merely Visic's natural progression from the research to the development phase.

The reaction was cold fury. Karp thought the purpose of the breakfast meeting was to thank him for doing a great job. He expected a bonus and a big raise. After blurting out his surprise, he said nothing more other than muttering, "I should have known better," and "I'll never forget this."

I'm an old hand at firing people, including chief executive officers. It's always sad and tough. I tried to get Karp to talk more, even to yell at me—anything to express his obvious rage. In reality, he had no option but to accept our decision or quit. The investors had the clear right, if not the duty, to have the best possible chief executive officer to run a company in which they had an investment of $11.5 million. He stonewalled us.

Our breakfast meeting was supposed to be confidential, a chance for Karp to face up to his fate over the weekend. He decided instead to go on the offensive. He arranged to meet with Federman that very morning and, as I learned later from Federman, portrayed our breakfast in a distorted, brutal manner.

Federman, himself a victim of investor wars, immediately sided with Karp and vowed to block our attempt to unseat him. Karp spent the rest of the weekend trying to line up support among key Visic employees. He sought their commitment to threaten to quit or walk out if we tried to fire him. The next two weeks were a nightmare.

Karp believed in his power and charisma and was certain he was widely supported among Visic employees. He was equally certain the investors would reverse their position when faced with the dire consequences of their perfidious action. Without employees, our investment would be worthless. Karp was dead right. He simply forgot that without our money, the company was also lost. That, I didn't forget.

I listened sympathetically to Federman's complaint that he was not invited to our breakfast meeting. I apologized for the way things turned out. He eventually accepted my reason for not informing him about the purpose of the breakfast meeting. He listened carefully to my version of what transpired, including the fact that even our new investors lacked confidence in Karp. He was surprised to learn that Karp wasn't actually fired but would remain as chairman. He had no idea that we badly wanted to retain Karp in the company. To his credit, Federman weighed the facts, ultimately supported our decision, and spent a lot of time trying to reason with Karp.

The palace coup failed badly. No one, not a single person, threatened to walk out. Smoldering, Karp finally agreed to be replaced "as long as it's with a top person." Unknown to me, he also created a lengthy enemies list divided in two parts. On the "A" list were those who promised him support and then didn't threaten to walk out. On the "B" list were those Karp believed had fed the board of directors damaging information about him. The two lists blurred over time into one roster encompassing nearly the entire organization.

We began the chief executive officer search. John Holman, a successful and highly resourceful headhunter, took the assignment and began churning up suitable candidates. After screening 25, we interviewed 3 or 4. A clear pattern developed. Karp liked the people everyone else thought inadequate. Karp disliked anyone we thought qualified.

The interviewing process consumed six months with many wasted weekends. By mid-year, after 18 months of operation, Visic's situation was badly degenerating for want of leadership.

One afternoon board meeting that ran well into the night was one of the most discouraging I ever attended for any company. The VTI/Visic relationship was strained to the breaking point. The first production run had a very low yield, 20 to 30 percent of usable chips instead of the expected 80 percent. Worse, most of the good chips were unstable when baked in (the standard industry practice of heating chips overnight at a temperature of 100 degrees centigrade).

Karp vehemently blamed VTI's sloppiness and John Reed's incompetence. He then attacked a number of manufacturing engineers. They blamed the process, pointing out that it was too difficult to get exactly right most of the time. The board spent hours wrangling over problems and solutions until it became clear to me that we needed to completely reengineer the process. This effort would delay our program for at least six months. Since Visic's burn rate, or monthly cash outlay, was $750,000, this delay meant we would need another $5 million, maybe more. In other words, we would have to spend nearly all the remaining money we had just raised without having met Milestone Two objectives. I began to realize we should have taken the extra $5 million and hidden it under a mattress.

Karp begged to plow ahead with the development program, hoping for the best. The board overruled him and ordered an immediate cutback in spending. Cash had to be conserved to develop a better process to improve both the yield and performance of the fast chips. All other development work was canceled including a second generation fast chip. This would hurt the future but would at least give the company a chance to have a future.

At this same meeting, Bagnell, citing a frenzy of customers clamoring for Visic chips, sided with Karp. After the meeting, however, Bagnell pulled me aside to say his support of Karp was solely to pacify him. Karp had become so unreasonable and irrational that he, Bagnell, didn't think Visic could survive. Bagnell said he agreed with the board's decision to cut back spending and focus on process development. I went home wondering if paranoia was contagious. Palace intrigue certainly was!

Two venture capitalists, part of the second round financing syndicate, came to this, their first Visic board meeting, as observers. They had questions about Karp's competence to run the business, but this was their first exposure to all the other problems. I could tell from looking at their faces they believed their investment was doomed a month after they had written sizable checks.

With Dave Strohm, a fellow venture capitalist and board member, I worked with Karp and Visic's chief financial officer to put together the layoff hit list, the 20 people that had to be fired. Acting quickly to avoid morale-destroying rumors or creating a panic, we told everyone who was leaving about his or her severance package, then held a general meeting for the remaining employees. Karp asked me to explain the layoff and what was to happen next. I stood before 60 stunned people and told them that Visic needed to focus all its resources on making the fast chip work, that I realized the cutback was a setback to the company's plans and horrible for the people laid off. I was confident Visic could succeed. I believed in what I told them and think that most of Visic's personnel thought we had taken the right action.

The luau celebration was now all but forgotten. Karp was grateful that I spoke to his people. He was always uncomfortable announcing bad news and gladly let me carry that message, clearly disturbed about the layoff and the failure it represented.

What a mess! Our chief executive officer search was futile. Visic needed Karp's genius but he was driving the organization mad. In desperation we hired a very talented consultant, Ken Yagura, a successful entrepreneur who had sold the semiconductor company he founded. He now worked only part-time and would only work with us three days a week. It was better than nothing. Besides, Karp liked him. That didn't last long.

More people quit Visic. Federman's protégé, the chief financial officer, quit over Karp's heavy-handed approach to financial accounting. In fairness, Karp was stretching reality to make Visic look worth saving, a mistake but a human mistake. The chief financial officer told me he found Karp's behavior unacceptable. When he heard this, it destroyed all the remaining confidence Federman had in Karp. He resigned as a director that same week. Karp's personal assistant quit or was fired after what I heard was a tumultuous fight between them.

Patiently and quietly, Yagura tried to hold Visic together. He constructed a realistic plan to develop a new process to produce chips. He cut back spending and laid more people off. Reed was brought back from Siberia and put in charge of process development. Miraculously, the company made tangible progress. The remaining people trusted Yagura and once again worked hard and seemed to enjoy what they were doing. Karp became increasingly petulant, however, and became most useful traveling around the world of semiconductors to find a buyer for Visic.

With all our problems and setbacks I knew we'd never raise another dime of venture money. Our only way out was to be sold. In a few months, four potential buyers surfaced at a price that was not only acceptable, but in my mind extravagant. Visic's monthly board meetings became calm and even pleasurable. Then, six months later, disaster struck. The new process worked, yields were up, and the majority of chips were fast. We were about to mass produce chips in the VTI foundry when we had a crucial revelation. There were no orders, not one single customer for our chips. Bagnell, our marketing guru, had never gotten beyond abstract discussions with potential customers. Everyone wanted to buy a fast chip. But he had not told us that absolutely no one wanted to redesign electrical circuits to accommodate the Visic nonstandard plug. It's like going to Europe with an American TV—you can't plug it in and it won't work if you try. The board meeting one year earlier had unanimously endorsed a nonstandard plug design to ward off competitors, calling it a brilliant strategy. It was a brilliant strategy and worked great except that it warded off customers!

It's funny that no one remembered having a role in approving the brilliant nonstandard plug design. Bagnell remembered being against the idea and the rest claimed to have been absent from the meeting. Once again, failure was an orphan.

Bagnell had not discovered the defect in the plug design in time to correct it. He had never actually asked for an order. Much to my horror, we learned that Bagnell talked only to hardware development people who wholeheartedly endorsed fast chips but had no say at all in using them in existing designs. "Yes," they told him, "introduce a new model, we might use the Visic chip." Redesigning a plug now would cost another year and millions of dollars. We had neither the time nor the money.

The buyers we had talked to ran for the hills. Overnight Visic, as a freestanding company, became a terminal case. I took the responsibility of selling Visic to any buyer at any price. This was a better solution than a liquidation in bankruptcy with no assets to pay off creditors and the remaining employees becoming instantly jobless.

Federman's company, Monolithic Memories, once an enthusiastic champion of Visic's technology, turned me down.

They'd had enough of Karp and his problems! The entire semiconductor industry was in the jaws of the worst recession in its history and Monolithic Memories had plenty of troubles of its own without taking on Visic. I was down to one buyer, VTI, so I pressed for a quick merger before they discovered they were the only game in town. Our lawyer, Larry Sonsini, did a masterful job of putting a workable and fair merger together.

VTI bought Visic. Despite all the backbiting and bickering, they still admired Karp's genius and Bagnell's marketing talent. VTI didn't care that the two of them were not speaking to each other. VTI bought the company for about fifteen cents on the dollar, a token amount for the investors. Visic disappeared into VTI. Most of the remaining employees kept their jobs. The Visic fast chip technology was ultimately useful and became an integral part of VTI's product line. The merger was a good deal for them.

Karp was difficult, volatile, and unpredictable. He was also a genius and Visic's most important asset. He had the vision and guts to create Visic. He nearly made it work. I know of no one else we might have hired who would have changed the outcome. I'm sure Karp will always believe that if we had followed his strategy in the first place, Visic would have succeeded. He might even be right. The Visic odyssey began in 1983 and ended in ignominy for me and our investors in 1987. I wish Karp and his colleagues well and hope their fast chip designs become a huge commercial success.

8

Not Exactly as Planned—Exac

I first heard about Erik Dahlin from my partner, Bill Hambrecht. By coincidence, these two men had met while sitting together on a flight from Stockholm to San Francisco and Dahlin had seized the opportunity to describe his idea for creating a new business. Hambrecht thought Dahlin might have something and turned the deal over to me.

Dahlin, a Swedish national living in Silicon Valley, was a Ph.D. physicist who once headed research and development for Measurex, a highly successful American company. Measurex made instruments to monitor and control machines used to manufacture paper. The company, the biggest in its field, was very profitable. Measurex stock had been a high flyer since going public in the 1970s.

With two colleagues from Measurex, Dahlin had left to seek his own fortune. By the time we met, Dahlin had designed and created a crude model of a unique liquid flowmeter. Worldwide, the food, chemical, and petroleum processing industries use flowmeters to control the proportions of liquid ingredients. Standard flowmeters were accurate to only 5 percent; thus 100 pounds of chicken soup might be as little as 95 pounds or as much as 105 pounds. Mixing errors are costly especially when raw materials are expensive. Misformulations might be totally rejected and worthless. When mixing chemicals, formulation errors could drastically slash profits and put marginal producers out of business. In some instances, these mixing errors could cause dangerous accidents.

Dahlin's company, which he named Exac, was based on a flowmeter with an accuracy of plus or minus 0.1 percent or 500 times better than industry standards. The Exac flowmeter technology utilized the physical phenomenon called the Coriolos effect, the force that makes water always go down a drain in a counterclockwise swirl (clockwise in the southern hemisphere). Dahlin discovered that running liquid counterclockwise through a loop in a transport pipe produced measurable Coriolos forces in perfect mathematical proportion to the amount of liquid passing through. The Exac instrument used a sensor to measure those forces precisely. The instrument was also capable of instantly calculating the exact mass, weight, or volume of the liquid flow.

The Exac product was designed to continuously record liquid flow and could be programmed to adjust the feed or flow rate of incoming materials. This feature enabled the user inexpensively to control formulations and the rate of chemical reactions. The Exac founders believed that for most users, these cost savings would pay back the price of the instrument in three to six months.

After carefully analyzing the bill of materials or components required to make the instrument, we knew we could profitably sell it for $10,000. There was no technical or manufacturing risk. All the raw materials and subassemblies were readily available and could easily be connected.

Another attractive aspect of this venture capital investment was that Exac needed only $2.5 million and 18 months to engineer the product and to begin to generate sales. Exac was expected to be profitable within two and a half years after which no additional capital would be required. The financing was structured so that the investors would own 60 percent, Dahlin and the other employees, 40 percent. If the plan were executed on time, the investors would easily make tenfold on their money.

After my initial meetings with Dahlin, it was apparent to me that if Exac succeeded we'd earn every penny of any profit. Dahlin was a dour man, crusty on every subject except for his absolute certainty that Exac would be a huge success. He always translated Exac's success into the share price at which Exac would go public. Every report he prepared was dominated by charts depicting price earnings ratios and market capitalizations as a multiple of sales revenues. In this fantasy, Exac, under Dahlin's stewardship, became a billion-dollar company in seven years though at the time it was merely three guys with guts and a crude prototype.

Dahlin wrote me glowing reports in the style of a Wall Street security analyst promoting publicly traded companies. Were he a playwright, he'd write the *New York Times* review of it before he wrote the play. Planning for the next month was of only passing interest to Dahlin. Accounting for delays was never worthy of comment.

Dahlin was such a difficult person that I nearly passed on the investment. My decision to invest in Exac was based on my confidence in the steadiness of his two colleagues, Fred Riander, an engineer with outstanding accomplishments in digital signal processing, and Alan Young, an experienced manufacturing manager. All three men had worked together successfully at Measurex. They promised they were ready to work together again to make Exac a huge winner. Ultimately I decided Riander's and Young's willingness to accept Dahlin's annoying idiosyncrasies was their trade-off for access to his inventive genius.

I became chairman of Exac's board of directors and became deeply involved in the operations of the company. Since Hambrecht & Quist was the sole investor, the original board was just Dahlin, Young, and me. With the investors holding a controlling interest in the company (60 percent), I wanted to use my role as chairman to ensure that we had the day-to-day routines in place to stay close to our business plan. Fat chance, I found out!

Most encouraging to Exac's potential was another start-up company called Micro Motion. They manufactured a rudimentary flowmeter also based on the Coriolos effect and, in just a few years, had generated sales of $20 million. Their success assured me there was a big market anxious for an even better flowmeter.

I was certain the Exac instrument, twice as accurate as Micro Motion's instrument, capable of process control, and with other sophisticated features, was demonstrably superior. I was absolutely right.

Exac was formed as a California corporation and began operations in January 1984 in the rear of a small building in Silicon Valley. There was barely enough space for a few desks, benches, and a tiny machine shop. A Rube Goldberg flow-measurement test stand was set up in the parking lot. It consisted of a weigh scale, two 100-gallon tanks, and some garden hose. It was crude but effective. The tanks were weighed before and after being filled with water. The gain in weight was compared with the reading from the Exac meter. In this setting we proved beyond any doubt that the Exac flowmeter worked with exquisite accuracy. We bought a Micro Motion meter and proved to my satisfaction that Exac had a vastly superior product.

With all this success, it was astonishing to see how fast the company became mired in squabbling between Dahlin and every other employee. He was oppressive, overbearing, inconsistent, punitive, and cruel to everyone including Riander and Young. Since they had worked together amicably in the past this development was very disappointing to me. We fell behind in our development schedule and overran our spending plan. Spending more time and more money than budgeted is the double destroyer of most start-ups. Time costs money and the delays help competitors. With each passing week Dahlin became more unreasonable and the stress drained everyone.

One aspect was upbeat. We made great progress in drafting our patents. Dahlin worked well with our patent attorney because he was pedantic and patient, a pleasant surprise. I was certain that Exac would be granted important patents on its technology and unique flowmeter design.

By mid-year morale had fallen dangerously low and key people were on the verge of quitting. I decided to fire Dahlin as president and changed his job to technical director. We needed his genius but could no longer afford to have him in charge. Dahlin hated me for deposing him and never got over the hurt and humiliation. I'm sure he'll always believe my move was not justified and caused irreparable harm to Exac.

I had the absolute right to make this decision, however. As the investor representative, I controlled the company and took full responsibility for the consequences of firing Dahlin as president. The rest of Exac's organization rejoiced.

In one of those wonderful coincidences, I found the perfect candidate for the job of running Exac, Keith Swanson. Like the other founders, Swanson had been a Measurex executive, the director of marketing. He had left Measurex to form his own start-up company. Three years later his venture capitalist had fired him because his company was not growing fast enough. He had failed to meet their expectations largely because his original projections were unrealistic and the potential market wasn't big enough.

After talking to a handful of references, I concluded that Swanson was very able and that no one could have done better than he in his start-up. I believed Swanson could succeed at Exac regardless of his past.

When a deal goes badly, emotions, especially anger, run high among venture investors. After I hired Swanson, I received an unsolicited telephone call from one of his former venture backers. I was told in vivid terms that Swanson was an incompetent fool, incapable of "running an ant farm."

I'll always remember that quote, said in such anger that its author, an immensely successful venture capitalist, didn't realize he wasn't making any sense. When I told Swanson about his booster club it made him even more determined to succeed in this, his second (and probably last) chance to be a successful entrepreneur.

Swanson took over Exac operations quickly and smoothly except for daily run-ins with Dahlin. Fortunately, Swanson not only had great patience and self-esteem but he also recognized that Exac needed Dahlin's genius, at least for the moment. Swanson revised the existing plans, speeding up the product introduction and redirecting the marketing effort. He canceled Dahlin's plans to sell flowmeters to places like SAS Airlines and a neighbor's cheese factory. Neither application made sense because in neither instance were precise flow measurements required.

The real market was the chemical processing industry. Swanson documented and detailed potential customers and how to sell them in the United States and abroad. There was an unexpected announcement of what we thought was great news. Micro Motion was acquired by Emerson Electric. Despite sales of only $20 million, Emerson paid $100 million to buy the company.

This generated two important benefits to Exac. Emerson Electric immediately announced plans to sell Micro Motion meters direct through its own sales organization. The entire Micro Motion distributor organization was to be dismissed. Exac could thus sign up a trained and vengeful selling network that knew exactly where all the customers were.

The second benefit of Emerson Electric's $100 million acquisition was that it helped establish the comparable value, or what someone should pay, for Exac. According to Dahlin, Exac was now worth more than $100 million because it had vastly superior technology. Good news produces instant euphoria, making it easy to believe in big-number fantasies. In reality, the purchase price is always what someone is willing to pay. The gap between the perception of value and what someone might pay is usually as large as the state of Montana.

After a year of operations, Exac introduced its flowmeter at an annual exposition of equipment, machines, and devices for the chemical industry. Exac's debut created tremendous excitement and interest. The company appeared to be spectacularly launched. Despite all our internal problems, real customers wanted our product badly.

The high lasted less than a week, at which time Emerson

Electric sued Exac for patent infringement, a devastating blow.

United States patent law is the most arcane part of our legal process. Patents are filed to obtain for inventors the exclusive right to use their ideas or principles. The concepts must be both novel and useful, otherwise they're not patentable. The best strategy for filing patents is to seek the broadest possible claims. An inventor of a better mousetrap should try to patent traps for all animals, not just mice. An even better strategy would be to patent all ways of capturing animals, not just with traps. This enables the inventor to cover everything from bengal tiger pits to roach motels. Such broad claims give the inventor sweeping control of all the possibilities, including unforeseen ones, surrounding his idea, thereby granting the maximum protection from competition. Solid patents also add considerable value to the company owning the patent.

Patents prevent others from copying not only the inventor's specific idea, but they also indirectly block copying similar ideas. In patent law this is called the doctrine of equivalence meaning that a patent on a technique for slicing bread blocks someone from slicing bologna the same way because both slicing techniques are obvious and therefore deemed equivalent. Violating the doctrine of equivalence is dealt with harshly in patent court, especially if it is proven that there was any intention to subvert or get around the patent.

As a result of the Emerson Electric patent suit, Exac was in a big mess. The plaintiff claimed we violated or infringed their issued patents. Here I was, chairman of the company, and up until then I hadn't a clue we had potential patent problems. It should have occurred to me that Emerson executives, after paying $100 million to buy Micro Motion, would be furious to discover an upstart company with a better product and would do everything possible to thwart our efforts.

It's tough to get clear answers from patent attorneys. Exac's patent lawyer assured me we had nothing to worry about, but he was equally quick to point out that it was impossible to predict what might happen in court. He then told me that the Polaroid/Eastman patent suit on instant cameras illustrated that the courts had become very sympathetic to patent holders and very harsh on infringers. For a man who was telling me not to worry, he gave me a lot to worry about.

"Infringers," that's what Emerson Electric publicly called Exac. We were accused of violating Micro Motion's specific patents as well as the doctrine of equivalence. After several intense meetings, our lawyer convinced me we were not guilty. This good news was, however, tempered by really bad news—it could cost Exac millions of dollars and several years to defend its innocence.

Emerson Electric was steadfast and resolute in its intention to see us in court. They rejected our formal and informal overtures to settle the matter amicably. They demanded absolute unconditional surrender which meant Exac would have to go out of business immediately. They were so steadfast in their win/lose attitude that I began to believe it was either a genetic defect or a blatant attempt to disrupt our business.

There were many more patent meetings. I always asked our growing array of lawyers, "What can Emerson's lawyers be telling them to make their position so immutable when you tell me we'll win?" I never heard a satisfactory or even reasonable answer other than they were trying to scare us. If that's all it was, it sure worked.

Exac, with a patent suit pending and needing millions of dollars for the defense, was never going to get another penny of venture capital money. A cardinal rule of venture investing is the money must go for building a company, not to a bunch of lawyers.

Rather than just surrender and saying farewell to $2.5 million dollars, I made an aggressive attempt to sell Exac, patent problems and all, to corporations with large chemical equipment businesses and deep pockets. We needed a buyer with cash, enthusiasm for our product, and the courage to take on a nasty patent suit.

In a matter of weeks we found three potential buyers, a wonderful validation of the importance and superiority of the Exac flowmeter. In the months that followed, each of these buyers examined the patent situation in excruciating detail. They all concluded that Exac would *probably* win in the end. All three positive patent opinions included the standard caution that Exac might lose. If it lost and if the judge believed Exac willfully disregarded the Emerson Electric patents, the patent court could award triple damages to the plaintiff. The penalty would be hundreds of millions of dollars and would put Exac out of business. Quite naturally, no corporation was about to write a check to buy a company with that much risk attached to it.

Luckily we conceived of a purchase strategy that solved the triple damages, willful disregard nightmare. We granted one of our suitors an option to buy Exac at a fixed price any time within the following two years. If Exac lost the patent dispute the buyer could walk away without any liability. If Exac won, because of the option the buyer had an absolute right to acquire Exac.

I was en route to Europe to complete negotiations with a German company that had proposed a joint venture as a way to avoid getting caught up in the patent problem. When I called my office from Heathrow Airport, I learned that an American company was ready to agree to our option purchase formula. The paperwork would take months to complete and the deal could abort any time during that period. The German deal was a sure thing but not nearly as attractive. The choice was mine and had to be made at once.

I met with the executives of the German company the following morning, listened to the details of their proposal, was taken to the president's home for a spectacular luncheon, and as I was leaving announced we would not accept their offer. I still got a ride to the airport in time to fly back to San Francisco, although the chill in the car matched the subzero temperature outside.

The American company was Monsanto, the second largest corporation in St. Louis. The third largest is Emerson Electric. (A brewery is first.)

A believable rumor began circulating shortly after Monsanto signed the option agreement with Exac, that the chief executive officers of Monsanto and Emerson made a $500 bet on the outcome of the patent suit. In my opinion, this country club wager fueled more emotion than any other business consideration in the turmoil that was to come.

I also believed the Emerson Electric executives responsible for the decision to buy Micro Motion for $100 million would rather see a patent suit go on for years than admit they hadn't carefully evaluated the patents and competition prior to their purchase. The longer the suit took, the longer they would be employed.

The next two years were very difficult. We tried to operate in a "business as usual" mode. That quickly became a joke as potential customers were threatened by Emerson Electric with a patent suit if they bought an Exac flowmeter. Emerson also used Monsanto's unwillingness to buy Exac outright as the best reason why no customer should dare buy Exac's meter. There was the specter of no service after we went bankrupt. Swanson moved quickly to indemnify customers against losses from any patent action, but many were too timid to get into a legal entanglement. Exac found it very difficult to sell meters. Despite our problems, we sold enough during this period eventually to break even.

The most attractive part of our Monsanto option was that they paid for all our patent defense legal costs. Monsanto became a magnificent supporter of Exac financially, intellectually, and emotionally throughout this horrendous time. Without it, Exac would never have been able to survive long enough to go to trial.

In addition to the patent problems, I had Dahlin to deal with. He became more embittered and was very destructive internally to Exac. He was especially hard on Swanson, holding him personally responsible for devaluing Exac. Dahlin believed he personally would make only a few million dollars now rather than the $50 million he had dreamed of. No amount of discussion would budge him from that belief.

By this time, one and a half years after starting up with

Dahlin's creation, the technical work was completed and he could be dismissed without any loss to the company. Monsanto was already weary of trying to work with Dahlin. His only value to Exac was help with the patent defense. We needed at least his goodwill when the case went to court.

With Monsanto's concurrence, I fired Dahlin outright but offered him a generous consulting agreement to keep his goodwill through the patent suit. We needed his testimony. He was hurt and angry, but accepted my decision and resigned as an employee. Though he was paid, I don't think he actually showed up for consulting work more than once or twice over the next year.

Emerson Electric began to subpoena Exac personnel for interrogatories (pretrial examination) and for copies of many of our files. They got to me early on. Monsanto hired a new patent lawyer to represent Exac. He was low key and extremely well prepared. In contrast, the Emerson lawyer was aggressive and theatrical. He introduced himself by reciting his perfect winning record in patent cases, including personally representing Polaroid in the famous Eastman suit. His action was a blatant attempt to scare me. It worked.

The thrust of his questions centered on finding evidence that I induced Exac to violate Emerson Electric patents. This would enable Emerson to sue me and Hambrecht & Quist as well as Exac. For once I was pleased—no, delighted—to admit to my own stupidity. I never knew anything about Micro Motion's patents. I didn't know those patents existed. After a day of badgering me, their lawyer concluded I was hapless. Despite being chairman of Exac, I didn't seem to know anything. I was never asked to testify again.

The legal process of discovery was very time-consuming and debilitating for the company. Just copying files was a full-time job. Preparing and coaching each employee who faced interrogation took weeks, not counting the actual formal testimony which took a month each for Dahlin, Young, and Swanson. Exac's attorneys retaliated by asking for tons of files from Emerson Electric, but that huge corporation had platoons of staff people to do the required work. Exac couldn't afford the luxury of a large staff. Swanson had to lead Exac at a killing pace, responding to the mountain of legal questions and effectively running the business. Otherwise it wouldn't matter who won in court, Exac would be no more.

Swanson's management style was based on teamwork. He was steady, reliable, and well liked. He lacked Dahlin's creative genius, but he made up for it with leadership. Without Swanson, the company would not have survived the terrible, draining effect of the patent suit and the incredible time required for our defense. This pressure overlaid all the normal problems every start-up company must face making life very difficult and anxious for Exac's employees.

Compounding these problems was another tragedy. Riander, one of the founders and head of manufacturing, died from a malignant brain tumor. It was not only a tragic loss, but a grim reminder of how powerless and vulnerable we all were.

On top of this pile of problems we had another nasty surprise. One meter failed our quality control pressure test by exploding. Since our meters were hooked up "in line" by customers, an exploding meter could cause a flood of potentially dangerous materials. We had to shut down production, find the cause of the failure, and fix the problem. We didn't know if we had a one-in-a-million problem or if every meter in the line was defective and had somehow squeaked by our quality control. We were grateful that we had pressure tested each and every meter. Our fears of customer problems with existing meters were minimal. We couldn't in good conscience, however, ship any more product until we were sure.

After a week of nail biting, we discovered the welding on the flange of the meter was defective because of contamination. This was a break for us because we could inspect all weldings by X-ray to determine which ones were bad. We screened out a few dozen bad flanges, repaired the defect, and were shipping safe meters within two weeks. That episode cost Exac about $300,000 in lost sales and unabsorbed overhead. A bigger problem would have destroyed the company.

The patent trial was delayed, then delayed again by Emerson Electric. I hoped and wanted to believe that this was the strategy of a litigant who wanted to stretch out Exac's pain as long as possible. I expected that Emerson would settle out of court just before the trial began.

A serious side effect of these delays concerned the trial date between Exac and our benefactor, Monsanto. When we signed the two-year option agreement, we all believed that was more than adequate time to settle the patent dispute. With the trial now scheduled right at the end of the option period, Monsanto wanted a six-month extension. Though I was enormously grateful for Monsanto's help, Exac's situation had changed for the better. We had reached cash-flow break-even and had most of the patent defense expense behind us. Exac could now go it alone and sell the company later at a higher price.

The solution I reached was to grant a six-month extension to Monsanto for an immediate, nonrefundable, payment of $1 million to all shareholders. We would all get some money back regardless of the patent outcome and Monsanto could still buy the company for the original option price. I might have been able to gouge Monsanto for more money but I felt we had struck a fair deal for everyone. I learned later that most of the shareholders thought I had a lot of moxie asking for more money considering all the company had been through. In retrospect they were right. I have a lot of moxie, otherwise I wouldn't be a venture capitalist.

As our court date approached, our lawyer got very jittery. In the beginning he predicted our chances of winning were 80 to 20. As the trial approached, he dropped the odds to 60 to 40. We finally went to trial in July 1987, flummoxing my pretrial settlement theory. During the three weeks of the trial our lawyer dropped the odds further to 40 to 60. I felt like dropping him out the window. He pleaded with us to seek a last-minute settlement. We refused because Emerson persisted in demanding unconditional surrender (plus $500 from Monsanto for the bet).

I would have given anything to know what Emerson's patent lawyers were telling their client. It was inconceivable to me that they believed Emerson was sure to win the case. I had enough legal opinions from enough different patent firms to know that only one thing was certain—there was no certainty.

The trial ended abruptly. The jury was unanimous on every count. Exac won the case. A few months later, Monsanto happily exercised its option to buy Exac for $14 million plus the legal fees they had expended.

The investors made three times on their money, much less than originally hoped for, but far more than they would have realized in the bankruptcy Exac faced for two of the three years it had operated.

Keith Swanson and most of the others are now Monsanto employees. I hear from Keith from time to time and know he's doing well. He was perfect for a tough job and carried out the assignment with dignity and sensitivity.

I always remind myself that though Dahlin has a bag full of personal flaws, he is truly a genius. He created the Exac concept, designed the flowmeter, raised money (from me) to turn his technology into a business, and developed a prototype that worked. None of the rest of us at Exac, including Keith Swanson, could have done that.

The combined legal fees for the patent dispute, with the two St. Louis giants slugging it out, exceeded $5 million not counting the cost of the incredible time wasted.

The Exac outcome was successful for all of us. It's a perfect example of there being no alternative except to succeed. In the case of Exac, we were almost eaten by a monster we never knew existed.

In the summer of 1990, three years after winning, Monsanto was retried on a narrow aspect of the patent. Emerson won that right on appeal. Monsanto lost the retrial and awaits a 1991 trial on damages before deciding whether or not to appeal. I was told that legal fees have now exceeded $10 million.

9

The Best and the Brightest—Ridge

David Folger, Hugh Martin, Edwin Baseheart, and John Sell, four exceptionally talented young men in their late twenties, joined together in 1981 to form a company to design and manufacture a minicomputer based on a new concept. They named their company Ridge after a popular ski trail. All Ridge products were to be named for ski trails. The metaphor was based on the skill required to successfully navigate through complex terrain at very high speed. No one noticed that all these ski trails also went downhill.

The four founders were whiz kids, brilliant, visionary, determined, and highly motivated. They were also very special because they had worked successfully together as computer jocks at Hewlett Packard. Two of them had been classmates and close friends in college.

Each man had his own special area of expertise in either computer hardware or software. By unanimous agreement, Folger, the feistiest among them, became Ridge's president. The other three, Martin, Baseheart, and Sell, each headed up technical development groups. All four men were elected to the board of directors. From the very beginning they were dedicated to operating as a team—one for all, all for one.

The Ridge business plan was to design and build a superfast

family of computers. Ridge computers would be faster and cheaper than any other data processing system available as measured by the cost per transaction. What made Ridge unique and able to deliver on this performance promise was a technology called reduced instruction set computation (RISC). RISC enabled the Ridge computer to complete complex mathematical calculations with a much simpler code or pathway. The Ridge RISC-based computer was designed to excel at fast, cheap number crunching.

Their market was a rapidly growing $2 billion readily identifiable segment—scientists and engineers. There are thousands of scientific and engineering uses for a high speed, inexpensive number cruncher or a "hot box" as insiders call it. Technologists needed fast, cheap number crunchers for countless and diverse applications such as gene synthesis, semiconductor circuit design, molecular modeling, mechanical design, architectural drawings, robotics, weather forecasting, and even for determining where to drill for oil.

The Ridge business plan was so compelling that it was readily capitalized with $3 million of start-up venture funding. Hambrecht & Quist was the lead investor. Art Rock, the master venture capitalist with an uncanny talent for picking extremely promising young people with winning ideas, was so attracted by Ridge's founders that he agreed to join their board of directors.

Rock, who will serve on only six boards at a time, has been a long-time board member of both Intel and Apple Computer. Because of his reputation he receives hundreds of invitations to join company boards. Having Rock join Ridge was the company's best reference. Ridge was thus considered by the venture community to be as close to a sure thing as they were likely to get.

Another break for Ridge came from Machine Bull, the France-based computer giant. In exchange for European marketing rights, Bull not only invested money in Ridge, but undertook costly development work solely for Ridge's benefit. The Bull relationship was a financial and technical bonanza for

Ridge and further validated the promise and viability of their RISC technology.

The key elements of Ridge's business strategy were to introduce a family of "hot boxes," with each successive system more powerful than the last, and to create a proprietary operating system designed to block competition.

Implicit in Ridge's strategy was the need to constantly optimize and improve the RISC technology to maintain leadership in cost-effective fast computations. This meant a long-term commitment to substantial research and development expenditures.

The company began operations in 1982. During the next two years the four founders and the 40 employees they hired expended a monumental effort. The first product, North Face, was introduced in 1984 right on schedule. One hundred key scientific users in prestigious research centers in the United States and France enthusiastically bought this first Ridge machine. Sales soared to $7 million in the first year of manufacture. During that time the company expanded to 100 employees to gear up manufacturing, expand the sales force, provide in-field service, and reinforce the technical development effort. Ridge had the look, smell, and profile of a big winner.

The $12 million in sales forecasted for 1985 looked conservative to both the company and the board of directors. Companies at this stage usually more than double sales year to year. With an increase from $7 million to a conservative $12 million in sales, Ridge would nearly break even for the year and actually achieve profitability in the fourth quarter. The equally conservative forecast of $20 million in sales for 1986 would make Ridge highly profitable. The next generation product, a more expensive but higher powered and faster machine, was being developed and would be introduced in late 1986.

The board agreed in the fall of 1985 that $5 million in additional financing was required to cover the expected 1985 operating losses and to provide working capital to support sales increases. The board decided to hire an investment banker to raise the money from financial institutions rather than from venture capitalists. This was called a mezzanine financing, the last money needed before Ridge went public and was the least dilutive alternative to the company. The term derives from the money used to build the mezzanine of a building, the last thing a company needs. Mezzanine financing in high-tech companies were bonanzas for investors during the 1982 to 1984 period. Companies quickly went public at two to three times the mezzanine share price.

Folger, Martin, Baseheart, and Sell continued to work together effectively and seemed immune to all the stress that goes with starting up a company. They stoically accepted the personal sacrifices, the 70-hour weeks, and the relentless pressure to meet milestones and deadlines. The rest of the work force caught their fever and excitement and matched the example set by their leaders.

With success they became cocky. As time went by, their record of success only—no failures—went to their heads. In 1984 when Evans & Sutherland, the Utah-based computer corporation, proposed a merger, the founders turned it down though they would each have made $1 million. Ridge, they believed, was destined to be worth ten times more. (Ironically, Evans & Sutherland later told me they would have scuttled the merger because they found the Ridge founders too cocky to work with.)

Ridge had its first major setback toward the end of 1985. Fourth-quarter sales stalled and the mezzanine financing completely derailed. The capital market for technology turned ice cold. Investors, on average, took a 40 percent haircut on publicly traded technology stocks during that year. There was no hoped-for recovery in the last quarter. Private companies, even those as classy as Ridge, lost their glitter overnight. Even with glib answers as to why Ridge sales stalled, the marked downturn in demand was a bright red caution flag to already jittery investors.

Ridge managed to raise only $2 million, less than half of the $5 million it needed. The board of directors realized that it was unlikely that a new financing could be attempted before the middle of 1986 and only then if there was a dramatic improvement in both Ridge and the technology sector.

There was endless debate among the founders over the circumstances leading to the failure to fully finance Ridge. If the investment banker had started to raise money two months earlier, the mezzanine financing would have worked. With adequate funding, Ridge would have continued to develop product enhancements on schedule. Competition would have remained far behind. No matter what the truth was, the debate was entirely irrelevant. What was so, was so, and no one could alter it.

When a company fails to raise money at a critical time there is never a financing alternative. It's impossible to reopen other means such as going back to the venture capital community. Investors look on a financing failure as a broadcast of defeat, an announcement that something is very wrong, so why bother to even look at it.

With insufficient funds, Ridge had to cut spending drastically. This meant layoffs, the worst possible morale buster for a start-up company. The people that get fired in these circumstances are always innocent.

Ridge development programs were delayed, cutting into the heart of its strategy to keep well ahead of competition. Despite these problems, the remaining Ridge employees distinguished themselves not only by accepting the cutbacks but also by unanimously agreeing to a 10 percent reduction in their salaries, an unprecedented action and an affirmation of their faith in the company.

For the next six months the company put their faith in the power of prayer. They waited in vain for a return of rapid sales growth. Everyone wanted to believe that the last quarter of 1985 was an aberration, that 1986 would be the year Ridge got back on a trajectory that would lead to annual sales of $100 million. In this scenario, though the plan was displaced by a year, the company would nevertheless still be the invincible leader in its field.

Unfortunately, 1986 was another chilling year. Sales forecasted to be $12 million reached only $9 million. So much for "conservative" forecasting. (Every time I hear a company president utter that word I cringe.) The money raised at the end of 1985 ran out. During the summer, the existing venture investors and Ridge's corporate partner, Bull Machine, dug down in their pockets and put up another $1.5 million, only enough to keep the doors open for three months, not enough to pay for badly needed development and engineering. Ridge was in the worst possible situation for a new company. Sales remained well below the $14 million level needed to break even. The $1.5 million the investors put up was entirely consumed by operating losses. At a time like this, merger discussions were fruitless. Other than divine intervention, there was no feasible alternative to Ridge going bankrupt.

It was devastating for the four founders and the dozens of employees to have worked so hard for five years only to face the horror that it was all for naught. The prospect of imminent failure utterly destroyed teamwork and camaraderie. Everyone remembered that two years earlier management nixed the chance to merge with Evans & Sutherland. Rage became the pervasive attitude with everyone from management to shipping clerks.

Folger and everyone else had been misled by Ridge's fast start—$7 million in first-year sales. The factor that drove the initial sales was Ridge's "hot box." Prestigious scientists in leading universities have the budget to buy one of anything that appears to be new and exciting. For Ridge or any other such company to succeed, the average scientist or engineer who comprises the bulk of its market must have the interest and the *budget* to buy something new. It's easy to be fooled by the enthusiasm of leaders into believing that admiration from luminaries will translate into universal sales.

To conserve the small amount of remaining cash, Ridge crunched the sales and marketing people. They were the ones who missed revenue goals. Heads rolled, good people quit, the organization was totally demoralized. None of the remaining technical people mourned their loss, however.

I decided to meet informally with the four founders to explore the alternatives to calling it quits. Folger suggested a beer and spaghetti dinner at his home. The evening was the first chance I had to see these four men in a more relaxed environment, free from the enormous tension and anxiety of the office. I learned that Folger loved cats, Martin went to the San Francisco Symphony the same night I did although we never saw each other. I realized how much I liked these men as human beings quite apart from their role in the fate of Ridge. I also reaffirmed my belief in RISC technology and the talent we had to make it work. That night gave me even more incentive to find a plan that would give Ridge another chance.

Not long after this meeting, Folger, the chief of the 1981 whiz kids, became the next target. Martin, Baseheart, and Sell turned all their anger and frustration on Folger, and demanded his head. The board of directors eventually concurred. In everyone's mind Folger was the architect of failed mergers, unrealistic goals, and flawed vision. A consummate engineer, he was deemed arrogant in believing he alone knew what customers wanted. Then he blamed potential customers instead of his own bad judgment when the orders dried up.

Hundreds of companies fail for the same reason, the myopia of brilliant engineers and scientists convinced they and they alone know what customers need and don't need.

Ridge laid off 30 more people affecting all areas, reducing the work force to just under 50. Development activity virtually stopped. Ridge, in this mode, was terminal.

During these doldrums I came up with a radical scheme to save Ridge. The employees, the board of directors, and outside consultants were steadfast in the belief that RISC was an important and valuable technology. Ridge, with all its problems, had tremendous talent and expertise in RISC. The problem was the company didn't have the money or leadership to make it work. I felt that maybe it wasn't too late.

My concept centered on hiring a well-seasoned computer executive to join Ridge as president. This person would revalidate the viability of the company and attract the money needed to restart the technical development effort. Most important, the new president would rekindle morale and the dedication to once again work tirelessly to enable Ridge to succeed.

Though disappointing, existing sales were $9 million, more than halfway to the level that would make Ridge profitable. In the worst case, our new computer-guru chief executive officer would help find a merger opportunity that would put Ridge with a well-financed corporation.

I knew just such a man, Bob Evans. After a distinguished career at IBM, he had taken early retirement. Widely known as the father of the IBM System 36, the billion-dollar bread-and-butter machine of the 1970s, he had run IBM's Federal Division and was later corporate director of technology. Evans was well known throughout the world of computers as brilliant, daring, honest, and hard working. He had won presidential awards and was a member of the prestigious National Academy of Engineering. A prominent IBM executive told me that Evans "knew more about everything than was knowable, more than the next five best people put together."

To those who knew him well, Evans was also stubborn, overly aggressive, and insensitive, all accented by a lightning wit. A lot of smart young computer jocks were fearful and contemptuous of Evans. In review meetings he trampled them when he believed they were wrong or foolish. He was often right, but few people wanted to hear his criticism, especially in the way it was delivered: "If you worked for me and did a dumb thing like that, I'd chain you to a log and throw you in the river." Evans never did understand why some people ran for cover when he showed up.

Evans had one crucial asset. He loved to mentor bright young engineers. Besides, he hadn't actually thrown anybody in the river. I believed he was perfect for Ridge. So did Martin, Baseheart, and Sell and the rest of the board of directors. Since he knew little about Ridge, Evans agreed to personally evaluate the company in intricate detail. He spent three months intensively studying the technology, products, and markets. He reported back with the following conclusions.

- The overwhelming reason for the shortfall in Ridge sales was the lack of application software converted to run on the special Ridge operating system. Millions had been spent to create a proprietary operating system to fend off competition but the result had been to fend off customers. Software suppliers were not interested in spending their time and money to adapt their products to the alien Ridge operating system. Without application software, customers were unable to use a Ridge computer even though it was the fastest "hot box" on the market. The Ridge North Face computer couldn't run the most popular CAD/CAM or geophysical or molecular modeling software.
- Ridge's technical leadership was substantial in 1984. Competition had caught up by 1986. By then the arena for fast scientific computers was crowded with new products. Ridge was way behind in its technical development and was now merely part of a big pack of competitors using alternative technologies to build a "hot box."
- The Ridge product strategy to introduce a new, higher-power, higher-capacity machine every two years was flawed. The new machine immediately made the old machine obsolete, rendering it nearly worthless. Potential customers were thus discouraged from buying an existing Ridge computer and encouraged to wait until the new model came out. Ridge made the situation worse. After announcing the next-generation machine, they canceled the development effort because of fiscal problems. It would be a very long wait for any new model.

The most ominous bit of information came from Art Rock. He showed me a survey taken of people who buy sophisticated computers. These potential customers were hopelessly confused by all the conflicting, competitive data and recommendations on what "hot box" to buy. The most stinging comment of all was they were glad to pay significantly more for hardware from an established corporation like IBM or Digital Equipment rather than take a chance on a start-up company.

In retrospect, giant killing was an immense problem for Ridge as well as for a dozen other fledgling computer companies. Venture capitalists could have saved a pile of money if they had recognized this problem earlier on.

They had a love affair with the potential of exciting new technology available in both computer hardware and software. Dozens of new companies overstated their capability, announcing machines well before they were able to deliver. Some never delivered. These premature announcements were partly due to the cocky passion of the entrepreneurs and partly to the need to hype the potential of their machines in order to raise money.

The unanticipated result was customers completely confused with dazzling alternatives and unqualified promises. Customer attitude turned into either wait and see or conservatism—buy what's proven from well-established companies.

The most important aspect of the Evans report on Ridge was that it outlined in exquisite detail the solutions to the problems and ways to correct the defects. First and foremost he immediately needed $7 million, then $5 million more in a year. Otherwise the lack of capital would scuttle Ridge. No one doubted that conclusion.

With the first $7 million in the bank, Evans would:

- Immediately switch the Ridge operating system to Unix, the industry standard platform. This move would make Ridge instantly compatible with all application software. In fact, unknown to Ridge, Machine Bull had already done all the work necessary to make the switch to Unix and was prepared to give it to Ridge at no cost. Evans discovered this development by chance in a discussion with Bull engineers. Folger had known of it all along but had ignored the development because he was so committed to a Ridge operating system. That technical windfall saved a year's work and $1 million. It was the first positive break for Ridge in three years. (I hoped the company was starting on a roll.)
- The renewed technical development effort would be directed toward the low-end, low-priced market. By a quirk, there was far less competition for inexpensive machines. Everyone was pursuing more expensive, souped-up versions. RISC technology was especially potent in lower-cost systems because it required less hardware to accomplish mathematical calcula-

tions. This sounded like a very sensible idea and so it proved to be.

- Evans made an obvious decision that all new Ridge products would be designed in modules. Customers could then simply connect a module and instantly upgrade old products with new improved capability. The fear of obsolescence would be eliminated. This was not a novel idea. Other computers had been made this way, but Ridge had never considered it before Evans.

Martin, Baseheart, and Sell pledged to work enthusiastically and energetically for Evans. They also pledged to continue to work like madmen. They were poised for this last grab at fame and fortune.

The Evans "recovery and turnaround" plan made sense to me and the rest of the board of directors. My partners at Hambrecht & Quist, however, were negative about putting up more money. After heated debate and soul searching, I ultimately put together the $7 million financing with $5 million coming from Hambrecht & Quist funds. We had a total of $7.5 million invested and owned two-thirds of Ridge. Our investment could be worth $50 million if I was right. We were out another $5 million (the original $2.5 million was long gone and written off) if I was wrong.

Within nine months sales and orders improved and new product versions were being developed for introduction. By the summer of 1987, the board knew that the $7 million would run out in three months. Unfortunately, the company did not quite catch the gold ring. Ridge remained unprofitable with sales reaching only $12 million, $2.5 million short of break-even, only 20 percent short of success. The market for scientific computers had become more crowded and confusing. Customers were even more wary. Sales never reached the break-even level.

Desperate, Evans personally solicited orders while trying to sell the company to any of a half dozen seemingly interested buyers, including Bull. It was exquisite torture. Every day there was heartwarming news, a big new order, an excited buyer, a trade magazine endorsement. No merger materialized. There was no clear path for Ridge to become profitable even though we were so close I could smell it.

When they saw no one lining up to finance or buy the company, the whiz kids lost heart and the will to keep trying. Eventually, they all quit. Ridge never got the second $5 million financing. I decided against putting in any more money. Evans had failed and left Ridge in ignominy as did I. The company was cut back to be a RISC research project in the hope its technology could be sold.

Ridge had a window of opportunity, a clear lead on competition, and the brightest talent around, but it failed to execute its plan. Ridge simply missed the train. There were no more chances. The venture capital business is heartless about repeated failure, as well it should be. I lost more money on Ridge than on any other investment. It hurts, not because my judgment was wrong and it was, but because such a talented group failed to realize its dreams.

There is no doubt in my mind that had the mezzanine financing succeeded in late 1985, Ridge would have succeeded. If time and money hadn't been wasted on a proprietary operating system and Unix had been used from the beginning, Ridge would have succeeded. I don't restate these factors as "couldas, wouldas, shouldas," but to point out that Ridge's destiny was in our own hands. Outside forces didn't make it a disaster. We did it ourselves.

Several companies have since successfully introduced computers based on RISC. IBM, the latest entry, has used RISC to build a low-end "hot box" precisely using Ridge's 1986 strategy. Ridge had the right idea but the wrong execution.

The investors lost $15 million on what in the beginning looked like a sure bet.

10

Getting It Right—Read-Rite

Jack Osbourne and Peter Bishof, two engineers from a company called Memorex, had an elegant idea in 1983. They believed it was possible to design a recording head that would greatly enhance the performance of a computer memory disk drive. With this improvement, computer memory could be manipulated more quickly and stored at higher densities. Confident that they would be able to find venture capital financing, Osbourne and Bishof quit their jobs and spent six months, tirelessly and without pay, developing a plan to design, manufacture, and sell a thin-film recording head. Their thin-film process was based on semiconductor technology and they planned to use it to make a head to read or write memory on a computer hard disk. They sought $3 million for start-up money from venture capital financing.

IBM, the only company to have mastered production of thin-film heads, used them for its own computers but refused to sell them to competitors. Two years earlier, three men had spun out of IBM to form a company called Cybernex to produce a product equivalent to the IBM head. They raised and spent $50 million of venture capital. Not surprisingly, they soon became defendants in a bitter lawsuit with IBM who claimed they had stolen its technology.

The Read-Rite founders were introduced to me by the president of a successful computer peripheral business. He vouched for Osbourne and Bishof saying they were honest, capable men, deeply committed to building a business based on their unique design. In subsequent meetings they convinced me that the Read-Rite thin-film head would be cheaper than and have superior performance to the Cybernex head. Since Read-Rite was well aware of the IBM/Cybernex lawsuit, they meticulously avoided making Cybernex's mistake and designed their product well outside of existing patents and proprietary technology.

The main attraction of thin-film heads is they double the density or the amount of data that can be packed on a disk for later retrieval. Since accumulating and storing information is nearly an obsession, doubling memory density with only a minor increase in the system cost is of great importance.

All computer or disk drive memory manufacturers, except IBM, used magnetic heads. Magnetic heads were cheaper, $5 versus $15 for Read-Rite heads, but Osbourne and Bishof believed that customers would pay the premium to get the double density benefit. Disk drives sold for $180 to $250 per unit and could absorb the cost increase for a high-performance head.

After months of study, Hambrecht & Quist, along with two other venture groups, put up $3 million in exchange for 60 percent of the company. All the investors understood that at least $10 million more would be required before the company became profitable. In addition, $5 million of lease-financed capital equipment would be needed to manufacture the product. The initial board of directors was comprised of the founders, me, and two other venture capitalists.

Once the start-up financing was in place, Osbourne and Bishof threw themselves into making prototype heads designed so that the device could be readily mass produced in a production assembly line. The factory they were planning to build would need to turn out five to ten million heads per year if Read-Rite were to succeed.

The business had to "ramp-up" quickly. Read-Rite's potential customers, disk drive manufacturers, would likely take their time evaluating prototype heads, but once they decided to convert from magnetic to thin-film heads, they would need tens of thousands of the devices overnight. The dilemma for Read-Rite was that disk drive manufacturers could test a device then order 10,000 in a matter of months, or they could take years to test before deciding to switch. It was a real dilemma. There was no way Read-Rite could foresee what might be needed and plan for production capacity accordingly. The customers were noncommittal.

There was, therefore, enormous pressure to design and build a full-scale factory quickly. Read-Rite needed production equipment and trained workers in place well in advance of receiving any firm orders. Customers who placed orders based on the performance of the prototypes insisted on testing devices made in production before committing to all-out use. Once they had made the changeover, they needed absolute assurance that the product would be reliable and abundantly available.

The process required to make a complete device took eight weeks and was incredibly complicated. From beginning to end there were 300 separate steps, some of which were very labor intensive. Each device was physically handled or touched more than 200 different times. Compounding the problem was the fact that the device couldn't be quality tested until the very last step was completed. If, for example, something went wrong in the first step, there was no way to know it until two months and 300 additional and costly steps later.

Why did I want to start or invest in such a complicated business? The answer was simple. The rewards would be big and fast. This was an original equipment manufacturer (OEM) business. We would be selling a subassembly to an OEM who could incorporate the Read-Rite device into a disk drive. There were only a few dozen potential buyers and therefore little marketing expense. The customers were sophisticated and welcomed innovation. Best of all, the market for disk drive memory was growing at 15 to 25 percent per year. Once accepted, high-performance thin-film heads could sweep the market. Read-Rite could be a $100 million company in five years. That's the stuff of high-valuation public offerings.

I also recognized that once established, Read-Rite would be insulated from competition. The thin-film technology was tricky as well as capital and labor intensive. If Read-Rite executed its plan, as challenging as it was, the shareholders would make a pile of money, more than ten times on their investment.

The technology Read-Rite was using was proven and had been used in other industries. There was no risk of "pushing the envelope" for Read-Rite. The process started with the production of plain vanilla semiconductor silicon wafers. Unlike the demands of making C-MOS chips with six-inch wafers and 1,000 lines and spaces per inch of circuitry, the Read-Rite process used three-inch wafers and 100 lines and spaces per inch. The wafers were sliced into hundreds of tiny chips followed by a multitude of cleaning and polishing procedures. The chips were then bonded to a multilayered substrate, surface etched, washed clean, bonded to other layers, and etched and cleaned again each time. The bonded chip was then glued to a metal holder. A wire harness was soldered to the assembly and the whole device cleaned one more time. Finally, after eight weeks in the production line, the wired device was attached to a fixture simulating a disk drive for testing. Up until this moment, there was no meaningful way to test the device.

The performance required of this tiny device was enormous. It had to "fly" at high speeds over the disk while maintaining a few thousandths of an inch gap perfectly. The head couldn't wobble at all. The electronics had to perform flawlessly.

Remarkably, the laboratory prototypes did perform perfectly. The yield or the percentage of good parts per wafer was 40 percent, far exceeding the expectations of the business plan. Though there was little time to rejoice, we all started to believe we could make Read-Rite into a big success.

Then the real world settled around us. Building the production plant turned into a nightmare. The process required sophisticated automation and a "clean room" environment. The air had to be stringently purified without the tiniest dust or dirt particles. Any contamination would ruin the performance of the heads. Even with workers dressed in surgical gowns, hair nets, masks, rubber gloves, and plastic bags over their shoes, human handling had to be minimized.

Despite the most modern robotics, the device still had to be handled or touched by human hands hundreds of times. Workers squinted at each part through microscopes on a dozen different occasions. They attached wires, glued the tiny pieces together, and placed the assembly in test fixtures. It was demanding, tedious work where the tiniest human error or microscopic contamination could ruin a head.

After six months of operations, Read-Rite was in serious trouble. None of the dozen customers who sampled prototype heads for testing was near a commitment to switch from magnetic heads to Read-Rite, though the prototype devices worked perfectly. There was little more Read-Rite could do except to wait it out and hope that we had guessed right about market acceptance.

At the same time we realized that the production plant was hopelessly delayed. During a plant tour through the rubble of construction in progress and idle equipment, I pointed out that "the good news is we don't have any orders." Lamentably, if we had, we wouldn't have been able to fill them. There were defects in the design of the clean air systems and delays in deliveries of important capital equipment. As a result of a new bureaucracy, permits to operate the facility were withheld by the town. Silicon Valley's elected officials, frightened by environmental lawsuits, had instituted new, often contradictory, regulations right in the middle of our plant construction.

Delays, whether market driven or production limited, always mean the same thing—more money than anticipated being spent for nothing. Spending additional money to get a company to where it was expected to be in the first place is very damaging. Even worse is the knowledge that some companies never get there despite gobbling up tenfold more money.

As a consequence, raising new money because of a capital overrun is always difficult. New investors are hard to come by and it requires a leap of faith by the initial investors, who live with the nagging fear that their entire investment will have to be written off if the company never meets its milestones. New money also means heavy dilution to employee shareholders.

Nevertheless, the existing investors put up another $2 million. By this time, however, all of us had lost confidence in Osbourne's ability to run the company. The investors unanimously demanded a new chief executive officer. I was asked to deliver the bad news to Osbourne which was especially difficult because I had grown to like and admire him immensely. After considerable discussion and reflection, Osbourne agreed to step down and help find the best possible person to run the company he had founded. Putting his disappointment aside, Osbourne, obviously hurt, had the heart and courage to work hard at finding his own replacement.

In less than two months (on average, finding a new chief executive officer takes six months) we found and hired the perfect candidate, Wade Meyercord. Our quick success was a big morale booster. Meyercord had had a distinguished fast track marketing career at IBM and operations responsibility at Memorex. Moreover, he had ten years experience in disk drives. Most important to me, the two founders liked him. We all believed he was honest, hard working, credible, and he had a proven record of leadership. Meyercord made a strong impression and had a charismatic personality. I was certain that the employees would readily follow his lead. It was a marriage made in heaven.

With the second venture financing completed and a new president in place, the production facility started up. Read-Rite began hiring workers and supervisors to run the facility. In about three months production was brought up to operating at a third of capacity. The heads when tested worked exceptionally well. The yield, the percentage of total parts made that performed to specification, was 30 percent, a reasonable level for this stage. The remaining seventy 70 were worthless. The Read-Rite business plan forecasted yields of 40 percent by the end of the first year of operation, building to 60 percent in future years as the engineers optimized the process and the workers became more adept.

Read-Rite would be profitable at 40 percent and doubly profitable at a 60 percent yield. In contrast, IBM operations were at an 80 percent yield. It appeared our company was headed toward becoming a $100 million plus company in a few years. All we needed was an order. Customers could now test production devices, eliminating that deterrent to getting them to convert from magnetic heads to Read-Rite.

With all the complex manufacturing problems, I spent most of my time during my weekly visits reviewing manufacturing results, inventory levels, spending, and cash balances. The last and shortest subject on my review schedule was the customer order status. It didn't take long because we didn't have any. Maxtor, one of the biggest disk drive makers, appeared to be close to switching but no other buyers seemed ready and no one at Read-Rite had any good ideas on how to promote an order.

Once more Read-Rite was slipping into a gigantic black hole. There was a huge factory overhead in place, a growing finished inventory of unwanted devices, and money was running out.

Then Maxtor came through with a huge order that not only cleaned out Read-Rite's inventory but also overwhelmed our production capacity. The company's world was suddenly turned upside down. We couldn't deliver fast enough. The board of directors chortled over "our high class problem." It sure beat the problem of no orders. The general feeling was it was time to break out the champagne and toast our collective genius. By this time in my life, I knew all I wanted to know about premature celebrations, but I did allow myself a few wishful thoughts and extrapolations.

The good news from Maxtor pulled us through a third

financing, $5 million, half of which came from new, eager investors. It was enough money to push Read-Rite over the top to cash-flow break-even.

Wrong again. Within a month of banking the new money, the company was in its biggest mess yet. The yield suddenly crashed from 30 percent to less than 20 percent. Somewhere during the previous eight-week production cycle, an undetected contaminant had found its way into most of the devices. There was a tiny peppering of a white powder, visible only under a microscope, on all the finished devices. It was spotted by Maxtor's incoming quality control. No one knew if the microscopic white powder would hurt the performance of a disk drive but Maxtor wasn't about to chance it. Read-Rite took all the contaminated parts back and junked them.

After an exhaustive analysis, the white powder was discovered to have originated in a cleaning step in the wafer slicing process. This had occurred early in the process which meant that for the next six weeks the contaminated production parts were still being worked on though they were useless. The problem was quickly remedied but it took two months to get acceptable parts through the line. All in all, we lost more than four months' production at an out-of-pocket loss of more than $1 million. Maxtor was sympathetic, but clearly jittery about Read-Rite's reliability.

We knew that the $5 million we had just raised wouldn't be enough to get Read-Rite over the top. Yet another financing would be required.

At this same time Cybernex, our only competitor, was about to go to trial with IBM. In an unprecedented move Cybernex approached Read-Rite to propose a merger to avoid the massive cost of litigation, a move they believed would receive IBM's blessing. After a frenzied 60 days of negotiations, a complicated settlement was reached with Cybernex and IBM. Cybernex and the patent problem would disappear within Read-Rite. For Read-Rite, it was a way to strengthen its competitive position and to acquire trained personnel and production equipment at a fraction of its replacement cost. The move was enthusiastically endorsed by our biggest customer, Maxtor. They believed it would give Read-Rite the extra talent and production capacity needed to become a reliable thin-film head supplier. They doubled their current orders and tripled their long-range purchase estimates. Even IBM was happy because Cybernex stopped benefiting from its secrets. The Read-Rite design did not violate IBM patents or use its technology.

The merger with Cybernex included new financing, another $6 million with half going to a new group led by the Hillmans, Cybernex's leading investor. A few Read-Rite investors were unhappy with the merger. Some saw little benefit; others too much dilution. They believed if we waited for a half year Cybernex would be out of business and we could pick up their customers and equipment for a song. I believed if we waited we could scare Maxtor away and encourage another competitor into the market. One Read-Rite investor had lost confidence in Meyercord completely and refused to back anything he endorsed. When companies have problems, fall behind in their plans, and overrun spending, investors get angry and frustrated. None of them has a clue as to how to solve the problems, but they often become negative and vindictive. With all our other problems we had to take on a court battle with some of our investors who objected to the merger.

I saw no alternative to Meyercord's merger plan and backed it to the hilt. In my mind, Meyercord had to succeed or the business would collapse. I was dead right.

Despite all the investor turmoil, Read-Rite was once again financed. For the first time, the company was fully staffed with the best available employees and consultants. The whole disk drive industry was poised to go our way. Most of them were actively planning to switch to Read-Rite within the next six months which would nicely coincide with a public offering.

The plant began to operate at nearly full capacity and yields started to edge up to 25 percent then 29 percent. Then another disaster struck. The heads started to delaminate. The manufacturing process included bonding or gluing layers together. For no apparent reason they started falling apart. As in the past this problem went undetected until final test and inspection. Virtually all the parts were worthless. The production line had to be completely shut down until the cause of the delamination was determined. Until then, no devices could be produced.

This time Maxtor was devastated by Read-Rite's problem. Eventually Maxtor had to curtail its own production and suffered huge financial losses which caused its stock to plunge.

The delamination incident cost Read-Rite millions of dollars. The disk drive industry withheld plans to switch to thin-film heads. Read-Rite became widely known as an unreliable supplier.

Making matters worse, the morale among former Cybernex employees plummeted. They felt like lost souls and second-class citizens and were regularly reminded of their status by some Read-Rite personnel. In every merger there is a polarization between winners and losers. In our case Read-Rite was a boastful "winner" and only gave lip service to assimilating the "losers." Amidst all the problems, Read-Rite's management failed to recognize and resolve this very bad situation.

After three tense weeks, we found that the quality problem was caused by a formulation change made by the glue supplier. Without informing Read-Rite, they had changed the chemistry of their glue. When we learned that the supplier couldn't go back to the original formula, we hastily conducted experiments and found a new glue that worked. The production line started up again.

During this frantic period, the entire Read-Rite staff, led by Meyercord, worked doggedly putting in Herculean hours to improve the performance of the company. Training for workers was intensified. Engineers were put on night shifts to be on the spot to help with problems. Personnel of the merged organizations began to know each other and work together effectively. Communication became the order of the day from daily "What's happening" meetings among all the foremen and section heads to hot dog roasts with Meyercord as the chief cook and cheerleader to the employees as they filed by to fill their plates. Morale soared; everyone began to believe the worst was behind us.

Two months later the yield crashed again. White specks came back, then the connecting wires mysteriously began to corrode.

Read-Rite had simply lost the recipe or technique for making quality parts. A year ago the process had worked. Now it no longer did and it wasn't getting fixed. This time, no one, not even me, believed the current management could make Read-Rite healthy and successful.

Meyercord, always a professional in his demeanor, was a natty dresser which annoyed some investors, especially during the bad times. He took his work and responsibilities seriously, always appeared calm, and was very articulate. Our last formal board meeting was electrifying to everyone but Meyercord. He listened to all the groaning about problems, the utter despair from certain investors, and after hearing everyone out proceeded to outline a plan to triple capacity, though he could not run the capacity already in place. Meyercord assumed by the time expansion was completed, the problems would be solved. It was a logical conclusion but no one, investors or employees, was going to back him at Read-Rite. The investors conferred privately later that day and by acclimation authorized me to get rid of Meyercord.

I fired him the following morning. He was, in part, the innocent victim of circumstance and gremlins. Read-Rite had been a break or two away from becoming a wonderful success. However, the reality of the venture business is you can't raise money around management that has failed. In many ways Meyercord had become the symbol of Read-Rite's failure.

I resigned as director shortly after firing Meyercord. I had outlived my usefulness to the company. My decision to hire and back Meyercord had been a big mistake. In hindsight, the merger was also a bad idea because we were unable to make it work.

Hambrecht & Quist brought in a turnaround team to take over operations. It was the spring of 1987, three and a half hard years since Read-Rite's inception. It took a year or more and a lot more money to salvage the situation. It was still worth the candle; a huge market still beckoned.

As of late 1989, Read-Rite remains operational and promising. Yields, while never consistent, have been sufficient to provide for a profitable business.

Oops—January 1990—the gremlins are at it again. The president and chief of operations have been summarily fired. The turnaround is still turning around. Maybe someday it will be all we hoped for.

11

Murphy's Law Redux—Salutar

Steve Quay, a young medical doctor and biochemist on the faculty of Stanford University, in 1984 formed a company he called Salutar. Quay had discovered, and later patented, the phenomenon that a metal combined with certain organic chemicals called rare-earth metal chelates greatly enhances the medical image taken of the body by magnetic resonance imaging (MRI). MRI is the exciting new technique that goes way beyond the capabilities of X-ray for use in medical diagnosis. The MRI process was pioneered by a successful venture-backed company called Diasonics, the founder of which introduced us to Quay. Rare-earth chelates, the basis for Quay's invention, are a mouthful of exotic chemicals made from an unusual metal, gadolinium, coupled with an organic substance called tetraacetic acid, a complex material the roots of which exist in vinegar.

These esoteric chemicals assist MRI in the same way barium helps medical X-rays. A barium "milkshake" tastes awful but it effectively helps radiologists to see what's happening in someone's stomach and intestines. MRI, a revolutionary new procedure, can be used to picture the brain, spine, heart, liver, and other organs opaque to X-ray. Before Quay's discovery the MRI images were fuzzy.

In tests on rabbits and dogs using Quay's chemicals, the images became sharp and well defined. Without the chemical, a rabbit brain looked like a hole in its head, a greyish mass with a few rivers running through. With the Quay chemical, one could clearly see blood pulsing through all the lobes and the major neurological centers. When I saw this, it left me with no doubt that Salutar's technology would enhance brain images and provide doctors an accurate picture of the size and location of brain tumors, trauma damage, and other abnormalities never before seen "in vivo" in the body.

The animal tests also proved that the chemicals Quay invented were perfectly safe and should be harmless to humans. The animals excreted all the chemicals within an hour or two which meant that, besides being nontoxic, they weren't around long enough to accumulate and cause side effects later on.

Nevertheless, since these substances would be injected into humans by radiologists prior to an MRI examination, they were, by Food and Drug Administration (FDA) regulations, automatically classified as pharmaceuticals, thus necessitating extensive, time-consuming, and expensive preclinical animal studies. If these animal trials were successful, extremely expensive and very time-consuming human trials would follow. To gain FDA clearance of Salutar's imaging chemicals both safety and efficacy had to be proved. Side effects, if any, had to be determined and evaluated.

On average, complete pharmaceutical clinical trials take seven to ten years and cost $25 to $75 million. Start-up companies always believe they can complete this work more quickly and cheaply than corporations. They assume they can complete the process in the theoretically shortest time. In fact, the well-documented history of clinical trials proves it always take two to three times longer in practice than in theory. Because of this overoptimism, start-up companies usually wind up taking shortcuts and eventually take even more time and spend more money.

To minimize the use of investor capital, Salutar sold the geographic marketing rights for some of the chemicals to three leading pharmaceutical companies in North America, Europe, and Japan. In exchange for marketing rights, Salutar received enough cash to theoretically pay for half the cost of the clinical trials. The market was expected to be $300 to $500 million so the marketing rights would be very valuable *if* Salutar's products worked in humans and received regulatory approval. At that early stage of development, those were very big ifs. In companies based on complex technology, venture capitalists and entrepreneurs alike always assume the products will work. A little self-delusion helps avoid panic attacks later on.

Since Salutar hired independent testing laboratories to conduct its clinical trials, the company needed only a modest-sized group of technically trained employees, 20 to 25 people. Salutar's business strategy was eventually to manufacture all the chemicals with the three corporate partners selling them in their designated geographical areas. While the products were advancing through clinical trials, the company planned to build a facility to mass produce and package the substances in dosage form. Each dose would sell for $100. Salutar had the potential to generate over $300 million in sales within five years of getting FDA approval.

Over the long range, Salutar expected to manufacture and sell second-generation products entirely on its own without competition from its corporate partners. Based on just a rough outline, Arthur Rock, Mohr-Davidow Ventures, and Hambrecht & Quist initially invested $2 million in exchange for owning 50 percent of the company. The rest of the shares went to Quay and other current and future employees. This valued the company at $4 million. There was no clear path to raising the additional $25 to $50 million it would take to build Salutar into a $300 million success. Though unspoken, the belief held by the investors was that Salutar would be sold to a pharmaceutical giant before all the money would be needed.

The employees were expected to spend most of their time developing the process of making, characterizing, and purifying the chemicals used to make the imaging drugs. Under Quay's close daily supervision, Salutar personnel were divided into four groups. Each group had a carefully detailed work plan including an optimistic schedule of completion dates for every task.

Despite this professional and highly organized leadership, there were massive problems and delays right from the beginning. Completing the experiments that led to important milestones turned out to be time-consuming and frustrating as it always does during the research phase. Quay began to show signs of stress, bouncing between optimism and rage when experiments went awry.

An important step was the selection of the most promising chemical formulation for use in the animal preclinical trials. The molecules made from gadolinium chelate could be chemically rearranged to improve their safety. These modifications dramatically reduced potential toxicity by lowering the time it took to excrete all the chemical. Once gone, it could do no harm. Unfortunately, lowering toxicity equally reduced the chemical's image enhancement quality. Balancing safety with effectiveness to achieve the optimum formulation was far more difficult than we had originally thought.

Paralleling the formulation effort, other Salutar personnel were seeking practical ways to make these exotic chemicals in large quantities. This meant scaling up from one-liter laboratory glassware to 1,000-liter then 10,000-liter reactors. Making rare-earth chelates even in small quantities was as hard as it sounds. The chemical reaction produces a mixture of what is desired plus hundreds of different impurities. Engineers had to learn how to refine the process to minimize impurities and then learn how to get rid of the impurities. The separation, purification, and concentration of the final product was far more complex than anyone planned for, though the procedures were always known to be difficult. In venture companies' overoptimism rules, delays are always the other guy's problem.

The next task was pharmacology. The optimized purified formulation had to be packaged in a stable, dosage form. Since the product was to be injected, the rare-earth chelate had to be diluted and must thereafter remain stable, not degrading for at least six months to provide an adequate shelf life. Finding the right diluent, preservatives, and buffers was incredibly elusive, compounded by the fact that the technical people forgot that a six-month test takes six months. Each time the formulation changed, the test had to start over.

The final task was supervising the clinicals and preparing the documentation necessary for FDA approval. Tens of thousands of data points had to be collected and statistically analyzed for eventual presentation to the FDA.

As required, the chemical was produced in an FDA-licensed facility and formulated in dosage form, both mandated before it could be called a drug. Clinical trials in animals were conducted as follows:

- The drug was fed to animals to determine the toxic level.
- The drug was injected in animals at 10 and 100 times the expected human dosage and the results determined and recorded.
- The drug was injected in animals at one to ten times the expected dosage and the excretions tested. The animals were then killed at one-hour intervals for up to 12 hours. All the organs were autopsied and tested for drug residues.
- The drug was injected in animals at the expected dosage levels daily for six months. Half the animals were then killed and autopsied, the other half injected for another six months before they also were killed and autopsied.

When the animal testing was completed, the data were submitted to the FDA with a request for approval to proceed to human clinical trials. It normally takes three to six months after submission to obtain approval. If and when approval is received (not all submissions are approved), Phase I clinics may legally begin. This involves testing one then 10 or 20 human volunteers at a low dosage, then repeating the experiment, if all goes well, at higher dosages. The thrust of this work is solely to determine safety. No attempt is made to see if the drug works.

Volunteers are given complete physicals before the experiment. After the experiment or being injected with the drug, they are checked for side effects daily for a week then monthly for three to six months. If there is the tiniest abnormality, it must be reported to the FDA and the entire trial may be disqualified or stopped altogether.

Salutar began animal testing in 1985. At the end of 1988 we were still waiting for FDA clearance to move on to Phase I human clinical testing. The work was tedious, time-consuming, and unpredictable, conducted in outside laboratories, not under Salutar's direct control.

Quay managed all four development groups and was in the middle of all the delays and disappointments. This exacerbated his already difficult management style. Quay was extremely intense and moody, and worked incredibly long hours, seven days a week for months at a stretch. A perfectionist, he was unforgiving of himself as well as everyone else, regardless of their level of responsibility. Worst of all, he expected everyone from the receptionist to the director of manufacturing to match his work habits. After a year of watching this, the board realized that Salutar needed someone else to run the company before everyone quit or someone murdered Quay.

After a six-month, exhaustive search, the board of directors hired John Diekman as president. Diekman, at the request of the board, worked as a consultant to Salutar for three months prior to the job offer to see if he could get along with Quay. He did and Quay, with a twinge of reluctance, said he knew they could work together.

Diekman had a Ph.D. in chemistry from Stanford. After graduating he worked in research then as an executive for Zoecon, an animal medicine company, and later for Sandoz, the Swiss pharmaceutical giant. He was bright, had a warm, sincere personality and a wide range of interests. He was an excellent tennis player.

If Quay was Dr. Death to the employees of Salutar, Diekman was Dr. Congeniality. Besides working at Salutar, he pursued a vigorous personal life on and off the tennis court. He enjoyed and wanted a life outside of the business. Diekman always managed to give more than enough time to the company, but far from all there was to give. Certainly not enough for Quay.

I never knew if it was purely Diekman's style that compelled Quay to lobby with certain board members to get Diekman fired within months of his being hired, or his natural resistance to having a boss other than himself. Within a year, Quay openly loathed Diekman. And though he tried harder to hide it, Diekman felt the same about Quay.

There was a vital second financing of the company during the spring of 1987. Six million dollars was snapped up by an array of existing investors along with four new groups. Salutar could easily have raised double that amount. At the time pharmaceuticals were a very promising area to investors and the company had the look of a hot deal, though it was at least four years away from an FDA-approved product. After this financing Salutar was valued at $18 million.

A month after closing the financing, right on cue for the new investors, there were a series of terrible setbacks. I always feel badly when new investors suffer unpleasant surprises right after investing at a higher price than the first investment. I try to honestly portray the state of a business to new investors, but invariably something unexpected goes wrong right after the closing.

By this time Diekman and Quay were openly at war, each criticizing the other in front of fellow employees, the board of directors, and even important external contacts. Quay blamed every mistake the company made on Diekman's work habits or stupidity. And the company made a lot of mistakes. As a director, I found it comical to observe Quay blaming his own mistakes on the tremendous distraction caused by Diekman's behavior.

For his part, Diekman punched away at Quay's maniacal style, reminding anyone who would listen that Quay had the personality of an excited cobra. Diekman saw himself as Salutar's only link to sanity and reasonableness.

During that same time, the company learned that a patent

issued to Schering, a German pharmaceutical company, contained claims that threatened Salutar's position. We also learned that when Quay filed Salutar's patents, he and his lawyer had somehow completely overlooked an issued Schering patent—an unprecedented, egregious oversight.

Diekman flogged Quay at every opportunity for this error. Quay, in turn, blamed Diekman. They both blamed the patent attorney. It was a bleak moment for the company, especially for the new investors. We hired a new patent lawyer.

After an exhaustive study, our new attorney concluded that most, if not all, of Salutar's chemicals were outside of the Schering patent. Learned counsel also concluded that the German company's patent was not valid. His words sounded warm and wonderful, but I also knew that our patent lawyer was paid by the hour and had no stake in Salutar's future. Over time, however, *ten* or more other law firms looked over the Salutar patent position and each drew the same conclusion.

I arranged a meeting with executives of Schering. From our discussions I concluded they believed their patent was valid and that their claims overlapped Salutar's technology. I left the meeting with a strong sense of dread. Our lawyers eventually put in writing that it was unlikely but conceivable that a court would declare Schering's patent valid and that Salutar was infringing. I would never put a patent to a test unless absolutely necessary. No sane person would because the only test is in patent court. I could only hope that Schering came to the same conclusion.

The patent was not Salutar's only problem. The company was a year or more behind in their schedule for clinical trials. Nothing adverse had happened. The development work simply took longer than anyone expected. A year's delay cost $5 million more than planned and Salutar didn't have the money. Our corporate agreements didn't provide for delays or increased costs. It was impossible to raise another $5 million just months after our last financing without severe dilution. In addition, a new financing would be adversely affected by the open Quay/Diekman war, the patent problem, and the delay which caused the need for more money.

The board of directors met frantically, formally and informally. We came to two conclusions. Diekman had to go. Quay was a handful but was also indispensable. It was time to sell Salutar rather than attempt to refinance and build it.

We would have a difficult, if not impossible, task to hire a new president. Who would want the job? In an attempt to insulate the organization from Quay's capriciousness, the board of directors elected one of its directors, Larry Mohr, chairman. A venture capitalist investor in Salutar, Mohr had already become the focal point of all policy, the arbitrator of disputes, and a father confessor. He had no management or pharmaceutical experience and was a stubborn, single-minded maverick but despite these traits, he did an exceptionally fine job as chairman. Without his skill and devotion, Salutar would have cratered on the spot.

Quay's personality was a nigh insuperable obstacle but he remained Salutar's most important asset. Without Quay, there was no Salutar.

Diekman was not totally surprised but he had hoped we would fire Quay. He saw his demise as a failure on his part to win enough votes on the board of directors. Mohr and I tried to convince him that his resignation was in the best interests of the company. Salutar needed Quay's genius to become successful and, after all, Diekman was a substantial shareholder and stood to gain a great deal of money if Salutar continued to increase in value.

Mohr and I agreed to give Diekman a positive reference to anyone seeking to hire him and asked in return his pledge not to bad-mouth the company or Quay. We gave Diekman a letter of understanding regarding his severance package, suggested he hire a lawyer to review our proposal, and concluded what was a fairly calm and reasonable meeting.

During the next weeks, while negotiating changes in the severance agreement with Diekman's lawyer, we hit a big snag. One of our directors leaked a bad reference regarding Diekman's work habits to a potential employer who, in turn, repeated the words to Diekman. He was furious and rightly so. He made repeated telephone calls to me, both at the office and at home at night, to be sure I understood his position. We eventually solved the problem by getting the board member to apologize in writing and to agree to remain mute on the subject of Diekman thereafter. After two wasted months of wrangling, Diekman signed his severance agreement.

It was a messy ending, but eventually achieved without litigation or open warfare.

Salutar was in a unique situation. Despite our difficulties, our technology was potentially valuable to five or six pharmaceutical companies, all of whom sold products to radiologists. One big obstacle was the patent problem. Most big companies shun buying into patent disputes because it's very difficult to predict the outcome. Another obstacle was the old marketing agreements with three separate companies. Any buyer would want to cancel or modify those agreements to benefit fully from the purchase by selling directly to radiologists.

Unexpectedly Salutar got a big break. Preoccupied as we were with our problems, we were all surprised the day Quay's patents were issued. Patents are applied for by filing applications with the U.S. Patent Office. After about six months the patent office usually takes some action, disputes claims, asks questions, or cites prior art (disclosures) that might invalidate the possibility of receiving a patent. In all, the process normally takes one to three years. The Salutar application was nearing the three-year mark when it was finally approved and issued as a valid patent. It gave everyone a much needed boost. Salutar now owned patents on what was believed to be the safest, most effective, known imaging agent. Deservedly, Quay was ecstatic. Not only did this help morale but we needed Quay in an elevated mood. The biggest downside in selling the company was the fear that Quay could become angry and blow out a potential buyer.

It was now just a question of choosing a purchaser and a price. The board of directors debated fiercely over the asking price for Salutar. Most of the directors favored "something north of $100 million." I was a $50 million man and would have taken $40 million for a quick sale. My reasoning was based on the fact that Salutar would have no product revenues before 1991. It was January 1988 and no product had yet made it to human clinicals. Pharmaceutical industry statistics predict that only one out of 12 products that enter human clinicals ever gets approved. The risks were still enormous.

My biggest concern was time. If Salutar didn't get sold and ran out of money, or if Steve Quay became absolutely intolerable, the value of the company would be zero. It was the worst case of the "prince or pig" syndrome I've ever seen. Salutar would either sell for tens of millions of dollars or be worthless.

After debating the selling price interminably the board decided to let the five or six potential buyers set the price. Within days, Quay preempted this wisdom by telling every buyer the price was $110 million. At least the auction had begun.

Several potential buyers walked away immediately. One of them, Mallinckrodt, told me they would consider $35 or maybe $40 million, but felt $110 million was absolute lunacy.

Even so, the company expected a quick sale, certainly by mid-year. By August 1988, with no offer in sight, the board began really to worry. Time was flying. Suddenly our best prospect, Eastman Kodak/Sterling Drug, the owner of Salutar's U.S. marketing rights, offered $55 million. After a quick deliberation, the Salutar board of directors accepted. Our high hopes were shattered six weeks later, however, when squabbling over contract terms scuttled the deal. By maneuvering to lower the purchase price, the buyer overnegotiated the deal.

Fortunately in a matter of days, Mohr, our chief negotiator, was able to get the last potential buyer, Nycomed, a Norwegian pharmaceutical company, to step into the exact deal we had proposed to Eastman Kodak/Sterling. They ultimately purchased Salutar lock, stock, and Steve Quay on April 1, 1989, for $55 million. Mergers take a long time, in this case more than one year. Hambrecht & Quist made $7 million or 14 times its original investment.

By the end of 1989, Quay was an important and successful executive with Nycomed. The merger looks like a big success for the acquiror. Eastman Kodak/Sterling is still very unhappy it lost the merger. The patent issue remains unresolved. John Diekman is the president of another venture-backed company.

It would be wrong to conclude that Quay sounds like someone to be avoided. He's a genius. I would back him in a minute in any reasonable new idea and would build another company around him. He would probably still be the same tyrannical pigheaded person he was at Salutar. I'd also probably make 14 times on my investors' money. It's important to remember that there are hundreds of people like John Diekman who can run a company but they seldom can create valuable companies. The Steve Quays come along but once a decade. I wish him well and remain his friend.

12

The Farmer in the Dell—Calgene

Calgene was founded in 1981 by a very wily guy named Norm Goldfarb. He created Calgene in the belief it would become the premier plant genetics biotechnology company in the world. What made Goldfarb's vision extraordinary was that he was an electrical engineer and his only work experience was in semiconductors at Intel. He had no experience or technical training whatever in either plants or biotechnology.

Goldfarb was a thinker. He read how Bob Swanson founded Genentech in 1976 by collaborating with Herb Boyer, a world-famous Stanford University gene splicer and microbiologist. Swanson, a great visionary, had, in a stroke of genius, telephoned Boyer cold and convinced him to join Genentech as a founder. By 1981, Genentech was the clear leader in pharmaceutical biotechnology. The company first pioneered genetically altered bacteria to produce human insulin. A virtual cornucopia of genetically engineered pharmaceuticals followed.

Goldfarb copied what he believed was the Genentech success formula except that he put the focus of Calgene entirely on genetically manipulating plants. He too made a cold call to Dan Cohen, a world-renowned plant geneticist who was then a tenured professor at the University of California at Davis. UC

Davis is the Harvard of agricultural science. Though perfect strangers, Cohen and Goldfarb immediately joined forces and formed Calgene.

Imitations seldom work. In this case, however, Calgene was promising despite Goldfarb's total lack of knowledge about plant biotechnology. Few people in the early 1980s really understood the science. Cohen was among that tiny group. Goldfarb quickly figured out what he thought it would take to turn plant biotechnology into a successful business. No one has ever matched his vision.

All by himself, Goldfarb put together a credible business plan, found start-up capital, and hired people to carry out the plan.

His original dream was perfect copy for readers of the science section of *Time* magazine. Biotechnology, he claimed, would enable scientists to genetically alter plants so they could grow nearly anything imaginable. The fantasy he created was that genes could be transplanted from a coffee tree to a blueberry bush. Coffee berries could be grown in backyards in New Jersey. Beefsteak tomatoes could be engineered to contain the same amount of protein as prime rib. Meat could come in a ketchup bottle.

"Yes," he opined, "there could be strawberries the size of pumpkins, apple trees growing drugs, and limes sprouting from tomato plants."

Biotechnology in reality has made only small steps toward thus thwarting Mother Nature. According to Cohen, one realistic possibility was to transfer to corn the genes alfalfa uses to "fix" nitrogen from air. If accomplished, this would eliminate the need for expensive and environmentally offensive fertilizers.

A second possibility was to genetically double the protein content of winter wheat from 2 to 4 percent. Though not quite beefsteak, it would improve human nutrition as well as its value as animal feed.

A third possibility was to make crops resistant to herbicides. Since the 1970s, before planting a field, farmers sprayed with herbicides as a "pre-emergence" weed killer. Herbicides such as Roundup would kill all the weeds. After planting, however, herbicides were no longer useful because they would kill the crop as well. Weeds then had to be removed by machine or human labor.

By a quirk of nature, one plant, Johnson Grass, is unaffected by herbicides. Calgene planned to discover the gene that made Johnson Grass herbicide resistant and transfer it to, for instance, tobacco or cotton plants. Herbicides could then be used to control weeds without harming the crop, a big plus for farmers as well as for herbicide producers.

Goldfarb incorporated these three goals into Calgene's business plan and used this blueprint to raise capital.

Allied Chemical, a major fertilizer producer, was determined to become a technology leader. By chance, Goldfarb contacted them at just the right moment. They put up $1 million along with the promise of $1 million a year for the next two years. Goldfarb personally put up $500,000, a large part of his and his siblings' trust fund. That was a bold move by a founder, unheard of the first time around.

One of Goldfarb's best talents was finding outstanding people and convincing them to join Calgene. One crucial recruit was Bob Goodman, a University of Illinois professor and world authority on the genetic manipulation of plants. To this day, I know of no one who can outthink Goodman in this field.

Goodman then attracted outstanding technical people to Calgene, people who believed in the practical application of plant genetics. Within a year, Goodman and his organization had mastered the transferral of genes from one species of plant to another. They developed a microinjection technique to transfer genes to germ plasm and used plant viruses as vectors or carriers of the basic genetic material, plant DNA.

The first Calgene model was the manipulation of the genetic structure of a tobacco plant. It was a perfect laboratory specimen, hardy and easy to grow indoors. Tobacco has a constant companion, the tobacco mosaic virus. This virus was readily available as a friendly genetic vector or carrier of a desirable gene.

Having spent all its start-up capital, Calgene needed new

financing by the summer of 1983. At that time no investor seemed interested in betting money on an esoteric plant research project. Even if it worked, it was years from commercialization. It was at this point that I heard about Calgene from Rob Jack, the company's lawyer from Wilson, Sonsini, Goodrich and Rosati, a venture-oriented law firm. Of those looking, I became the only venture capitalist who liked the company. My enthusiasm was based entirely on the economic importance of plant technology and the high quality of Calgene's research team. I was confident that if it were doable, these were the people to do it.

I undertook to raise $3 million. Right in the middle of this financing, Allied reneged on its commitment to make further investments. They abandoned their corporate strategy of becoming a technical leader and dropped the Calgene project without notice. They even fired the man who sponsored the original investment. Very few potential investors were astute enough to see this move for what it was—corporate capriciousness. Everyone thought that Allied had discovered something very negative about Calgene. Just because no one could figure out what didn't mean it wasn't something awful. J. H. Whitney and Venrock, two premier venture capital groups, dropped out. I showed the deal to two dozen more without any luck. Few venture capitalists wanted to play especially when they found out about Allied and learned that Whitney and Venrock passed. There's a snowball effect in being turned down and it's all downhill. The three investors I finally corralled were a ragtag group. The individual partners at Lazard, the New York-based investment bank led by Goldfarb's college roommate and long-time friend, Peter Roberts, comprised the largest new investor unit.

When Hambrecht & Quist became the lead investor with $1.5 million, half the total, I went on the board of directors. This entailed driving one and a half hours from San Francisco to Davis nearly every week since I believe in close contact with any company of which I am a director.

One of my first acts as a director was to ratify hiring a

marketing manager. Calgene would never become a real company without a viable marketing strategy. Questions such as how to make money out of corn that doesn't need fertilizer or has resistance to herbicides needed to be answered.

Calgene hired Roger Salquist, a Stanford MBA with 15 years experience in the high-tech agricultural business. And as a recently failed entrepreneur he had guts and had learned humility.

From the very first day, Salquist demonstrated he was bright, enthusiastic, articulate, knowledgeable, and a bundle of energy. The Calgene organization was immediately drawn to his style, decisiveness, and leadership. Salquist was gregarious, funny, had wide interests, and loved to travel. He was a perfect counterpoint to Goldfarb who was Mr. Enigma and damned proud of it. Goldfarb held back all he could. Salquist was unable to hold back anything.

The company consistently made breathtaking scientific progress. Goodman's scientists successfully transferred the herbicide resistant gene from Johnson Grass to a tobacco plant. For the first time we had tangible proof that genetic manipulation really worked in a crop, not just in a test tube.

A rapidly growing biotechnology bag of tricks enabled Calgene to produce a tomato containing a third less water and therefore a third more solids. Shipping costs would therefore be cut and ketchup and soup would need fewer tomatoes.

The most amazing scientific advance Calgene invented in 1985 involved plant oils. Plants make or grow oils in molecules containing two carbon-based couplets. Edible oils, such as corn, peanut, or soy, have one or two couplets. After the harvest, oils are pressed out of the fruits and sold wholesale for eight to ten cents a pound.

More valuable oils, such as coconut or cocoa, have two to four carbon couplets and sell for premium prices, double that of soy. Exotic oils, such as palm and castor, have five to ten couplets and sell for sixty cents to two dollars per pound. They are used in cosmetics and as industrial lubricants.

Each plant species is genetically coded to make oils with a

specific number of carbon couplets. Calgene scientists demonstrated that the genetic code could be changed to make certain plants produce any desired number of carbon couplets without noticing the difference. Instead of producing an edible oil worth ten cents a pound, the genetically altered plant could make the same weight of oil worth one dollar or more per pound.

The farmer could grow the genetically altered plants the same way he grew soy or canola. This very valuable crop could then be pressed to recover the new oil in exactly the same manner as a food oil. No new capital investment was needed to process these high carbon couplet oils.

As is always the case, not everything worked. Corn plants genetically altered to fix nitrogen didn't need any fertilizer. Unfortunately, the plant was so busy making its own fertilizer it didn't make any corn either. Nature gave a choice—make corn or make fertilizer.

Higher protein wheat never made it out of the laboratory. It didn't germinate in field trials. The species was too weakened by its genetic manipulation. Even if it worked, as Salquist pointed out, Calgene would be able to sell only one crop year's worth of altered wheat. Farmers would simply store their own seeds from then on and wouldn't need Calgene.

This was a vitally important insight. Calgene had to have a way of controlling genetically altered plants. Corn, tomatoes, and tobacco could be hybridized. Their seeds wouldn't produce a second-generation seed so farmers would have to buy them each year from Calgene. The oils business was perfect because Calgene could grow and own the crop, thereby controlling the special seeds.

It was clear to me that Calgene now had the technology to create a profitable business. Its array of scientifically feasible projects included herbicide-resistant cotton and tobacco, high solids tomatoes, and high value oils.

It was 1985. The company had all this valuable technology and a clear path to becoming a large, profitable business, but the process would take time and a lot of money. The technical effort alone would cost more than $3 million a year.

One major hurdle was that farmers, already plagued by natural risks such as weather, insects, and soil pathogens, who traditionally make a meager living, pathologically resist innovation. Anything new is viewed with suspicion and cynicism. The industry's rule of thumb was it took seven crop years to accept something new and then only if the field trials were perfect. Calgene would have to be lucky to succeed in as little as seven years. That pushed profitability ahead to no earlier than 1992.

Despite Calgene's incredible scientific progress, no new group wanted to invest any money. I put up another $1 million of Hambrecht & Quist's funds on top of the $1.5 million already in. The Lazard partners also doubled up. The rest of the existing investors put up as little as possible, about $150,000.

Right after the meager financing closed, Bob Goodman calmly announced at a board meeting that he was planning to accept a position as dean of the Graduate School of Natural Sciences at the University of Illinois. He wanted to return to academia and his wife wanted to leave Davis and live in the Midwest. Naively, he said he had waited until the financing was over before resigning, "so as not to interfere with the business of raising money." The meeting turned ugly and chaotic. I grabbed Goodman and took him for a very long facts-of-life walk. I appealed to his sense of responsibility and made blunt threats about the consequences of withholding material information prior to a financing. Goodman, a very decent fellow, recanted his resignation. The board reassembled and moved on to consider where we might get the money we needed for Calgene.

Fortunately Calgene received nearly $3 million over three years in contract research from Rhone-Poulenc and Nestles in exchange for marketing rights to certain specific technology. It still wasn't nearly enough money, however.

On top of our cash crisis, there was a minipalace coup. The entire senior management, overdosed with stress and frustration, rebelled at Goldfarb's phlegmatic management style. They gave me a "him or us" ultimatum. Ordinarily I stonewall ultimatums. In this case, I knew they were right. Goldfarb had outlived his usefulness as chief executive officer.

I took him to lunch at my favorite San Francisco Chinese restaurant. Right after the mushu pork I told him he was no longer chief executive officer and would be replaced at once by Salquist.

Goldfarb was devastated by my action, but the trip back to Davis gave him time to accept the change. Upon his return he endorsed Salquist as his successor. Goldfarb spent the next two years as chairman of the board and vigorously assisted Calgene in every way possible. He even put more personal money into the company.

He got high marks for character from everyone. He told me later, however, that he lost his taste for Chinese food that day.

As president, Salquist did a magnificent job of selling Calgene to additional corporate sponsors. Contract research reached $5 million per year. Without this money, Calgene might well have perished. Another big plus was endorsement by large companies such as Rhone-Poulenc, Nestles, and Campbell's Soup. It was as if they were announcing that Calgene had something very special.

By late 1986, we were once again out of money and on the brink of financial disaster. After weeks of soul searching, I put up another $1 million. It was a close decision. I almost gave up and let it go under. In the end, I supported the company because I still believed in the economic importance of its technology and Calgene deserved a chance to succeed.

At the end of the first quarter of 1987 there was clearly something special in the air. Investors showed a sudden interest in Calgene. With new and renewed corporate sponsors, the company was on the cusp of breaking even. Procter & Gamble, after a year of study, finally came through. They put up $2.5 million for the rights to the use in cosmetics of oils from genetically altered plants. The market for new public offerings began to heat up. Underwriters actually courted Calgene. The board of directors picked Paine Webber and Hambrecht & Quist to take Calgene public.

After a whirlwind road show, or talks to groups of institutional investors, Calgene blew out their public offering and easily raised $25 million which valued the company at $85 million. A year earlier we had struggled to raise money at a $20 million valuation. My investment, nearly written off six months earlier, was suddenly a big success. On paper I had earned four times on the $3.5 million I had invested.

I resigned from Calgene's board of directors a year later. I believe a venture capitalist needs to get off public boards and get back to helping new companies start up.

Venture capitalists don't make much money for their investors by remaining on public company boards. They stay because they are having a good time basking in their success as an early investor, or because they fall in love with management having scaled so many mountains together, or they believe they are protecting their investor/shareholders' interests. The only good reason to stay is the last one, the shareholders, but that seldom works. Board members have a tough time selling their stock in a company without trashing the price or being sued for acting on inside information (a few stay on boards precisely for that advantage). It was hard for me to leave Calgene and I visit the company from time to time to see how my chickens are roosting.

At the end of the 1980s, after nine years in operation, Calgene is waiting for the mid-1990s when it expects to become a huge, profitable business. Salquist remains as enthusiastic and ebullient as ever. Calgene has completed four additional acquisitions, has started a joint venture in the Pacific Rim, and has raised another $25 million in public markets.

Goldfarb, the plant biotechnology novice, saw his dream come true and he (and his siblings) made a lot of money. Cohen still teaches at UC Davis but takes more time off to fish for salmon. Calgene throws out any textbook formula for success. And for this company, the best is yet to come.

13

To Be or Not to Be

The difference between a resounding success and total bankruptcy is the length of a gnat. If you listen to war stories, it's easy to conclude that a company's success is the result of the heroics and brilliance of one person—usually the person telling the story. Beware! You're likely to encounter any number of claimants who'll tell you he is that one.

It's not surprising that failure is always an orphan. I've never heard anyone claim he contributed to a failure. Almost to a man, participants see failure as entirely the result of external forces—the "we got screwed" syndrome.

What really causes a company to fail? In my experience failure is caused by delays in execution, bad decisions, and misfired actions by entrepreneurs in collaboration with their venture capitalists. In hindsight most of these mistakes could have been avoided or at least mitigated. Success is always the result of a team effort. A lot of people make it work. More things go right than wrong which means that good luck also plays an important role in any success. Baby companies are simply too fragile to survive if everything that can go wrong does.

There are two separate constituencies within the structure of a company that must get it right—the employees and the board of directors.

The environment for employees shifts dramatically during the various stages of a company's growth and development. In the early days of a start-up, a handful of people do all the work. They build and test prototypes, answer the telephones, install equipment, and lock up at night after emptying the wastebaskets.

At this stage the president leads the tiny employee group without the need of structure or formality. Everyone knows what everyone is doing by osmosis. Goals or objectives are clear and very expensive in terms of both money and personal sacrifice.

Within months of the start-up, anguish usually sets in. Though everyone has worked hard, no important goals have been met, at least not those that would reduce the fragility of the business. During this time new people have been hired and no one has had time to integrate them into the company's work plan. The boss has continually set unrealistic and unachievable goals and everyone has bought into them. The employees have done their best but after a while they start to grumble. Prototypes don't work and need to be reengineered quickly. If anything, there seems to be more, not less, risk, more questions, fewer answers. The 60- to 80-hour workweek takes a physical and mental toll. Life outside of work takes a real licking.

Some companies never escape this hellhole. After six months to three years of banging away, they run out of money and go south. Millions of dollars are lost by venture capitalists and all those smart, hard-working employees who made monumental sacrifices are suddenly unemployed.

Though they may be staggering, those who tough out this first stage can reach the second stage. At this point the company learns how to manufacture its products, arranges for customers to test the products, gains regulatory approvals, develops the systems, and plans to scale up production. The employee head count rises from 5 or 10 to 50 people. The boss, despite what he thinks, can no longer run the organization out of his hat. With the help of the board, a hierarchy is established on paper. In practice it works imperfectly. Communications are of the utmost importance but are seldom effective. New people hired in haste don't know what's expected of them. Everything has the highest priority. Everything is scheduled for completion by month's end. By this time everyone knows the goals are cockeyed and the emperor has no clothes. Finger pointing sets in and cabals form. Tempers get short and blowups occur with increasing frequency.

Near the breaking point, the boss holds a company-wide meeting, fervently promises to improve communications, apologizes for all the confusion, thanks everyone for their hard work, and reschedules goals. Everyone is hopeful and enthusiasm returns. Unfortunately, it's usually short-lived.

Few entrepreneurs have the personality or the skill to lead a large organization effectively. In many instances that's why they become entrepreneurs in the first place. They hate structure, authority, and bureaucracy. When they create a 50-person organization, they fail to realize that it takes all three of these elements to function efficiently.

Organized chaos characterizes many companies at this second stage. Only in rare cases does a former chief executive officer remain effective. In the majority of venture capital-backed companies, entrepreneur presidents get fired or pushed aside at this stage. They may stay on as chairman or director of technology, but they are no longer chief executive officers. In every one of these cases the board wishes it had acted six months or a year sooner, a feeling that further alienates it from the deposed president.

Since few companies have anyone in the organization to take over, a new chief executive officer has to be hired from the outside. This change of leadership is the *single most critical development* in the life of a baby company. The time spent hiring the new chief executive officer, the shock to the organization when the changeover takes place, the lack of direction in the interim, the quality of the new person hired, and the speed with which he or she seizes command, all impact heavily on the health and potential of the company.

In the best of circumstances replacing a chief executive

officer is a wrenching experience and companies can easily fail at this juncture. Delays, poor product planning, incompetent or poorly directed management, bad morale, good people quitting, bad people staying, stress overload, running out of money, program cutbacks can all happen and usually do. This litany of disasters can result in companies becoming terminal, a conclusion not often discovered until more millions of dollars have been spent. When a company fails, its assets are sold off at bargain prices or it goes bankrupt. In this situation venture capitalists lose $3 to $20 million and 50 people become unemployed.

Those companies that survive enter the next stage of development, called ramping-up. Products are now routinely made and sold in ever growing volumes. The burn rate, or total monthly cash outflow, skyrockets, often peaking at more than $500,000. (The term "burn rate" comes from the fact that if a company fails, the venture capitalist might just as well have burned his money.) Eventually the losses diminish (or it's lights out) as sales revenues grow to a profitable level. The company's organization expands rapidly including factory workers, sales and customer service, accounting, and a personnel department. Hierarchy and bureaucracy work efficiently and a new generation of management starts to develop from within the ranks. Manufacturing capacity is sold out more quickly than expected and the parking lot overflows with cars.

During this time the company and its board contemplate IPOs and mergers. Employees no longer work quite so hard. There is a receptionist overseeing a large flow of visitors waiting in a glamorous area. (There is a sense among top management that "you have to look like a winner to be a winner.") In this stage, the third to seventh year of existence, the companies seldom fail outright and shareholders often make a bundle. Failure at this stage after all the heavy spending to cover losses and pay for production facilities would result in catastrophic losses to investors.

The Board Room

The board of directors is another constituency that influences the company's success or failure. Technically, the board is responsible for protecting the shareholders' interests but in practice it operates as the boss of the chief executive. I've been on dozens of boards and have seen little in common among them. Most support the chief executive officer's decisions right up until the moment they fire him. I've seen a few boards where outside directors bully management, are always confrontational, and are destructive. There are other boards of directors that blindly back a chief executive officer's every whim and are equally destructive.

A typical board of directors for a start-up company consists of five people—the chief executive officer and one other representative from management, usually both founders of the company; two directors who are venture capitalists, the lead investor and one other; and a fifth director selected at large. Ideally the fifth director is a widely recognized expert in an area directly related to the company's interest, perhaps a retired business executive, a successful entrepreneur, or a university professor. More often than not, this fifth director is, or quickly becomes, a crony of the chief executive officer.

The purpose of the "outside" or nonmanagement director is to be helpful. This means offering solutions to problems, interviewing job candidates (I interview them all at this stage and later on all direct reports), providing advice and counsel on strategy and operational issues, raising capital, or arranging corporation partnerships. I believe that the directors should challenge the chief executive officer but not smother him.

A useful board member needs two assets—the experience to gain credibility from the chief executive officer and the time it takes to understand the company. Board meetings are monthly or bimonthly. Directors must visit the company at least twice a month, not only to talk to the chief executive officer but with key employees as well. There's no other way to grasp what's going on. Unless board members have direct knowledge about the company, their opinions carry little weight. On the other extreme, unless outside directors work in the company on a daily basis, they are never qualified to "call the shots" and be the boss.

When the venture capitalist director is an associate fresh out of "B" school, he or she can't provide much help, not having the experience to be believable. The chief executive officer tolerates such associates only because they will be needed to write checks in the future. Some chief executive officers cuddle up to novice venture capitalists, becoming father and mentor. Others develop a thinly disguised loathing. (I beat up on venture capitalist associates in part because they're half my age and twice as smart.)

Monthly board meetings focus on the previous month's results versus the business plan, with particular emphasis on spending versus budget. As delays and disappointments occur, most chief executive officers glibly rationalize and externalize the roots of their problems. The chief executive officer personally manages to remain a hero during these difficulties. Overspending is always a hot board topic. Most of the discussion centers on why it happened. Unfortunately, little time is spent on the consequences, that is, running out of money.

Venture-backed companies are usually financed around milestones. For example, $2 million is invested to *develop a prototype*. When that's completed $5 million more is raised from existing and new investors to *build a pilot factory* and *sell the first product*, then $15 million is raised to *build a full-scale factory* and to provide working capital to support achieving *$10 million in worldwide sales*.

Blowing through all the cash before reaching a milestone is big trouble. When this happens, the existing venture capitalists are the only source of new cash except at distressed prices. When spending overruns occur, venture capitalists become unhappy with both the company and its chief executive officer (and even with the other venture capitalists). If all the venture capitalists lose confidence and don't invest "make-up" money, the company goes under immediately. If half the venture capitalists refuse to pony up, the others must put up twice their fair share in order to keep the company going. When all the venture capitalists invest their pro rata share, the company keeps going but there is a big residue of malice toward the chief executive officer. The board of directors must set such feelings aside and redouble its efforts to ensure that the company meets its milestones before the next financing.

Each successive financing usually brings money from new venture capitalists at a higher price per share than previous financings. One of the new investor venture capitalists joins the board of directors and almost from day one has a different agenda than the veteran board members. As he or she discovers more about the company, the surprises are seldom pleasant. There is a residue of feeling that information was withheld prior to writing the check. If problems cause a need for an unexpected financing, the new venture capitalist might push for special treatment and may very well deserve it. All this adds up to a potential polarization among the venture investors, adding to the turmoil already existing in a troubled company between management and the outside directors. My partner and I figure two venture capitalists on a board works fine, three or more inevitably result in trouble.

During the development stage of a company, the board of directors often faces replacing the chief executive officer and hiring other key employees. The recruiting process chews up lots of time but all directors can and should participate and be helpful. Strategy, product planning, meeting regulatory requirements, even making customer contacts are other vital tasks of the board during this phase in the life of a company. By this time the business is moving fast and has become complex. Outside directors must therefore spend several days a month working on behalf of the company. Otherwise they are not competent to make judgments and should avoid gratuitous comments. Uninformed directors at this juncture should either spend enough time to become informed or not waste management's time. Meetings with the company should be well organized, with an agenda to minimize management's time, which at this stage is far more valuable than that of an outside director.

When things go badly, the relationship between the outside directors and the chief executive officer can often go into free fall. Directors no longer believe in forecasts, estimates, or the explanation of delays. Chief executive officers become very cagey when communicating bad news. Company presidents would rather die by inches than make a full breast of a disaster so they spoonfeed problems to directors. This may extend the chief executive officer's life expectancy but it minimizes the board's ability to help. I've seen many chief executive officers who wait until the end of a four-hour meeting to say to everyone already standing to leave, "By the way . . . ." That always means there's a horrendous problem.

Entrepreneurial chief executive officers often lobby one-on-one with outside directors hoping to ingratiate themselves or at least to soften them up. Initially this polarizes the board and soon it causes a loss of confidence in the chief executive officer who has told each director something different, the same story but with a different emphasis and set of facts. Eventually directors compare notes, invariably leading to a loss of trust and confidence in the chief executive officer.

Firing entrepreneurial chief executive officers is a horrific task. I always involve myself in the actual firing to be certain the person in question knows it's really over. Most board members are reluctant to say "You're fired," and the chief executive officer leaves the meeting thinking that at worst he's been given a stern warning.

Discharging him is always sad and difficult. The fallen chief executive officer has worked like a madman for one to three years. He externalizes everything that has gone wrong and takes pride in everything that's right. He feels betrayed by both the board and the coworkers who refuse to stand by him.

There are compensating factors. The president has stock vested in the company and logically should want those shares to appreciate in value even if it means finding a new chief executive officer. Many entrepreneurial chief executive officers swallow their personal failures because of their stock but they all harbor grudges. If the company eventually fails, they will go to their graves believing it wouldn't have happened on their watch.

Unless entrepreneurs make a lot of money (because of the failure rate, this seldom happens) they eventually turn their anger and disappointment into loathing both their replacement and the venture capitalists who put him there.

During the ramp-up stage, the board of directors changes its focus. New outside directors are added in preparation for a near-term IPO. An investment banker, a lawyer, and a luminary or two are elected to the board. By this time, the investor group owns the majority of the stock and controls the board. The chief executive officer knows he's working for the investors. Everyone begins to smell payday.

The One-Third Rule

Another venture capital dictum is that one-third of the companies fail, one-third succeed, and one-third manage to hang on neither succeeding nor failing. The latter are called the walking dead, barely profitable, fed small amounts of cash from investors from time to time to keep going. The employees earn a living and the venture capitalist avoids a write-off, enabling him to earn his management fee based on the value he assigns to the company.

The third of the companies that crater go down in one of two ways. The first failure is in the start-up stage. Financially this is the most painless loss—$1 to $3 million, depending on how many dollars the venture capitalist pumped in to cover spending overruns. In this failure, there is the least residue of anger and recrimination. The investment was a good idea but the product just didn't work. Too bad.

The worst loss is failure during the ramp-up stage. Not only is the write-off $5 to $20 million, but many venture capitalists have valued their initial investment up by two or three times thereby magnifying the eventual write-down. Venture capitalists commonly feed money into the ramp-up stage companies for years knowing the business is terminal just to avoid the write-down, squandering millions of additional dollars.

In this situation, the chief executive officer has usually been fired, his replacement given one to two years to succeed, and the company still fails. The employees have worked hard and are now unemployed with no severance pay and a pile of worthless stock. The venture capitalist is embarrassed by his financial loss and his decision to invest in the company in the first place. The venture capitalist nets the loss against gains from other investments thereby diminishing eventual profits. Blame gets passed around to everyone in sight. Sometimes there are lawsuits by ex-employees, angry creditors, or landlords. Acrimony a mile high, that's what failure means at this stage.

Walking dead is a more palatable alternative for everyone but the actual cash investors who are represented by venture capitalists. Even investors represented by money managers may benefit short-term: They can be kept happy with an inflated fund value. On the face of it, perpetuating the walking dead is wrong although some very successful venture capitalists argue that someday the walking dead will become valuable. There may be either a hot market for anything that breathes or a merger opportunity with a corporation looking for precisely that product. Many venture capitalists bailed out weak portfolios in the 1982 to 1984 market run-up, proving the walking dead theory can work or every dog has its day, so they say. Maybe so but the perpetuation of losers in the hope of passing the problems on to someone else won't work very often. It's not an easy call because of all the conflicts of interest. I suspect that over time few venture capitalists will ever financially justify the money spent to keep lost causes on respirators.

Another look at the "to be or not to be" question is the scorecard on the seven companies I described earlier. In summary, the results are as shown in Table 13.1.

TABLE 13.1 *Seven Companies's Scorecard*

Company	Founding CEO Status	Total Equity Investment	Other Capital*	Destiny	No. Years to Exit	Shareholder Cash Realization
Agrion	Fired	$10.0	$20.0	merged	7	$ 65.0
Visic	Fired	15.0	10.0	failed	3	1.0
Exac	Fired	2.5	10.0	merged	4	14.0
Ridge	Fired	20.0	7.0	failed	7	0.0
Read-Rite	Fired	12.0	10.0	turnaround	4	Nil
Salutar	Slid Through	7.0	15.0	merged	5	55.0
Calgene	Fired	9.0	25.0	IPO	6	85.0
		$75.5	$97.0			$220.0

*Capitalized leases, bank loans, guarantees, third-party payments, corporate contracts.
Note: Dollar amounts are in millions.

Agrion, Visic, and Ridge represent the classic venture capitalist's dilemma. How much new, unanticipated money should be invested because of company spending overruns? On two separate occasions, had I abandoned Agrion it would have quickly failed. Ridge failed despite my three extra financings. If Visic had been refinanced, it may have succeeded, but a "second chance" failure would have cost another $10 million.

Salutar was a big winner but if the merger had aborted, it might have literally imploded and failed. Since the odds of success are low for any merger, the Salutar win was aided by good luck.

Exac would certainly have failed if we'd lost the patent suit. Even then I would have abandoned and written off Exac had it not been for the support (OPM) from Monsanto. We made money, but had we not been sued, Exac might have been a $50 to $100 million company.

Calgene may someday become a billion-dollar company but it would have died without my $2 million investment during its development phase. I almost pulled the plug.

One problem that goes unnoticed is the speed with which venture capitalists must decide to "fish or cut bait," one of the milder clichés used on these occasions. Companies run out of money and can't meet payroll or pay their rent. There's no time to procrastinate, either more money goes in or the telephones get cut off. Venture capital is not a business for the faint of heart.

Don't Plan on Long Vacations

Venture capitalists have to keep a bunch of balls in the air and it's easy to get overextended. Here's what I did in 1987, for the seven companies I wrote about plus others I was deeply involved in:

AGRION The chief executive officer was fired, I became acting chief executive officer, the board was restructured, a major financing was completed; and merger discussions were started.

VISIC The company cut back operations, laid off half its employees, I fired the chief executive officer, hired a new chief executive officer, and sold the company.

EXAC The company won its patent case and was merged into Monsanto.

RIDGE A radical new plan was developed and implemented, the president was fired, and a new chief executive officer hired; a major financing was completed.

READ-RITE The company merged with its competitor, grappled with quality problems, I became chairman of the board, fired the chief executive officer, and then resigned.

SALUTAR I was involved in firing the president, the negotiation of a merger, and the resolution of its patent problems.

CALGENE The company went public, I became chairman of the board.

BP Evaluated a major investment in an Israeli company.

INTELLIGENT SURGICAL LASERS Started an evaluation of a major investment in a laser company (completed in early 1988).

ADVANCED SURGICAL INTERVENTION Completed the financing and became a board member of a start-up company in the area of urology.

LIFE SCIENCE TECHNOLOGY FUND Formed a new $27.5 million venture partnership fund.

If I tried to write about a typical day in the life of a venture capitalist, it would inevitably be too melodramatic (and self-serving). It would read like a combination of Clark Kent, Wyatt Earp, Svengali, and Ghengis Khan. A more useful portrait of the venture capitalist's job is a detailed examination of my tasks during the development of every company in which I invest in chronological order from the beginning through success or failure. The work load begins with my positive investment decision and writing that first check.

Negotiating and structuring the initial financing, including the review of legal documents for closing, occupy far more time than I ever intended or is warranted. At first everyone, investors and entrepreneurs, becomes jumpy and grumpy then, worn down by the sheer weight of documents, they slide into being benignly fatalistic: "It will happen if it happens" replaces high anxiety. At last there's money in the bank. I know of one case in which everyone forgot to open a checking account and the company president wound up going to his local branch bank just as it was closing on a Friday afternoon to open a new, corporate checking account with a $1 million deposit (a story the branch manager will tell his grandchildren).

There is a potpourri of easily forgotten administrative matters that must be acted upon at once—creating the payroll, obtaining a tax ID number, setting up employee and casualty insurance, arranging for a safe but high-yield deposit of cash not needed for 30 days, check-writing signature cards (always two signatures required), arranging for telephones and office equipment, furniture, stationery, PO forms, business cards, company logo, signing the lease, and so on.

Personnel planning is an early, key action. Three to six people are usually hired immediately and the plan to do so—want ads, headhunters, telephone calls to friends—must be started at once. Other action plans—precisely what each founding employee is going to do during the next week—must be recorded, tracked, and updated. These work plans become the heartbeat of the business as it develops. At this point, the first day in business, there will always be an incredible disparity between what must be done versus what can be done. Triage is the only way to establish priorities though most entrepreneurs prefer promising that they will do it all! (They never even come close.)

In the beginning I interview every candidate prior to hiring, from secretaries to executives. As the business develops, I confine my interviews to key management jobs.

If and when headhunters are employed, I participate in their selection and compensation, and get regular progress reports. Headhunters must know the job specs and our company's standards, but they assimilate the business's needs only by constant reminders and prodding. The company must demand to know which person will conduct the search, especially if that individual is other than the headhunter who negotiated the deal. As viable candidates are surfaced by the search, management and I must find the time to conduct interviews. Entrepreneurs often have no interviewing experience, especially outside their area of expertise. Consequently, as part of the hiring process I help the founder check references and once we've made our mind up, help sell the chosen candidate on the job.

As a board member I vote on salary and stock awards for new employees as well as help draft offer letters, including the all important matter of relocation. For more senior people, relocation costs can easily run $25 to $50,000. They are not all automatically reimbursed as they would be in a corporation. As companies hire new people, personnel policies must be written covering essential matters such as insurance, vacations, holidays, delegation of authority, safety, secrecy, business hours, travel expense, and so on. There are never any retirement plans as everyone understands that the stock is in lieu of a pension. Usually entrepreneurs hate policies but I insist on establishing basic policies outlining to employees their rights and obligations. Entrepreneurs would settle for just having a tacit understanding that all employees are expected to work 60 to 80 hours a week!

Another important organizational matter is the establishment of a business reporting system. As a minimum this must include spending, tracking purchase orders, cash balances, and payroll. Later on, these reports must translate into profit and loss statements, cash-flow balance sheets, and tax returns. Right from the first day of production, there must be a manufacturing cost system in place, an inventory control, order entry, payables and receivables system as well as an endless list of other accounting systems, all of which require computer power. Companies should buy the lowest cost variety of off-the-shelf software to go with proven hardware. Baby companies have no business whatever trying to be computer systems pioneers. There are plenty of other things to go wrong in these companies without creating a problem with a too-sophisticated computer. For some inexplicable reason (perhaps it's a death wish), entrepreneurs often become obsessed with the latest leading-edge computer system. One company in my portfolio is still waiting for its system to work *one year* after installation though there were a dozen old-fashioned systems that would have been up and running in 30 days. Meanwhile, this company has miscalculated its manufacturing costs by 50 percent.

Space is also a formidable organizational matter. Based on bitter experience, I am deeply involved in pushing the company to acquire cheap, ugly, inadequately sized space to get started as quickly as possible. Apart from the cost, companies can't afford to wait the six months it takes to build a Taj Mahal. Six months to a year after starting, as the business takes form and feels that it might survive, it's time to move to oversized, pleasant, and more expensive space. At this point the space should accommodate reasonable expectations for growth for the next two to three years. None of the early space should be wasted on trappings—elaborate offices or conference rooms, atriums, reception areas, and storage (all storage space gets used up no matter how large it is).

Board meetings during the first year should be frequent and informal, approving resolutions to enable the CEO to hire people, buying equipment, signing contracts and leases. These formalities should take very little meeting time as they are the natural outcome of the hiring, work plans, progress reports on milestones, strategy discussions, technology, and market and competition updates discussed on a weekly basis. As a prelude and postlude to board meetings, I remain intimately involved as a full partner or helper in these meetings and discussions.

After about one year in operation, I become consumed with plans to raise the next round of financing. There is no more important task for me than getting the financing organized and completed at this point in the life of the company. This effort includes developing a detailed business plan, the cornerstone of which, with other important information, must be the cash needed to achieve long-range milestones. In most financings pricing is always a struggle. Entrepreneurs want high share prices to minimize their personal dilution. I want the highest price that will attract the money. The entrepreneur and I are usually apart by a factor of two and the only way to resolve the difference is to let new investors set the price. Once the formal financing project is launched, it takes on a life of its own. Some financings go fast (the entrepreneur then says, "We priced it too low"), some drag out, some are severely compromised ("We failed to raise the money we believe we needed"). The going business must track its business plan all during this period before closing the financing, an aspect often overlooked. The fastest way to lose credibility with new investors is to fail to achieve the goals of the very plan used to raise money.

The frustration of raising money is a killer because of the anxiety involved. Since venture capitalists are prime movers in raising money, if they fail, the company, with all its hopes and dreams, fails. In one case Ted Greene, the founder of a very successful company called Hybritech, cashed in and left to become a venture capitalist only to quit a year later entirely because of his disdain for the heavy burden of raising money for his portfolio companies. Financing can be a tremendous time sink, frustrating, and with an unpredictable outcome. Nevertheless, no venture capitalist job is more important than raising the money needed to build the company.

Raising money becomes a serious diversion for management. I try to organize meetings with potential investors at a convenient time and I attend the meetings to help keep them focused and efficient. It's also useful to me in assessing genuine investor interest, separating the tire kickers from qualified leads. In addition, I try to make suggestions for improving management's presentation and the quality of its answers to questions. Because there is a large "show biz" component to a financing presentation, I rehearse the presentations and check the details of the visual aids. Entrepreneurs desperate to please (and raise the money) often overstate the business or focus too much on the distant future. Trivial perceptions can turn off a prospective investor. For example, one investor turned down one of my companies, I later learned, because the presenter's facial flush was taken as proof the man was an alcoholic. He was actually suffering from an allergy and despite this investor's turndown, the company became a big success.

For me, the most difficult and disappointing part of being a venture capitalist is participating in firing management and in layoffs. All firings mean that I failed in my judgment that the person involved was appropriate for the job.

I never fire anyone without a deep feeling for his or her loss. I have often grown to know the personal side, the families and the dreams of the people I fire. It's horrible for me, but far worse for them. After the firing ceremony the deposed person must see in writing the precise severance terms and agree to sign a letter of understanding. If the person is a top executive, he'll need a lawyer to advise him. No legal advice is ever given without a try for a better deal followed by a threat of litigation. I always make fair settlement offers and have never lost in litigation but neither have the lawyers because they always know how to get paid for their work. That's the system. The person who's fired gets bashed, then bashed again by his lawyer dragging it out. Already hurt, he then gets mad, even vengeful. Venture capitalists must learn to live with this anger. Inevitably some people will hate venture capitalists for reasons real or imaginary. When a company goes off the rails or fails, everyone gets angry. Living with anger is part of the venture capitalist's job and it's impossible to overestimate how tough that is.

Strategy is part of every discussion I have with the company management. It's not possible to spend too much time developing, reviewing, revising, and reevaluating strategy. Product planning for manufacturing companies is the centerpiece of strategy—pricing, design, precise function or performance, improvements, costs, reliability, specifications, documentation, quality assurance, and even the product name. Entrepreneurs come up with some astonishing names like "the 6XRY1" which was the computer entry code to retrieve the document that described the product. The company president thought this was real catchy until we explained that no customer would have any idea what the product was. Strategy also means how to market, sell, and service the product and plans for development of follow-on or entirely new products. Few one-product companies ever succeed.

The deployment of resources is another important strategic consideration. How much should be spent on research and development versus marketing versus cost control. The strategy for manufacturing capability and production capacity is one of the toughest calls—balancing the economics of scale versus demand, putting capacity in place in advance of demand, or paced with or lagging behind demand. Ramping-up also includes the questions of training one shift of workers versus multiple shifts and later on, the all important consideration of overseas production. I always take part in these strategic decisions pushing management to conform strategy to working within the budget. Nothing is more destructive to a baby company than pursuing a strategy without the money or people to get the job done.

Another important part of my job as a venture capitalist is to keep management focused on the company's strategy and to constantly revise and freshen the details. All strategies must funnel down to helping build the business toward the ultimate strategy—the exit.

All my portfolio companies have one common touchstone, proprietary technology that makes these companies special and valuable. I spend all the time necessary encouraging management to take every conceivable action to protect the secrecy of their company's technology. Competent patent attorneys must be hired and force-fed all the relevant details of invention and discovery. Patent files need regular review, submissions must be carefully studied, continuations used to strengthen claims, foreign rights acted upon on a timely basis, and a careful watch or study of relevant third-party patents must be made. The board of directors must be well informed about all the patent activity in the company's area of business. One company in which I am a director licensed a university patent that became the basis for a $100 million business and beat all the competitors to the punch because the company had an excellent patent watch and was able to make an immediate offer to license. Diligence and speed in licensing new technology are important ways a baby company can outscramble a corporation.

If that accursed day comes when one of my companies is put on notice by a competitor that we are infringing an issued patent, I have to be ready to help management formulate a plan of action. The company needs a patent litigator now rather than a patent originator. They are two very different kinds of patent lawyers. The originator embroiders, the litigator comes out swinging. Furthermore, the board of directors needs to be assured that the company is not willfully disregarding an issued patent; otherwise heavy punitive damages could be awarded the plaintiff. The company, in collaboration with its lawyer, must develop a patent infringement defense based on validity or noninfringement or both. No company should be caught unawares about patent conflicts but should be on top of potential problems and have a standby response already in place if and when needed. I prod the company to take these patent actions because management is usually so buried in the day-to-day details of its survival that they just can't take the time and they almost never have the expertise.

Beyond patents, I encourage my companies to protect their technology by having every employee sign a well-crafted confidentiality agreement. I also urge them to make visitors, suppliers, and consultants sign binding secrecy agreements and (this is the toughest part) insist on the company maintaining a low profile or even invisibility until there is a reason to seek publicity. Some entrepreneurs love to talk about their companies especially if a reporter from the *New York Times* calls. But loose lips sink businesses. Publicity enables competitors to get an edge or an inspiration.

There's a highly personal part of my job as a venture capitalist: Handling human frailty. Sometimes management commits a serious fraud-theft, spying, forged research data, or phony accounting. I have to watch for these problems and act quickly and decisively to clean them up or else I run the risk of becoming part of the problem. Cover-ups, looking the other way, and other forms of make believe will certainly lead to the inevitable destruction of the company.

Sexual escapades can be another problem. There's nothing like the intimacy of an 80-hour week as foreplay to blatant office affairs. Sometimes these relationships cause terrible problems in an already stressed organization—favoritism, disappearing acts, tolerance of poor performance, and loss of efficiency. There is seldom a need to be sanctimonious, but skillful action is required to solve this problem. Inaction because of sensitivity or embarrassment is irresponsible. I find that I'm often a father confessor.

Tyranny is another common situation. When the boss is a bully, the people who sign checks, the venture capitalists, and those on the board of directors are the only hope of preventing the horrendous morale problems that follow in the wake of tyranny. I have to be tough enough to challenge the bullies and to keep them from irreparably harming the organization. I also have to be quickly available to help resolve conflicts. Some bullies are simply insensitive and can be taught to manage without using a club. Others are sadists and need to be sequestered or fired. This action may destroy the company. It's always a nasty problem but one that can't be ducked.

A venture capitalist's role in the activities of a company requires experience, credibility, endurance, and understanding, adding up to an exciting but very stressful job. I handle six to eight companies at a time, each one multiplying the problems of the others. All require immediate and constant attention and the skill to simultaneously juggle 20 or 30 life-or-death issues. At least I never get bored.

The "to be or not to be" question has no clear answer except in hindsight. Financial support is vital but isn't everything. Product acceptance, regulatory approval, manufacturability, timeliness, valid patents, and reliability are also important factors. So is luck. The older I get, the more I believe in luck, even when one of my companies succeeds.

14

What's Next—Venture Capital in the 1990s

In 1983 Stan Pratt, the very canny head of *Venture Economics*, said he never knew a venture fund that lost money. Now, less than a decade later, he is saying that he rarely sees one that's making money. A venture capitalist enters the 1990s faced with the prospect of an acute shortage of cash to start new companies while straining to keep up with the financing needs of his existing portfolio. The downside of the law of supply and demand is always merciless.

Investors who poured $20 billion into venture funds from 1983 to 1989 have been bitterly disappointed with their returns and the worst is yet to come. Many venture funds begun after 1983 are permanently under water and most will be lucky to earn a 5 percent return.

No wonder investors who were promised a 50 to 100 percent annual return are furious. Since venture funds have a ten-year life expectancy, a 100 percent annual return on a $100 million fund is $100 billion, a mathematical absurdity, but some investors, eager to be a part of the boom, bought into the fantasy anyway. A perfectly executed $100 million fund with its entire portfolio liquefied in six years would return $6.4 billion at 100 percent, $1.1 billion at 50 percent, and $381 million at 25 percent—very few funds will.

What went wrong? Too much money chased too many deals. Too many companies were formed to conquer the same markets. I remember it well. I was a full-fledged part of the problem. Venture capital success was so publicized that the process looked easy to investors, venture capitalists, and entrepreneurs.

The excesses of the 1980s will result in important structural changes in the way venture capital works in the 1990s. My predications won't be popular with everyone but change is inevitable and necessary. My horoscope says: Returns on existing funds will be battered with little good news to cheer up investors. Most of the remaining cash in funds will be conserved for existing portfolios and investments in new companies will sharply decline. The venture capitalist will reduce his participation in new financings for existing companies while simultaneously trying to curtail spending by his portfolio companies. The financing problem will be complicated by a lack of broad syndication during the 1980s by the lead venture capitalists who pursued a strategy of "hogging" all the good deals for themselves. In the 1990s this narrow investor base will further reduce the supply of cash for new financings.

The results of cash conservation among individual funds will be disappointing because the whole venture industry will follow the same course. Financings will be difficult to complete and far less money than is needed will be raised. As a consequence, equity pricing will sharply decline resulting in massive dilution for management as well as for those investors unwilling or unable to invest further. "Down and dirty" financings, where share prices are devalued as much as ten for one by new investors, will become conspicuous. Venture capitalists will inevitably be forced into more portfolio write-offs, worsening the already dismal results of their fund's performance.

Shortchanging companies by inadequate financings will demoralize management by dilution, lay-offs, and further reductions in spending. These undercapitalized companies will fail to reach their potential. Important programs will be canceled, companies will be sold prematurely at lower than expected prices, and bankruptcies will increase, all causing lower valuations of the venture capitalists' portfolios.

Besieged by poor results, venture capitalists will hastily dig foxholes from which they will greatly increase communication with their investors. Handholding and explaining away bad results will become a time-consuming preoccupation. I've already seen some venture capitalists detach themselves from their poor performance by becoming reporters to their investors rather than fund managers. "What could anyone expect with all this money running around?" or "Jeez, 80 disk drive companies, no wonder no one made any money." He usually forgets to mention that he himself invested over $30 million in eight different disk drive companies.

A born-again venture capitalist, who has performed poorly but is ready to sin no more, will bring down from the mountain a new set of Ten Commandments for the 1990s:

- Return to basics and invest only in great ideas and people who have proven they are able to create companies that will sell products into market niches.
- Invest no longer in start-ups because the risks are too high and cashing in takes too long.
- Syndicate financings with other strong venture capitalists expecting them to be there with both assistance and money during any tough times for the company.
- Invest in very few companies and work hard to make them succeed.
- Avoid investing in companies that have technical risks or need costly, time-consuming regulatory approvals.
- Do not invest in companies that are either capital or labor intensive.
- Do not allow portfolio companies to waste money on trappings, extravagant salaries, or too much space and equipment.
- Invest at the lowest possible price.
- Value your portfolio conservatively and avoid unexpected write-offs.
- Support vigorously a substantial cut in, or elimination of, capital gains taxes.

These commandments may not affect the future behavior of venture capitalists but will soothe the relationship with their investors—handholding while hoping for the best.

Investors Will Strike Back

Some investors will take action to force a venture capitalist to cut his management fee and, in certain cases, will fire him. Most venture funds are legally structured to give investors the right to make these changes. And they will when they realize that poorly performing funds are being further decapitalized by the 2½ percent annual management fees that could continue to be a drain for another five to ten years. A $100 million fund, for example, will be deflated by $25 million over a ten-year period.

A venture capitalist can hasten his own demise by holding on to distributions for cash to bail out teetering portfolio companies and to pay himself his management fee. When an investment in a company liquefies via a merger, public offering, or sale of assets, the cash is normally distributed to the investors net of the venture capitalists' override. Most venture partnerships allow the venture capitalist, at his discretion, to withhold distributions. Investors will gradually figure that withholding distributions is not in their interest and "fix" the problem.

A new breed of money managers will be created when some institutional investors decide to divorce their venture capitalists. A "work-out" venture capital fund manager will be needed immediately by investors to supervise portfolio companies formerly managed by the deposed venture capitalist. These new kids on the block will further scale back financings and prod their companies to sell or shrink, inevitably leading to even more write-offs. It is a sure ism that the newly appointed venture capitalist will never like the first guy's deal. He'll soon recognize that it's in his best interest to write off everything in sight. Investors should be prepared for the worst and they will surely get it. Firing the venture capitalist is not the path to improved returns.

Some investors are going to renege on "cash calls," their commitment to put additional money into venture funds. During the 1980s, an important investor strategy was to split the cash given the venture capitalists into three or four parts called "take-downs." Contractually committed to invest $6 million in total, the investor puts up only $2 million in cash at the outset of the fund, another $2 million two years later, and the last $2 million two years after that. Some investors, their eyes bulging from the gold rush of 1980 to 1983, actually counted on getting distributions back in time to pay for the second or third take-down.

In practice, the venture capitalists needed money faster than expected and made cash calls (forcing a take-down) in one year instead of two and distributions (if any) were delayed or deferred. Some investors will refuse to answer a cash call. While waiting for the courts to sort out the legal issues, the venture capitalist will have even less cash to invest, compounding his troubles.

With existing venture funds struggling, raising new funds will be nearly impossible especially from traditional venture investors. Unless they employ an institutional money manager with chutzpah and a strategy to invest countercyclically, most institutions—insurance companies, endowments, and pension funds—that invested in venture capital in the 1980s will be relieved to work their way out of current investments and won't line up for new ones. Only those venture capitalists with excellent track records will have a source of new money, although a few newcomers with distinguished careers as corporate executives, entrepreneurs, or investing bankers will be able to raise funds.

Where will the new money come from? One source of new cash for a venture capitalist will be corporations trying to expand their horizons by participating in the venture capital process. Many corporations cut development spending to maximize short-term profits or pay down debt. They will be especially interested in a cheap fix. Corporations learned in the past that they could not operate an in-house venture fund. Investing in traditional venture funds seldom introduced corporations to companies that were of interest. They believe they paid too much for publicly traded emerging companies, and are regularly reminded of their largess by security analysts and shareholder suits. Intrapreneurship, or internal ventures, didn't work as well as advertised. Since corporations always need new ideas and products, investing in specialized venture funds dedicated to their specific areas of interest will become very fashionable and, therefore, a large source of new money.

By matching its venture fund strategy to its area of interest, a corporation will get acquainted with innovative baby companies—pharmaceuticals for Bristol-Meyers Squib, environmental systems for Exxon, chemicals for DuPont, for example. They can then more easily merge with these baby companies or license new products from them. Unlike the goals of institutional investors, financial returns are secondary to corporations investing in dedicated funds.

There are formidable obstacles to the success of dedicated venture funds. Exciting companies created by entrepreneurs are threatening to the new-business development bureaucracy that exists within corporations. I've seen research and development people criticized by corporate executives, "Why weren't you guys smart enough to come up with this?" No wonder they feel threatened.

A second problem for corporations in realizing the potential of venture investments is lack of a pathway or entry into their own organization. There is no person or group dedicated to assimilating an entrepreneur-run company, to nurturing and supporting it without smothering it. It is not easy, especially in the early stages, or as one executive aptly put it, "We can't buy that company, our overhead will kill it."

Some investors will, however, continue to back venture capitalists with new funds and will continue to pay the same fees for the privilege. Investors will be seeking a venture capitalist who looks, acts, and smells like a winner—a money management macho. Any venture capitalist willing to take a cut sounds like a wimp, unworthy of managing money. Besides, a successful venture capitalist earns every dime he makes.

There are institutions in the United States and abroad with other motives to invest, such as getting money out of the country or gaining access to technology. And there is a shopping list of companies with no 1980s venture experience now ready to get in the hunt. This is particularly true of the Pacific Rim countries. Venture capitalists trying to raise money will work hard to find these virgins.

Turnaround funds, money to restart failing companies, already exist and will continue to expand. Many baby companies run into problems and delays and are ultimately abandoned by their original venture capitalist. In what amounts to a voluntary bankruptcy, the company is sold to a rescue or turnaround fund for pennies on the dollar. Creditors who would have lost everything in bankruptcy reluctantly agree to meager settlements. Existing shareholders get diluted out. It's gut wrenching but it beats locking the doors. There are dozens of these failing company situations at any one time. The trick is to figure out which ones are worth saving and which ones deserve to go south.

Investing in low tech is an old idea that's periodically dragged out, like estranged relatives at funerals. Simply stated, low tech means something anyone can do, not proprietary or special. Making vinyl for shower curtains, formed styrene drinking cups, and glue for plywood are low-tech businesses. As commodity businesses mature and start to die out, entrepreneurs buy the remnants, cut overhead, and make modest profits but live well on the cash flow.

Few of these situations meet the standards, such as building value then cashing in, of traditional venture investments. Such commodity consolidations are better suited to bargain-purchase leverage buy-outs targeted by megafunds organized to provide enormous capital in the form of both debt and equity. Given the scale of venture capital, $1 to $5 million invested as equity in high-growth businesses, there's little room to play in leverage buy-outs. Besides, investors aren't going to pay high fees to venture capitalists for joining in a $300 million leverage buy-out syndication. Someone will ask, "Where's the value added?" Low tech became popular in the late 1980s when venture capitalists losing their shirts in high tech talked it up in the financial press. It won't work in the 1990s either.

No tech means a fashion business such as "in" restaurants, pet rocks, trendy boutiques, and fad food products. The rare winners are so dramatic that unsophisticated investors ignore (if they hear about) the legions of losers. Few venture capitalists know anything about fashion—just look at how we dress. Financial success for the uninformed is the result of sheer luck and backing a strictly OPM business. Using other people's money to finance a dozen different fast-food concepts might produce an occasional winner to brag about later.

The irony of the venture capital process in the first half of the 1990s is obvious but will be largely ignored. As new venture money dries up, returns will rise. Those bold enough to invest will receive superior returns and later become known as gutsy visionaries.

Throughout the 1990s there won't be any shortage at all of wonderful investment opportunities for venture capital. My unequivocal confidence is based on the certainty that technical advances will not only continue unabated, but will do so at an ever-increasing pace, thus ensuring change and opportunities for visionaries and innovators. Entrepreneurs will always be able to benefit from these opportunities because they work harder, faster, and smarter than corporations.

Dramatic changes will evolve in the process of venture capital in the 1990s. Funds will be created to buy existing baby companies. Since the crash of 1987, many publicly traded emerging companies are substantially undervalued. Some have an abundance of cash on hand and are profitable, but simply fail to excite the stock market. Often the senior management of these companies has been in place for seven to ten years living with the disappointment of under-water stock prices and unfulfilled dreams. They are getting old enough to start thinking about cashing in, estate planning, and avoiding paying taxes. An acquisition fund will buy out the management and enough additional shares to gain control of the company. The fund manager will then restructure and revitalize the company with an eye toward a corporate merger.

Buy-out funds will be created to purchase, at a discount, investor positions in under-water venture capital funds, or to purchase the entire fund thereby taking out all the investors. One immediate benefit will be that the former investors won't have to fire their venture capitalist and go through the process of finding a new one. The new owner from the buy-out fund will do that for them. The original investors will also have immediate liquidity and can take solace in the greater fool theory: "A greater fool than I for buying it in the first place, bought me out."

An investor buy-out fund will work because it meets investor needs. After years of disappointing results in illiquid investments, institutions are mad and weary. Selling their position at a "reasonable" discount is the only way some institutions believe, they can cut their losses and end the nightmare, a tactic widely practiced in banking. Without this concept, there is no formal way of arranging for investors to get out. A popular misconception about venture capital is that investors lose everything in a poorly performing, or underwater, fund. Venture capital is not a dry well. Some investments succeed and investors, in the worst case, receive distributions and will get back most of their original cash. They just won't earn a return.

Maturing venture portfolios are probably deceptively undervalued. If the losers have been written off and the winners are yet to be realized, the remaining portfolio will have a big upside. Few people have the wisdom, experience, and skill to properly value someone else's portfolio, but the venture capitalist who can figure it out and act on it will create a whole new business and earn superior returns for his investors.

Despite the downside from the excesses of the 1980s, benefits will be realized in the consolidation of crowded niches.

Because it will benefit many constituencies, cash will be used to force the merger of two or three profitless companies into one adequately financed successor. Consolidations dispose of the "living dead" with minimal face-saving recovery for the original venture investors who get some paper in the new company. The merger lessens competition, provides a chance to streamline the organization, and acquires low-cost manufacturing capacity and inventories. When it works, a merger reduces operating expenses while holding on to most of the sales revenues. The new company becomes profitable overnight, increases in value enormously, and makes a pile of money for the people who put the merger together.

Mergers among complementary baby companies can, however, be nothing more than combining dead whales with white elephants resulting in even bigger losses. Few people have the vision to sort out the winners from the whales or the ability to make these mergers-of-convenience work.

Another opportunity resulting from the excesses of the 1980s lies in the thousands of companies that were created and remain in hundreds of venture portfolios. Most venture capitalists were bent on making a killing in an IPO and never fully explored their company's acquisition by a corporation as a viable exit strategy. Most venture capitalists I've met don't know how to put such a deal together. In the past, the venture capitalist relied on mergers and acquisitions artists to do this work but, for the most part, these half-hearted attempts usually misfired. The Wall Streeters don't understand baby companies and the fees were too small to get any real attention.

Corporations, therefore, will not only invest in dedicated venture funds but will also put money in the hands of venture capitalists to buy positions in a few of the vast array of available portfolio companies with an eye toward eventually buying those companies. The role of the venture capitalist will be to handle the interface between company and corporation, avoid conflicts of interest, and encourage a partnership between two disparate entities. Some will end in marriage, some in divorce, but in all cases the relationship will evolve deliberately rather than result in the usual attempt to smash a merger together.

Geographic Dispersion

There was a major effort in the 1980s to create venture capital business in new geographic areas. It didn't work very well. Geographic dispersion of venture capital activity in the United States will gradually evolve but only in areas that have all the necessary ingredients—technology from universities or research centers, a social setting that encourages entrepreneurs, corporations to supply talent and ideas, experienced venture capitalists willing to spend time in the area, and lawyers who know how to put the deals together. In order to add value a venture capitalist must be physically present and available when needed.

Nationwide, state governments have tried to stimulate venture capital growth by creating low-cost industrial "parks" to encourage the formation of venture-backed companies. States have made outright financial grants to attract new companies as well as investing heavily in venture capital funds dedicated to their state. I don't think any of these measures will be very effective. States should help fund research at universities and vigorously compete to lure corporations. Technology and a pool of potential employees make venture capital work, not empty buildings. The rest will take care of itself but over a long time period. I don't know of any way to speed up the evolution.

There is a chicken/egg problem with geographic dispersion that can only be resolved with the passage of decades. Venture capital builds on its own success. Start-up companies cluster with later-stage companies. Entrepreneurs like to confer with each other, borrow a cup of sugar, and steal employees.

Creating a commercial development center on a Nebraska wheat field or a Montana cattle ranch, politically popular in 1985, won't work in the decade of the 1990s. Venture capital is catching on, however, in the Washington, D.C., area, as well as in Texas and Arizona. It's very slow to develop in Midwest urban areas. It's cheaper to get started in Detroit, but there is a nagging concern that auto workers' union wages have set standards that will make local manufacturing too expensive. In addition, the Midwest culture is basically risk averse. The biggest indictment is that the vast majority of technical people from the Big Ten graduate schools move to either coast. They don't stay in the middle.

A surprisingly important element in developing venture capital is experienced lawyers. Lawyers terrific at contracts or trusts who can't grasp the needs of little companies waste valuable time and money. I've seen 200 pages of legalese which cost $50,000 to memorialize a simple agreement. Most of the words cover the disposition of assets in the event the company fails. There are no assets when the company fails and the $50,000 would have come in handy for other purposes. The delays caused by novice lawyers can be fatal to a start-up. The company isn't funded until contracts are signed. Months can be lost without any benefit and may give committed investors second thoughts about going ahead.

Experienced lawyers first guide entrepreneurs through the mine field of what rightfully belongs to their former employer and what belongs to them. They have a good feel for what can be financed and they are a vital part of a venture capitalist's network as a source of deal flow. They must be quickly responsive to the legal needs of the new company and its board of directors. Lawyers are also vital to both mergers and IPOs. They can't be a thousand miles away and operate effectively even when they promise they love to fly.

Learning from the Past

The venture capital industry has learned that too much money results in too many start-ups spending more money than necessary. It's the surest way to poor returns on investments. This truism only applies to the "other guy's deals," however. Venture capitalists and entrepreneurs still don't consider the possibility that their company isn't special and won't easily outdistance competition. They still ignore the statistical imperative that only one-third of new companies succeed and only one in 100 is a big winner. Neither the failure rate nor the overoptimism will change in the 1990s.

What will be different is that venture capital won't finance companies that will ultimately require a tremendous amount of capital, $20 to $100 million, to become successful. Unless there is a clear, doable path to financing a capital intensive company, venture capitalists will pass on the investment. Companies will thus merge out at a much earlier stage and for a much lower profit. There will be fewer billion-dollar standalone companies and more dependence on corporate partners.

Business writers have already begun to forecast that venture capitalists, besieged by poor results, will be forced to accept lower management fees and high hurdle rates in order to qualify for a participation in profits. A few venture fund managers have already publicly announced voluntary cutbacks in carried interest from the current 25 percent to 20 percent. That's not exactly belt-tightening.

Veteran venture capitalists trying to raise new money have a different problem. Venture capitalists with poor records won't be able to raise money regardless of management fees or carried interest. No investor would be induced to place money in the hands of a failed venture capitalist just because his fees are low.

Meanwhile, the few venture capitalists with attractive performance records will get all the money they want without reducing fees or carried interest.

With the shortage of venture money and a diminished expectation that he will build value, the venture capitalist, except for the superstars, will also find his role diminished. Investors won't pay high management fees for poor performance. They will expect returns of 10 to 15 percent before giving venture capitalists a share of the profit. Investors will shun 1980-style megafunds, those sized $100 million or more. Some venture capitalists who are running giant profitless funds and taking management fees in large bites will be fired by the investors. Workout venture capitalists will be hired to salvage the remaining value.

With fewer start-ups financed, the natural selection process will become an important investment screen. Only the most attractive new companies will get the available money. This will result in venture capital operating at a much lower velocity and, therefore, with much less drain on the reservoir of both good ideas and aspiring entrepreneurs. The upside of the law of supply and demand will logically be triggered and venture capital will become much more profitable in the second half of the 1990s. It's axiomatic that money floods in at the top and evaporates at the bottom of the venture cycle. Profit is obviously the reciprocal of that investor folly.

Venture Capital Abroad

I have a tremendous bias against the potential of venture capital elsewhere in the world. There are formidable fundamental problems and negative attitudes.

One country, Canada, is attractive but only as an adjunct to the United States. Canada has smart people and good technology but no market. The government has funded venture capital programs and encouraged entrepreneurship but with little success within the country. Ultimately, to get venture backing, a new Canadian business must migrate south.

For more than a decade the United Kingdom has tried hard to make venture capital work. The United Kingdom has excellent technology, smart people, and generous government subsidies for venture capital but only a few winners have been produced. The best global strategy for venture capital is to back start-ups in the United Kingdom and then immediately transfer the business to the United States. That's a clever way of upstreaming the traditional "brain drain." The market in the

United States is vast compared to the United Kingdom and more accessible than that of the European Economic Community (EEC). High-priced exit strategies are therefore far more achievable resulting in far greater returns to investors.

On the downside, however, few people in the United Kingdom will work 60 to 80 hours a week. They do want perks—company cars, pension plans, and five-week vacations. Venture capital only succeeds when the baby company operates twice as fast as, and at half the cost of, a corporate competitor. Otherwise the corporation's nearly unlimited resources will always win out. I don't see enough margin coming from entrepreneurs now or in the near future in the United Kingdom.

Germany and Japan have amazingly similar deterrents to venture capital. The governments and banks in these two countries control and regulate the markets. Only a token public stock market is available to emerging companies. Not only do corporations never cooperate with baby companies, they despise them. Existing venture capital funds are therefore invested in second-rate opportunities and have no clear path to liquidity. Culturally, employees like to work their entire professional life for the same large corporations. Venture capital is just talk in these countries. Leaders claim they want venture capital to work but in the same way as virtue—in theory, not in practice.

Currently there is great interest and activity in venture capital in places like Taiwan, Singapore, the Philippines, and Mexico. Venture capital is used in these area to create low-cost manufacturing factories for Japanese and American companies. Investors will make money but not through the venture capital paradigm. These manufacturing companies quickly become prisoners of their foreign customers. What's called venture capital competes directly and indirectly with local government subsidies. No local exit strategy is available and profits, if any occur, can be frozen in the country or subject to double taxation.

The radical changes in many eastern countries have already

brought forth the call for venture capital to stimulate the economy and help free enterprise flourish. Entrepreneurs and government capital are needed to create modernized fundamental businesses offering goods for domestic consumption as well as export. American-style venture capital, based on new technology and envisioning IPO or merger strategies in six years, won't work.

Organized venture capital will continue to flourish in the United States. Entrepreneurs will create new companies with venture capital backing. The venture capital process will create new jobs and improved goods and services. Some venture capitalists will become more "pro-active" or involved in the process. Some canny ones believe they can create deals rather than wait for business proposals to come to them. They can spot trends, create a business plan to serve the new opportunity, finance the start-up, and hire the people to run it. Brook Byers of Kleiner Perkins Caufield & Byers, the West Coast venture wizards, took a six-month sabbatical to visit universities around the country to find out what was hot, then formed a few companies around his findings.

Missing from this do-it-yourself equation are the passion and zeal of the founder entrepreneur, the madness that propels the creator and can produce a winner. I don't think many venture capitalists will find their own deals better than those evolving from the traditional deal flow. What they are demonstrating is a positive example of adding value. Venture capitalists who don't add value to their new companies won't be around for very long.

A big change in investor strategy will come from the dilemma caused by the huge size and velocity of the investment business. One brutal lesson that investors have learned is it's much easier to make money in a $50 million venture fund than in a $500 million fund. Large funds force too much money into too many deals managed by too many inexperienced people. Megafunds have been established just to collect large management fees without regard to, or an expectation of, ever making profit. Investors don't realize that funds have a long investment cycle and won't be profitable for five years or more. Over a five-year period, a $500 million fund is decapitalized by over $60 million in management fees.

The dilemma is that the big institutions manage huge pools of money and must put hundreds of millions of dollars to work in venture capital to impact the overall return on their funds. A $5 billion fund, for example, might have $2 billion in the stock market, $2 billion in bonds, $800 million in short-term securities, and $200 million in venture capital. Two hundred million dollars is huge for venture capital but barely enough to impact the total return on the institution's $5 billion cash pool.

Beyond the danger of megafunds living off management fees there are further complications. Investment banks that manage venture funds are riddled with conflicts of interest between portfolio investments, corporate finance transaction fees, and research recommendations on publicly traded companies in which they have venture investments. The argument to separate principal and agency in venture investing is very compelling and will be considered by investors.

The same is true of cherry picking. A venture capitalist must avoid investing his personal money in the "hot deals" to the exclusion of investors. Even worse is personally investing in the first round, or start-up, when the stock is cheap, then using the funds to buy the expensive stock later.

Another insidious problem is the venture capitalist who raises funds for a venture capital partnership then quits to raise his own fund. The investors in the original partnership are left to deal with a stranger, often without experience, hired to replace the venture capitalist who resigned.

Where Are the Watchdogs?

The National Venture Capital Association (NVCA), whose membership includes most venture capitalists, has bylaws as follows:

1. Membership in NVCA implies support of venture capital development, advancement of technology, productivity, and the creation of opportunity.
2. Members will conduct their business in a professional way and will not engage in practices which would be damaging to the image of the venture capital industry.
3. Members will avoid financing enterprises or participating in activities which are inimical to these goals.
4. Members will know the true source of all significant investment capital in their funds and will not represent major "blind" pools of capital. Members will not seek investment capital from foreign governments or sources deemed to be hostile to the United States by the State Department of the United States.
5. Members will take a long-term view of the economy and venture capital industry to build value over a period of time, rather than engage in short-term speculations.
6. Members will be accountable to their investors with fully disclosed operating and financial reports.
7. Members will abide by decisions of the Professional Standards Committee designated by the NVCA Board of Directors.

The venture capital industry would benefit from a meaningful code of conduct to minimize unethical behavior. Otherwise, this vital industry could suffer the horror of being regulated by a government agency.

I expect that in the 1990s the recovery from the excesses of the 1980s will include a venture capitalist code of conduct set forth by both national public accounting firms and the National Association of Venture Capital. This voluntary code could then be adopted by all venture capital investors and would go a long way to eliminate or avoid abuses. Unlike the nouveau venture capital Ten Commandments, the venture capital code would include:

- Accounting standards for the valuation of investments
- Restrictions on the use of bridge loans

- Standards for distributions, including stock in illiquid companies
- Elimination of cherry picking
- Disclosure of transaction fees earned
- Restrictions on intercompany relationships that have common investors
- Separation of venture capital investments from ties to investment banks

The venture industry should spend more energy in self-policing than in gratuitous lobbying for lower capital gains taxes. I see no reason whatsoever to have a differential in capital gains between investments and ordinary income. Entrepreneurs seeking capital *never* consider the tax rate as a factor in plunging ahead. Institutional and corporate money flows into venture capital either untaxed or below corporate tax rates. Venture capitalists are and will continue to be glad to get funds regardless of tax rates. The decline in money flowing into venture capital is the result of poor performance, not a higher capital gains tax. And poor performance means no one has to worry about capital gains taxes in the first place.

Despite all the problems, I love my work. My job is always fascinating. My investments enable very smart people to create businesses out of important ideas and for me to be part of them.

In 1986 I helped create a fund focused entirely on the life sciences, products for medicine and agriculture. Life sciences have always been an important interest and back in 1985 I guessed right about the need for dedicated venture capital activity in this area. Our first fund, formed in 1986, will be one of the few winners of that time period. Since I now make investments exclusively in medicine and health care, it's especially gratifying to me that these companies are expected to benefit humankind as well as make a profit for my investors. I truly believe I'm privileged to be able to do this work.

I also have been around enough to admit that constantly

living with promise, uncertainty, and the proximity to failure is both exhilarating and depressing. My professional life is always a telephone call away from disaster or a breakthrough. One or the other happens every week, often every day.

I wrote this book not as an exposé but to share some of the texture and flavor of venture capital, to demystify the process, and to give one venture capitalist's point of view.

Venture capital will continue to be an important, exciting factor in this country's economic growth and well-being in the years to come. I salute everyone brave enough to participate.